A ZOLA DICTIONARY

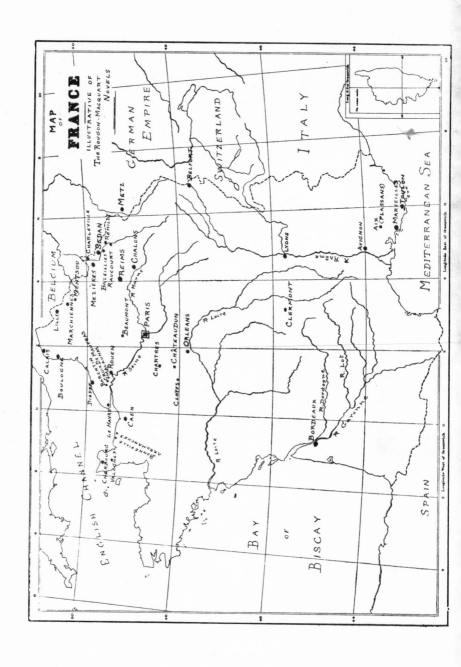

A ZOLA DICTIONARY

THE CHARACTERS OF
THE ROUGON-MACQUART NOVELS
OF ÉMILE ZOLA

With a Biographical and Critical Introduction,
Synopses of the Plots, Bibliographical
Note, Map, Genealogy, etc.

BY

J. G. PATTERSON

LONDON
GEORGE ROUTLEDGE AND SONS, LIMITED
NEW YORK: E. P. DUTTON AND CO.
1912

REPUBLISHED BY GALE RESEARCH COMPANY, BOOK TOWER, DETROIT, 1969

Library of Congress Catalog Card Number 68–27179

PREFATORY NOTE

In the preparation of my Introduction I have, of course, relied for information on the recognized Biographies of Zola, namely, *Notes d'un Ami*, by Paul Alexis (Paris, Charpentier) ; *Émile Zola, a Biographical and Critical Study*, by R. H. Sherrard (London, Chatto & Windus, 1893) ; *Émile Zola, Novelist and Reformer* : An account of his Life and Work, by Ernest Alfred Vizetelly (London, John Lane, 1904). Reference has also been made to Mr. Arthur Symons' *Studies in Prose and Verse*, and to articles in the *Fortnightly Review* by Mr. Andrew Lang, in the *Atlantic Monthly* by Mr. Henry James, and in the *Contemporary Review* by M. Edouard Rod, as well as to articles in the *Encyclopædia Britannica* and in the *Dictionnaire Universel des Contemporains*.

By kind permission of Messrs. Chatto & Windus it has been possible to include the diagram of the Rougon-Macquart Genealogical Tree, which appears in the Preface to their edition of *Doctor Pascal*, and to make use of their translations in the preparation of the Dictionary. In compiling the latter, Zola's own words have been adopted so far as possible, though usually they have required such condensation as to make direct quotation difficult. This difficulty was increased by the fact that occasional use was made of different translations of the same book, and that frequent references to the original were found necessary.

The Synopses of the Plots of the novels are arranged in the order in which the books should be read, as indicated by their Author in *Le Docteur Pascal*, and confirmed by his biographer, Mr. E. A. Vizetelly.

J. G. P.

Edinburgh, *May, 1912.*

CONTENTS

INTRODUCTION

ÉMILE ZOLA was born at Paris on 2nd April, 1840. His father, François Zola, was a man whose career up to that time had not been a success, though this was not due to any lack of energy or ability. Zola *père* was of mixed nationality, his father being an Italian and his mother a Greek, and it is not unlikely that his unrest and want of concentration were due to the accident of his parentage. When quite a young man, François fought under the great Napoleon, after whose fall he became a civil engineer. He spent some time in Germany, where he was engaged in the construction of the first tramway line in Europe, afterwards visiting Holland and possibly England. Failure seems to have accompanied him, for in 1831 he applied for and obtained an appointment as lieutenant in the Foreign Legion in Algeria. His career in Africa was, however, of short duration; some irregularities were discovered, and he disappeared for a time, though ultimately he came forward and made up his accounts, paying the balance that was due. No prosecution took place, and resignation of his commission was accepted. Nothing more was heard of the matter till 1898, when his son Émile identified himself with the cause of Dreyfus, and in the campaign of calumny that followed had to submit to the vilest charges against the memory of his father. The old *dossier* was produced by the French Ministry of War, the officials of which did not hesitate to strengthen their case by the forgery of some documents and the suppression of others. In view of these proved facts, and of the circumstance that François Zola, immediately after his resignation from the Foreign Legion, established himself as a civil engineer at Marseilles and prepared a scheme for new maritime docks there, and that in connection with this scheme he visited Paris repeatedly, obtaining private audiences with the King and interviewing statesmen, it must be held that the charges against him were of a venial nature, in no way warranting the accusations brought forward by the War Office nearly seventy years later to cast discredit on his son. Nothing came of the Marseilles harbour scheme, and the same fate attended subsequent plans for the fortification of Paris. Zola *père*, who by this time had married, then turned his attention to a proposal to supply water to the town of Aix, in Provence, by means of a reservoir and a canal. He removed thither with his wife and child, and after many delays and disappointments ultimately signed an agreement for the construction of the works. Even then further delays

ix

took place, and it was not till three years later that the work could be commenced. But the engineer's ill fortune still attended him, for one morning while he was superintending his workmen the treacherous mistral began to blow, and he took a chill, from the effects of which he died a few days afterwards.

The young widow, with her son Émile, then a child of seven, was left in poor circumstances, her only fortune being a claim against the municipality of Aix. Fortunately her parents had some means, and came to her assistance during the years of fruitless struggle to establish the rights of her dead husband. Émile had up to this time been allowed to run wild, and he had spent most of his time out of doors, where he acquired a love of the country which he retained in later years. Even when he was sent to school he was backward, only learning his letters with difficulty and showing little inclination for study. It was not till 1852, when he was twelve years old, that his education really began. By this time he was able to realize his mother's financial position, and to see the sacrifices which were being made to send him as a boarder to the *lycée* at Aix. His progress then became rapid, and during the next five years he gained many prizes. Throughout all these years the struggle between Madame Zola and the municipality had gone on, each year diminishing her chance of success. In the end her position became desperate, and finding it impossible to continue to reside at Aix, the little family removed to Paris in 1858. Fortunately Émile was enabled by the intervention of certain friends of his late father to continue his studies, and became a day pupil at the Lycée St. Louis, on the Boulevard St. Michael. For some reason he made little progress there, and when he presented himself for his *baccalauréat* degree he failed to pass the examination. A later attempt at the University of Marseilles had the same result. As this examination is in France the passport to all the learned professions, Zola's failure to pass it placed him in a serious position. His mother's resources were by this time entirely exhausted, and some means of support had to be sought without delay. After many attempts, he got a place as clerk in a business house at a salary of twenty-six pounds a year, but the work proved so distasteful that after two months of drudgery he threw it up. Then followed a period of deep misery, but a period which must have greatly influenced the work of the future novelist. Wandering the streets by day and, when he could find money to buy a candle, writing poems and short stories by night, he was gaining that experience in the school of life of which he was later to make such splendid use. Meantime his wretchedness was deep. A miserable lodging in a garret, insufficient food, inadequate clothing, and complete absence of fire may be an incentive to high endeavour, but do not render easy the pathway of fame. The position had become all but untenable when Zola received an appointment in the publishing house of M. Hachette,

of Paris, at a salary beginning at a pound a week, but soon afterwards increased. During the next two years he wrote a number
of short stories which were published later under the title *Contes
à Ninon*. The book did not prove a great success, though its
undoubted ability attracted attention to the writer and opened
the way to some journalistic work. About this time he appears
to have been studying Balzac, and the recently published *Madame
Bovary* of Flaubert, which was opening up a new world not only in
French fiction, but in the literature of Europe. He had also read
the *Germinie Lacerteux* of Edmond and Jules de Goncourt, on
which he wrote an appreciative article, and this remarkable book
cannot have been without its influence on his work. The effect
was indeed immediate, for in 1865 he published his next book,
La Confession de Claud, which showed strong traces of that departure from conventional fiction which he was afterwards to
make more pronounced. The book was not a financial success,
though it attracted attention, and produced many reviews, some
favourable, others merciless. Influenced by the latter, the Public
Prosecutor caused inquiries regarding the author to be made at
Hachette's, but nothing more was done, and it is indeed doubtful
if any successful prosecution could have been raised, even at a
period when it was thought necessary to indict the author of
Madame Bovary.

Zola's employers had, however, begun to look askance at his
literary work ; they may have considered that it was occupying
too much of the time for which they paid, or, more probably, they
were becoming alarmed at their clerk's advanced views both on
politics and literary art. As Zola afterwards explained the matter,
one of the partners said to him, " You are earning two hundred
francs a month here, which is ridiculous. You have plenty of
talent, and would do better to take up literature altogether. You
would find glory and profit there." The hint was a direct one,
and it was taken. The young author was again thrown upon his
own resources, but was no longer entirely unknown, for the not
unfavourable reception of his first book and the violent attacks
on his second had given him a certain position, even though it may
to some extent have partaken of the nature of a *succès de scandale*.
As he wrote at the time, he did not mean to pander to the likes or
the dislikes of the crowd ; he intended to force the public to caress
or insult him.

Journalism was the avenue which now appeared most open,
and Zola got an appointment on the staff of a newspaper called
L'Événement, in which he wrote articles on literary and artistic
subjects. His views were not tempered by moderation, and when
he depreciated the members of the Salon in order to exalt Manet,
afterwards an artist of distinction, but then regarded as a dangerous
revolutionary, the public outcry was such that he was forced to
discontinue publication of the articles. He then began a second

story called *Le Vœu d'une Morte* in the same newspaper. It was intended to please the readers of *L'Événement*, but from the first failed to do so, and its publication was stopped before it was half completed. Soon afterwards the *Événement* was incorporated with the *Figaro*, and Zola's connection with it terminated. A time of hardship again began, and during the year 1867 the wolf was only kept from the door by unremitting toil of the least agreeable kind. In the midst of his difficulties Zola wrote two books simultaneously, one supremely good and the other unquestionably bad. The one was *Thérèse Raquin*, and the other *Les Mystères de Marseille*. The latter, which was pure hack-work, was written to the order of the publisher of a Marseillaise newspaper, who supplied historical material from researches made by himself at the Marseilles and Aix law courts, about the various *causes célèbres* which during the previous fifty years had attracted the most public attention. These were to be strung together, and by an effort of legerdemain combined into a coherent whole in the form of a novel. Zola, desiring bread, undertook the task, with results that might have been anticipated.

Thérèse Raquin is a work of another kind, for into it Zola put the best that was in him, and elaborated the story with the greatest care. It is a tale of Divine Justice, wherein a husband is murdered by his wife and her lover, who, though safe from earthly consequence, are yet separated by the horror of their deed, and come to hate each other for the thing they have done. The book is one of remarkable power, and it is interesting to note that in the preface to it Zola first made use of the word *naturalisme* as describing that form of fiction which he was afterwards to uphold in and out of season. A violent attack in the *Figaro* gave opportunity for a vigorous reply, and the advertisement so obtained assisted the sales of the book, which from the first was a success. It was followed by *Madeleine Férat*, which, however, was less fortunate. The subject is unpleasant, and its treatment lacks the force which made *Thérèse Raquin* convincing.

Up to this time Zola's life had been a steady struggle against poverty. He was terribly in earnest, and was determined to create for himself a place in literature ; to accomplish this end he counted no labour too arduous, no sacrifice too great. His habits were Spartan in their simplicity ; he was a slave to work and method, good equipment for the vast task he was next to undertake. He had long been an earnest student of Balzac, and there is no doubt that it was the example of the great *Comédie Humaine* which inspired his scheme for a series of novels dealing with the life history of a family during a particular period ; as he described it himself, " the history natural and social of a family under the Second Empire." It is possible that he was also influenced by the financial success of the series of historical novels written by Erckmann-Chatrian, known as the *Romans Nationaux*. It was not, however, the past about which he proposed to write; no period was more suitable for his purpose than that in which he lived, that Second Empire whose *régime* began in blood and continued in corruption. He had there, under his own eyes and within his personal knowledge, a suitable *mise-en-scène* wherein to further develop those theories of hereditary influence which had already attracted his attention while he was writing *Madeleine Férat*. The scheme was further attractive in as much as it lent itself readily to the system of treatment to which he had applied the term *naturalisme*, to distinguish it from the crudities of the realistic school. The scientific tendency of the period was to rely not on previously accepted propositions, but on observation and experience, or on facts and documents. To Zola the voice of science conveyed the word of ultimate truth, and with desperate earnestness he set out to apply its methods to literary production. His position was that the novelist is, like the scientist, an observer and an experimentalist combined. The observer, he says, gives the facts as he has observed them, fixes the starting-point, lays the solid ground on which his characters are to walk and his phenomena to develop. Then the experimentalist appears and starts the experiment, that is to say, he makes the personages in a particular story move, in order to show that the succession of events will be just what the determinism of phenomena together with study demand that they should be. The author must abstain from comment, never show his own personality, and never turn to the reader for sympathy; he must, as Mr. Andrew Lang has observed, be as cold as a vivisectionist at a lecture. Zola thought the application of this method would raise the position of the novel to the level of a science, and that it would become a medium for the expression of established truths. The fallacy of the argument has been exposed by more than one critic. It is self-evident that the "experiments" by the novelist cannot be made on subjects apart from himself, but are made by him and in him; so that they prove more regarding his own temperament than about what he professes to regard as the inevitable actions of his characters. The conclusion drawn by a writer from such actions must always be open to the retort that he invented the whole himself and that fiction is only fiction. But to Zola in the late sixties the theory seemed unassailable and it was upon it that he founded the whole edifice of *Les Rougon-Macquart*. The considerations then that influenced Zola in beginning a series of novels connected by subject into one gigantic whole were somewhat various. There was the example of Balzac's great *Comédie Humaine*; there was the desire of working out the theories of heredity in which he had become interested; there was the opportunity of putting into operation the system which he had termed *naturalisme*; and there was also the consideration that if he could get a publisher to agree to his proposals he would secure a certain income for a

number of years. His original scheme was a series of twelve novels
to be written at the rate of two a year, and he entered into a contract with a publisher named Lacroix, who was to pay him five
hundred francs a month as an advance. M. Lacroix would, however, only bind himself to publish four out of the twelve novels.
The arrangement could not be carried out, and at the end of three
years only two volumes of the Rougon-Macquart series had been
published, while Zola found that he had become indebted to the
publisher for a very considerable sum.

The first novel of the series was begun in 1869, but was not
published till the winter of 1871, delay having occurred on account
of the war with Germany. Zola was never a rapid writer, and
seems to have regulated his literary production with machine-
like uniformity. As his friend and biographer Paul Alexis writes :
" Only four pages, but four pages every day, every day without
exception, the action of the drop of water always falling on the
same place, and in the end wearing out the hardest stone. It
seems nothing, but in course of time chapters follow chapters,
volumes follow upon volumes, and a whole life's work sprouts,
multiplies its branches, extends its foliage like a lofty oak, destined
to rise high into the air and to remain standing in the forest of
human productions."

His literary creed at the time he began the Rougon-Macquart
series may be conveniently summed up in a few words from an
article which he had only a month before written in the *Gaulois* :
" If I kept a school of morals," he says, " I would hasten to place
in the hands of my pupils *Madame Bovary* or *Germinie Lacerteux*,
persuaded that truth alone can instruct and fortify generous souls."

In *La Fortune des Rougon*, then, Zola set out to plant the roots
of the great family tree which was to occupy his attention during
the next twenty years of his life. His object was to describe the
origin of the family which he had selected for dissection in his
series, and to outline the various principal characters, members
of that family. Mr. Andrew Lang, writing on this subject in the
Fortnightly Review, points out that certain Arab tribes trace their
descent from a female Dog, and suggests that the Rougon-Macquart
family might have claimed the same ancestry. Adélaïde Fouque
came of a race of peasants who had long lived at Plassans, a
name invented by Zola to conceal the identity of Aix, the town in
Provence where his youth had been spent. She was undoubtedly
an undesirable ancestress, for she was highly neurotic, with a
tendency to epilepsy, but from the point of view of the naturalistic
novelist she offered many advantages. When a mere girl she
married a man named Rougon, who died soon afterwards, leaving
her with a son named Pierre, from whom descended the legitimate
branch of the family. Then followed a *liaison* with a drunken
smuggler named Macquart, as a result of which two children
were born, the Macquarts. Adélaïde's original neurosis had by

this time become more pronounced, and she ultimately became
insane. Pierre married and had five children, but his financial
affairs had not prospered, though by underhand methods he had
contrived to get possession of his mother's property, to the ex-
clusion of her other children. Then came the *Coup d'État* of 1851,
and Pierre, quick to seize his opportunity, rendered such services
to the Bonapartist party as to lay the foundation of the family
fortune, a foundation which was, however, cemented with treachery
and blood. It was with these two families, then, both descended
from a common ancestress, and sometimes subsequently united
by intermarriage, that the whole series of novels was to deal.
They do not form an edifying group, these Rougon-Macquarts,
but Zola, who had based his whole theory of the experimental
novel upon the analogy of medical research, was not on the outlook for healthy subjects ; he wanted social sores to probe. This
is a fact much too often overlooked by readers of detached parts
of the series, for it should always be kept in mind that the whole
was written with the express purpose of laying bare all the social
evils of one of the most corrupt periods in recent history, in the
belief that through publicity might come regeneration. Zola was
all along a reformer as well as a novelist, and his zeal was shown in
many a bitter newspaper controversy. It has been urged against
him that there were plenty of virtuous people about whom he
could have written, but these critics appear to forget that he was
in a sense a propagandist, and that it was not his *métier* to convert
persons already in the odour of sanctity.

La Fortune des Rougon was not particularly successful on its
publication, but in view of the fact that the war with Germany
was barely concluded no surprise need be experienced. Zola's
financial position was, however, by the arrangement with his
publisher now more secure, and he felt justified in marrying. This
he did, and settled down into the quiet bourgeois existence in
which his life was spent.

The next book was *La Curée*, a study of the mushroom society
of the Second Empire. The subject—the story of Phædra adapted
to modern environment—is unpleasant and the treatment is
daring ; but despite a slight *succès de scandale*, its reception by the
public was no more favourable than that of *La Fortune des Rougon*.

La Curée was followed by *Le Ventre de Paris*, which reached a
second edition. It contained some excellent descriptive writing,
but was severely attacked by certain critics, who denounced it as
the apotheosis of gluttony, while they resented the transference
of a pork-butcher's shop to literature and took particular exception to a certain " symphony of cheeses."

Next came *La Conquête de Plassans*, an excellent story, to be
followed by *La Faute de l'Abbé Mouret*, one of Zola's most romantic
books, and the first to attain any considerable success. He next
wrote *Son Excellence Eugène Rougon*, in which he dealt with the

political side of the Second Empire and sketched the life of the
Imperial Court at Compiègne. For this task he was not particularly
well equipped, and the book was only moderately successful.
Then came *L'Assommoir*, and with it fame and fortune for the
writer. It is a terrible story of working-class life in Paris, a
study of the ravages wrought by drink. Again to quote Mr.
Andrew Lang, " It is a dreadful but not an immoral book. It is
the most powerful temperance tract that ever was written. As
M. Zola saw much of the life of the poor in his early years, as he
once lived, when a boy, in one of the huge lodging-houses he
describes, one may fear that *L'Assommoir* is a not untruthful
picture of the lives of many men and women in Paris."

In order to heighten the effect, Zola deliberately wrote the whole
of *L'Assommoir* in the *argot* of the streets, sparing nothing of its
coarseness and nothing of its force. For this alone he was attacked
by many critics, and from its publication onwards an unexampled
controversy arose regarding the author and his methods. Looking
backwards it is difficult to see why such an outcry should have
arisen about such a masterpiece of literature, but water has flowed
beneath many bridges since 1877, and, largely by the influence of
Zola's own work, the limits of convention have been widely extended. At the time, however, the work was savagely attacked,
and to the author the basest motives were assigned, while libels
on his own personal character were freely circulated. Zola replied
to these attacks in a manner so calm and so convincing that quotation may be permitted. " It would be well," he said, " to read my
novels, to understand them, to see them clearly in their entirety,
before bringing forward the ready-made opinions, ridiculous and
odious, which are circulated concerning myself and my works.
Ah ! if people only knew how my friends laugh at the appalling
legend which amuses the crowd ! If they only knew how the
blood-thirsty wretch, the formidable novelist, is simply a respectable bourgeois, a man devoted to study and to art, living quietly
in his corner, whose sole ambition is to leave as large and living a
work as he can. I contradict no reports, I work on, and I rely on
time, and on the good faith of the public, to discover me at last
under the accumulation of nonsense that has been heaped upon
me." This statement is absolutely in accordance with fact, and
when it is realized that the writer of the Rougon-Macquart novels
was merely a hard-working, earnest man, filled with a determination to complete the vast task which he had planned, and not to
be turned from his ideas by praise or blame, it will go far to
promote a better understanding of his aims and methods. It is
necessary too, as has already been said, that the various novels
forming the Rougon-Macquart series be considered not as separate
entities, but as chapters of one vast whole.

L'Assommoir was an immediate success with the public, and
the sales were unusually large for the time, while now (1912) they

amount to one hundred and sixty-two thousand copies in the original French alone.

In 1878 Zola published *Une Page d'Amour*, the next volume of the series, a simple love story containing some very beautiful and romantic descriptions of Paris. Then followed *Nana*, to which *L'Assommoir* was the prelude. *Nana* dealt with the vast *demi-monde* of Paris, and while it was his greatest popular success, was in every sense his worst book. Of no subject on which he wrote was Zola more ignorant than of this, and the result is a laboured collection of scandals acquired at second-hand. Mr. Arthur Symons, in his *Studies in Prose and Verse*, recounts how an English paper once reported an interview in which the author of *Nana*, indiscreetly questioned as to the amount of personal observation he had put into the book, replied that he had once lunched with an actress of the Variétés. " The reply was generally taken for a joke," says Mr. Symons, " but the lunch was a reality, and it was assuredly a rare experience in the life of solitary diligence to which we owe so many impersonal studies in life." The sales of the book were, however, enormous, and Zola's financial position was now assured.

Publication of the Rougon-Macquart series went steadily on. *Pot-Bouille*, a story of middle-class life, was followed by its sequel *Au Bonheur des Dames*, a study of life in one of those great emporiums which were beginning to crush out the small shopkeepers of Paris. *La Joie de Vivre*, that drab story of hypochondria and self-sacrifice, was succeeded by *Germinal*, the greatest, if not the only really great, novel of labour that has ever been written in any language. After *Germinal* came *L'Œuvre*, which deals with art life in Paris, and is in part an autobiography of the author. We now come to *La Terre*, around which the greatest controversy has raged. In parts the book is Shakespearian in its strength and insight, but it has to be admitted at once that the artistic quality of the work has been destroyed in large measure by the gratuitous coarseness which the author has thought necessary to put into it. Even allowing for the fact that the subject is the brutishness and animality of French peasant life, and admitting that the picture drawn may be a true one, the effect has been lessened by the fact that nothing has been left to the imagination. On the other hand there has, since Shakespeare, been nothing so fine as the treatment of Père Fouan, that peasant King Lear, by his ungrateful family. It has been urged that Zola overdid the horrors of the situation and that no parent would have been so treated by his children. By a singular chance a complete answer to this objection may be found in a paragraph which appeared in the *Daily Mail* of 18th April, 1911. A few days before, a peasant woman in France had entered her father's bedroom and struck him nine times on the head with an axe, afterwards going home to bed. The reason for the crime was that the old man two years previously had divided his property between his two daughters on condition that they paid him a monthly allowance. His elder daughter was always in arrear with her share of the pension, and, after constant altercations between father and daughter, the latter extinguished her liability in the manner indicated. Now this tragedy in real life is the actual plot of *La Terre*, which was written twenty-four years before it occurred.

In accordance with the author's usual plan, whereby a heavy book was followed by a light one, *La Terre* was succeeded by *Le Rêve*, a work at the other extreme of the literary gamut. As *La Terre* is of the earth, earthy, so is *Le Rêve* spiritual and idyllic, the work of a man enamoured of the refined and the beautiful. It has indeed been described as the most beautiful book written in France during the whole of the nineteenth century.

La Bête Humaine, the next of the series, is a work of a different class, and is to the English reader the most fascinating of all Zola's novels. It deals with human passions in their elemental forms, with a background of constant interest in the railway life of Western France. The motives are always obvious and strong, a criticism which can by no means be invariably applied to French fiction.

Next appeared *L'Argent*, which is a sequel to *La Curée* and deals with financial scandals. It was inspired by the failure of the Union Générale Bank a few years before, and is a powerful indictment of the law affecting joint-stock companies. To *L'Argent* there succeeded *La Débâcle*, that prose epic of modern war, more complete and coherent than even the best of Tolstoi. And to end all came *Le Docteur Pascal*, winding up the series on a note of pure romance.

Regarded as a literary *tour de force* the work is only comparable to the *Comédie Humaine*. It occupied nearly twenty-five years in writing, consists of twenty volumes containing over twelve hundred characters, and a number of words estimated by Mr. E. A. Vizetelly at two million five hundred thousand.

There can be little doubt that Zola's best work was expended on the Rougon-Macquart series. With its conclusion his zeal as a reformer began to outrun his judgment as an artist, and his later books partake more of the nature of active propaganda than of works of fiction. They comprise two series : *Les Trois Villes* (Lourdes, Paris, Rome) and *Les Quatre Évangiles*, of which only three (Fécondité, Travail, and Vérité) were written before the author's death. Politics had begun to occupy his attention, and from 1896 onwards he increasingly interested himself in the Jewish question which culminated in the Dreyfus case. His sense of justice, always keen, was outraged by the action of the authorities, and on 13th January, 1898, he published his famous letter, beginning with the words *J'accuse*, a letter which altered the whole course of events in France. It is difficult now to realize the effect of Zola's

action in this matter ; he was attacked with a virulence almost
unexampled, a virulence which followed him beyond the grave.
Four years later, on the day after his death, the Paris correspondent
of *The Times* wrote : " It is evident the passions of two or three
years ago are still alive. Many persons expressed their joy with
such boisterous gestures as men indulge in on learning of a victory,
and some exclaimed savagely, ' It is none too soon.' The un-
seemliness of this extraordinary spectacle evoked no retort from
the passers-by." The feeling of resentment is still alive in France,
and it is necessary to take it into account in the consideration of
any estimates of his literary work by his own countrymen. It is a
mistake to attribute Zola's campaign for the rehabilitation of
Dreyfus to mere lust of fame, as has been freely done. He certainly
was ambitious, but had he wished to gain the plaudits of the crowd
he would not have adopted a cause which was opposed by the
majority of the nation. As a result of the agitation, he was obliged
to leave France and take refuge in England, till such time as a
change of circumstances enabled him to return.

On 29th September, 1902, the world was startled to learn that
Émile Zola had been found dead in his bedroom, suffocated by the
fumes of a stove, and that his wife had narrowly escaped dying
with him. A life of incessant literary labour had been quenched.

The reputation of Zola has suffered, it is to be feared, in no small
degree from the indiscretions of his friends. In England he was
introduced to the notice of the reading public by Mr. Henry
Vizetelly, who between 1884 and 1889 published a number of
translations of his novels. The last of these was *The Soil*, a translation of *La Terre*, which aroused such an outcry that a prosecution followed, and Mr. Vizetelly was sentenced to three months'
imprisonment. Without raising any question as to the propriety
of this prosecution, it is difficult to avoid pointing out that Mr.
Vizetelly was singularly ill advised not to have taken into account
the essential differences between English and French literature,
and to have seen that the publication of this particular book in its
entirety was an impossibility under existing conditions. It is
regrettable also that Mr. Vizetelly, who though a gentleman of the
highest character, was no doubt anxious to make the most possible
out of his venture, did not duly appreciate that the word
" Realistic," which was blazoned on the covers of the various
books issued by him, was in the early eighties invariably inter-
preted as meaning pornographic. Presumably nothing was further
from Mr. Vizetelly's wish—his defence at the trial was that the
books were literature of the highest kind—but it is unquestionable
that the format was such as to give the impression indicated, an
impression deepened by the extremely Gallic freedom of the
illustrations. There can be little doubt that had the works been
issued in an unobtrusive form, without illustrations, they would
have attracted less attention of the undesirable kind which they

afterwards received. The use of the term "Realistic" was the more remarkable as Zola had previously invented the word *Naturalisme* to distinguish his work from that of the Realistic school. But if Zola's reputation in England suffered in this way, it is right to refer here to the debt of gratitude to Mr. E. A. Vizetelly under which the English public now lies. Some time after the prosecution of his father, Mr. Vizetelly began to publish, through Messrs. Chatto & Windus, a series of versions of Zola's works. The translations were admirably done, and while it was found necessary to make certain omissions, the task was so skilfully accomplished that in many cases actual improvement has resulted. These versions are at present the chief translations of Zola's works in circulation in this country; but while their number has been added to from time to time, it has not been found possible to include the whole of the Rougon-Macquart series. In 1894-5, however, the Lutetian Society issued to its members a literal and unabridged translation of six of the novels, made by writers of such eminence as Havelock Ellis, Arthur Symons, and Ernest Dowson. These are the only translations of these works which are of any value to the student, but they are unfortunately almost unobtainable, as the entire edition was restricted to three hundred copies on hand-made paper and ten on Japanese vellum.

A charge not unfrequently brought against Zola is that he was a somewhat ignorant person, who required to get up from text-books every subject upon which he wrote. Now there seems to be little doubt that it was in the first instance due to the indiscretion of his biographer, M. Paul Alexis, that this charge has arisen. Impressed by the vast industry of his friend, M. Alexis said so much about "research" and "documents" that less friendly critics seized the opportunity of exaggerating the importance of these. Every novelist of any consequence has found it necessary to "cram" his subjects, but says little about the fact. James Payn, for instance, could not have written his admirable descriptions of China in *By Proxy* without much reading of many books, and Mr. Rudyard Kipling has not been blamed for studying the technicalities of engineering before he wrote *The Ship that found Herself.* It is open to question even whether Mr. Robert Hichens acquired his intimate knowledge of the conditions of life in Southern Europe and Northern Africa entirely without the assistance of Herr Baedeker. Zola undoubtedly studied his subjects, but far too much has been made of the necessity for his doing so. His equipment for the task he undertook was not less complete than that of many another novelist, and, like Dickens, he studied life in that school of a "stony-hearted stepmother," the streets of a great city.

Zola's literary method may be described as a piling up of detail upon detail till there is attained an effect portentous, overwhelming. He lacked, however, a sense of proportion; he became so carried away by his visions of human depravity, that his characters developed powers of wickedness beyond mortal strength ; he lay under an obsession regarding the iniquities of mankind. In dealing with this it was unfortunately his method to leave nothing to the imagination, and herein lies the most serious blemish on his work. There is undoubtedly much coarseness in some of his books, and the regrettable feature is that it is not only unnecessary, but in many cases actually lessens the effect at which he aimed. It is doubtful whether he was possessed of any sense of humour. Mr. Andrew Lang says that his lack of it was absolute, a darkness that can be felt ; Mr. R. H. Sherrard, on the other hand, indicates that his work " teems with quiet fun." On the whole, truth seems to lie with Mr. Lang. M. and Madame Charles Badeuil, in *La Terre*, may seem Dickensian to an English reader, but there is always the Gallic point of view to be reckoned with, and it is doubtful if Zola did not regard these persons merely as types of a virtuous *bourgeoisie*.

It was in the treatment of crowds in motion that Zola chiefly excelled ; there is nothing finer in literature than the march of the strikers in *Germinal* or the charges of the troops in *La Débâcle*. Contrast him with such a master of prose as George Meredith, and we see how immensely strong the battle scenes in *La Débâcle* are when compared with those in *Vittoria ;* it is here that his method of piling detail on detail and horror on horror is most effectual. " To make his characters swarm," said Mr. Henry James in a critical article in the *Atlantic Monthly* (August, 1903), " was the task he set himself very nearly from the first, that was the secret he triumphantly mastered."

" Naturalism " as a school had a comparatively brief existence— Zola himself departed largely from its principles after the conclusion of the Rougon-Macquart series—but its effects have been far-reaching on the literature of many countries. In England the limits of literary convention have been extended, and pathways have been opened up along which later writers have not hesitated to travel, even while denying the influence of the craftsman who had cleared the way. It is safe to say that had *L'Assommoir* never been written there would have been no *Jude the Obscure*, and the same remark applies to much of the best modern fiction. In America, Frank Norris, an able writer who unfortunately died before the full fruition of his genius, had obviously accepted Zola as his master, and the same influence is also apparent in the work of George Douglas, a brilliant young Scotsman whose premature death left only one book, *The House with the Green Shutters*, as an indication of what might have sprung from the methods of modified naturalism. M. Edouard Rod, an able critic, writing in the *Contemporary Review* (1902), pointed out that the influence of Zola has transformed novel writing in Italy, and that its effect in Germany has been not less pronounced. The virtue of this in-

fluence on German letters was undoubtedly great. It made an
end of sentimentality, it shook literature out of the sleepy rut into
which it had fallen and forced it to face universal problems.

One must regret for his own sake that Zola was unable to avoid
offending those prejudices which were so powerful in his time.
The novelist who adopts the method of the surgeon finds it
necessary to expose many painful sores, and is open to the taunt
that he finds pleasure in the task. On no one did this personal
obloquy fall more hardly than on Zola, and never with less reason.
It may be that he accumulated unseemly details and risky
situations too readily; but he was an earnest man with a definite
aim in view, and had formulated for himself a system which he
allowed to work itself out with relentless fatality. The unredeemed
baseness and profligacy of the period with which he had to
deal must also be borne in mind. As to his personal character,
it has been fitly described by M. Anatole France, himself a distinguished novelist. Zola, said he, "had the candour and sincerity
of great souls. He was profoundly moral. He has depicted vice
with a rough and vigorous hand. His apparent pessimism ill
conceals a real optimism, a persistent faith in the progress of
intelligence and justice. In his romances, which are social studies,
he attacks with vigorous hatred an idle, frivolous society, a base
and noxious aristocracy. He combated social evil wherever he
encountered it. His work is comparable only in greatness with
that of Tolstoi. At the two extremities of European thought the
lyre has raised two vast cities. Both are generous and pacific;
but whereas Tolstoi's is the city of resignation, Zola's is the city of
work."

It is still too soon to form an opinion as to the permanent value
of Zola's writings, for posterity has set aside many well-considered
judgments; but their influence has been, and will continue to be,
far reaching. They have opened up new avenues in literature, and
have made possible to others much that was formerly unattain-
able.

NOTE ON THE FRENCH EDITIONS AND ENGLISH TRANSLATIONS OF THE ROUGON-MACQUART SERIES

(The works of Émile Zola in the original are published in the Bibliothèque Charpentier by Fasquelle, Paris.)

1. *La Fortune des Rougon*, 1871. Forty-second thousand on sale in 1911. Translations : " The Fortune of the Rougons " (London, Vizetelly & Co.) ; " The Fortune of the Rougons " (London, Chatto & Windus).

2. *La Curée*, 1872. Fifty-seventh thousand on sale in 1911. Translations : " The Rush for the Spoil " (Vizetelly & Co.) ; " La Curée," translated by A. Teixeira de Mattos (Lutetian Society).

3. *Le Ventre de Paris*, 1873. Fifty-third thousand on sale in 1911. Translations : " Fat and Thin " (Vizetelly & Co.) ; " The Fat and the Thin " (Chatto & Windus).

4. *La Conquête de Plassans*, 1874. Thirty-ninth thousand on sale in 1911. Translations : " The Conquest of Plassans " (Vizetelly & Co.) ; " The Conquest of Plassans " (Chatto & Windus).

5. *La Faute de l'Abbé Mouret*, 1875. Sixty-second thousand on sale in 1911. Translations : " Abbé Mouret's Transgression " (Vizetelly & Co.) ; " Abbé Mouret's Transgression " (Chatto & Windus).

6. *Son Excellence Eugène Rougon*, 1876. Thirty-sixth thousand on sale in 1911. Translations : " His Excellency Eugène Rougon " (Vizetelly & Co.) ; " His Excellency " (Chatto & Windus).

7. *L'Assommoir*, 1877. One hundred and sixty-second thousand on sale in 1911. Translations : " The Assommoir " (Vizetelly & Co.); " The Dram Shop" (Chatto & Windus); " L'Assommoir," translated by Arthur Symons (Lutetian Society); " Drink " (Greening & Co.).

8. *Une Page d'Amour*, 1878. One hundred and twelfth thousand on sale in 1911. Translations : " A Love Episode " (Vizetelly & Co.); " A Love Episode " (London, Hutchinson).

9. *Nana*, 1880. Two hundred and fifteenth thousand on sale in 1911. Translations : " Nana " (Vizetelly & Co.); " Nana," translated by Victor Plarr (Lutetian Society).

10. *Pot-Bouille*, 1882. One hundred and second thousand on sale in 1911. Translations : " Piping-Hot " (Vizetelly & Co.); " Pot-Bouille," translated by Percy Pinkerton (Lutetian Society).

11. *Au Bonheur des Dames*, 1883. Eighty-fifth thousand on sale in 1911. Translations : "The Ladies' Paradise " (Vizetelly & Co.); " The Ladies' Paradise " (Hutchinson).

12. *La Joie de Vivre*, 1884. Sixty-first thousand on sale in 1911. Translations : " How Jolly Life is ! " (Vizetelly & Co.); " The Joy of Life " (Chatto & Windus).

13. *Germinal*, 1885. One hundred and thirty-second thousand on sale in 1911. Translations : " Germinal " (Vizetelly & Co.); " Germinal " (Chatto & Windus); " Germinal," translated by Havelock Ellis (Lutetian Society).

14. *L'Œuvre*, 1886. Seventy-first thousand on sale in 1911. Translations : " His Masterpiece " (Vizetelly & Co.); " His Masterpiece " (Chatto & Windus).

15. *La Terre*, 1887. One hundred and sixty-second thousand on sale in 1911. Translations : " The Soil " (Vizetelly & Co.); " La Terre," translated by Ernest Dowson (Lutetian Society).

16. *Le Rêve*, 1888. One hundred and thirty-second thousand of Charpentier's Edition on sale in 1911. Translation : " The Dream " (Chatto & Windus).

17. *La Bête Humaine*, 1890. One hundred and eighth thousand on sale in 1911. Translation: "The Monomaniac" (Hutchinson).

18. *L'Argent*, 1891. Ninety-sixth thousand on sale in 1911. Translation: "Money" (Chatto & Windus).

19. *La Débâcle*, 1892. Two hundred and twenty-ninth thousand on sale in 1911. Translation: "The Downfall" (Chatto & Windus).

20. *Le Docteur Pascal*, 1893. One hundred and first thousand on sale in 1911. Translation: "Doctor Pascal" (Chatto & Windus).

DIAGRAM OF THE ROUGON-MACQUART GENEALOGICAL-TREE.

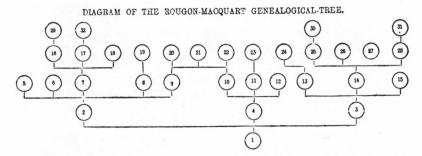

First Generation.

1. ADÉLAÏDE FOUQUE, called AUNT DIDE, born in 1768, married in 1786 to Rougon, a placid, lubberly gardener; bears him a son in 1787; loses her husband in 1788; takes in 1789 a lover, Macquart, a smuggler, addicted to drink and half crazed; bears him a son in 1789, and a daughter in 1791; goes mad, and is sent to the Asylum of Les Tulettes in 1851; dies there of cerebral congestion in 1873 at 105 years of age. Supplies the original neurosis.

Second Generation.

2. PIERRE ROUGON, born in 1787, married in 1810 to Félicité Puech, an intelligent, active and healthy woman; has five children by her; dies in 1870, on the morrow of Sedan, from cerebral congestion due to overfeeding. An equilibrious blending of characteristics, the moral average of his father and mother, resembles them physically. An oil merchant, afterwards receiver of taxes.

3. ANTOINE MACQUART, born in 1789; a soldier in 1809; married in 1829 to a market dealer, Joséphine Gavaudan, a vigorous, industrious, but intemperate woman; has three children by her; loses her in 1851; dies himself in 1873 from spontaneous combustion, brought about by alcoholism. A fusion of characteristics. Moral prepotency of and physical likeness to his father. A soldier, then a basket-maker, afterwards lives idle on his income.

4. URSULE MACQUART, born in 1791, married in 1810 to a journeyman-hatter, Mouret, a healthy man with a well-balanced mind. Bears him 3 children, dies of consumption in 1840. An adjunction of characteristics, her mother predominating morally and physically.

Third Generation.

5. EUGÈNE ROUGON, born in 1811, married in 1857 to Véronique Beulin d'Orchères, by whom he has no children. A fusion of characteristics. Prepotency and ambition of his mother. Physical likeness to his father. A politician, at one time Cabinet Minister. Still alive in Paris, a deputy.

6. PASCAL ROUGON, born in 1813, never marries, has a posthumous child by Clotilde Rougon in 1874; dies of heart disease on November 7, 1873. Innateness, a combination in which the physical and moral characteristics of the parents are so blended that nothing of them appears manifest in the offspring. A doctor.

7. ARISTIDE ROUGON, alias SACCARD, born in 1815, married in 1836 to Angèle Sicardot, the calm, dreamy-minded daughter of an officer; has by her a son in 1840, a daughter in 1847; loses his wife in 1854; has a natural son in 1853 by a work-girl, Rosalie Chavaille, counting consumptives and epileptics among her forerunners; remarried in 1855 to Renée Beraud Du Chatel, who dies childless in 1864. An adjunction of characteristics, moral prepotency of his father, physical likeness to his mother. Her ambition, modified by his father's appetites. A clerk, then a speculator. Still alive in Paris, directing a newspaper.

8. SIDONIE ROUGON, born in 1818, married at Plassans in 1838 to a solicitor's clerk, who dies in Paris in 1850. Has, by a stranger, in 1851 a daughter Angélique, whom she places in the foundling asylum. Prepotency of her father, physical likeness to her mother. A commission agent and procuress, dabbling in every shady calling; but eventually becomes very austere. Still alive in Paris, treasurer to the Œuvre du Sacrement.

9. MARTHE ROUGON, born in 1820, married in 1840 to her cousin François Mouret, bears him three children, dies in 1864 from a nervous disease. Reverting heredity, skipping one generation. Hysteria. Moral and physical likeness to Adélaïde Fouque. Resembles her husband.

10. FRANÇOIS MOURET, born in 1817, married in 1840 to Marthe Rougon, who bears him 3 children; dies mad in 1864 in a conflagration kindled by himself. Prepotency of his father. Physical likeness to his mother. Resembles his wife. At first a wine-merchant, then lives on his income.

11. HÉLÈNE MOURET, born in 1824, married in 1841 to Grandjean, a puny man, inclined to phthisis, who dies in 1853 ; has a daughter by him in 1842 ; remarried in 1857 to M. Rambaud, by whom she has no children. Innateness as in Pascal Rougon's case. Still living, at Marseilles, in retirement with her second husband.

12. SILVÈRE MOURET, born in 1834 ; shot dead by a gendarme in 1851. Prepotency of his mother. Innateness with regard to physical resemblance.

13. LISA MACQUART, born in 1827, married in 1852 to Quénu, a healthy man with a well-balanced mind. Bears him a daughter, dies in 1863 from decomposition of the blood. Prepotency of and physical likeness to her mother. Keeps a large pork-butcher's shop at the Paris markets.

14. GERVAISE MACQUART, born in 1828, has three sons by her lover Lantier, who counts paralytics among his ancestors ; is taken to Paris, and there deserted by him ; is married in 1852 to a workman, Coupeau, who comes of an alcoholic stock ; has a daughter by him ; dies of misery and drink in 1869. Prepotency of her father. Conceived in drunkenness. Is lame. A washerwoman.

15. JEAN MACQUART, born in 1831, married in 1867 to Françoise Mouche, who dies childless in 1870 ; remarried in 1871 to Mélanie Vial, a sturdy, healthy peasant-girl, by whom he has a son, and who is again *enceinte*. Innateness, as with Pascal and Hélène. First a peasant, then a soldier, then peasant again. Still alive at Val-queyras.

Fourth Generation.

16. MAXIME ROUGON, *alias* SACCARD, born in 1840, has a son in 1857 by a servant, Justine Mégot, the chlorotic daughter of drunken parents ; married in 1863 to Louise de Mareuil, who dies childless the same year ; succumbs to ataxia in 1873. A dissemination of characteristics. Moral prepotency of his father, physical likeness to his mother. Idle, inclined to spending unearned money.

17. CLOTILDE ROUGON, *alias* SACCARD, born in 1847, has a son by Pascal Rougon in 1874. Prepotency of her mother. Reverting heredity, the moral and physical characteristics of her maternal grandfather preponderant. Still alive at Plassans.

18. VICTOR ROUGON, *alias* SACCARD, born in 1853. Adjunction of characteristics. Physical resemblance to his father. Has disappeared.

19. ANGÉLIQUE ROUGON, born in 1851, married in 1869 to Félicien de Hautecœur, and dies the same day of a complaint never determined. Innateness : no resemblance to her mother or forerunners on the maternal side. No information as to her father.

20. OCTAVE MOURET, born in 1840, married in 1865 to Madame Hédouin, who dies the same year ; remarried in 1869 to Denise Baudu, a healthy girl with a well-balanced mind, by whom he has a boy and a girl, still too young to be classified. Prepotency of his father. Physical resemblance to his uncle, Eugène Rougon. Indirect heredity. Establishes and directs ' The Ladies' Paradise.' Still alive in Paris.

21. SERGE MOURET, born in 1841. A dissemination of characteristics ; moral and physical resemblance to his mother. Has his father's brain, influenced by the diseased condition of his mother. Heredity of a form of neurosis developing into mysticism. A priest, still alive at St. Eutrope.

22. DÉSIRÉE MOURET, born in 1844. Prepotency of and physical likeness to her mother. Heredity of a form of neurosis developing into idiocy. Still alive at St. Eutrope with her brother Serge.

23. JEANNE GRANDJEAN, born in 1842, dies of a nervous complaint in 1855. Reverting heredity, skipping two generations. Physical and moral resemblance to Adélaïde Fouque.

24. PAULINE QUENU, born in 1852, never marries. An equilibrious blending of characteristics. Moral and physical resemblance to her father and mother. An example of honesty. Still alive at Bonneville.

25. CLAUDE LANTIER, born in 1842, married in 1865 to Caroline Hallegrain, whose father succumbed to paraplegia ; has by her, prior to marriage, a son Jacques, who dies in 1869 ; hangs himself in 1870. A fusion of characteristics. Moral prepotency of and physical resemblance to his mother. Heredity of a form of neurosis developing into genius. A painter.

26. JACQUES LANTIER, born in 1844, killed in an accident in 1870. Prepotency of his mother. Physical likeness to his father. Heredity of alcoholism, developing into homicidal mania. An example of crime. An engine-driver.

27. ETIENNE LANTIER, born in 1846. A dissemination of characteristics. Physical resemblance, first to his mother, afterwards to his father. A miner. Still alive, transported to Noumea, there married, with children, it is said, who cannot, however, be classified.

28. ANNA COUPEAU, *alias* NANA, born in 1852, gives birth to a child, Louis, in 1867, loses him in 1870, dies herself of small-pox a few days later. A blending of characteristics. Moral prepotency of her father. Physical resemblance to her mother's first lover, Lantier. Heredity of alcoholism developing into mental and physical perversion. An example of vice.

Fifth Generation.

29. CHARLES ROUGON, *alias* SACCARD, born in 1857, dies of hæmorrhage in 1873. Reverting heredity skipping three generations. Physical and moral resemblance to Adélaïde Fouque. The last outcome of an exhausted stock.

30. JACQUES LOUIS LANTIER, born in 1860, a case of hydrocephalus, dies in 1869. Prepotency of his father, whom he physically resembles.

31. LOUIS COUPEAU, *called* LOUISET, born in 1867, dies of small-pox in 1870. Prepotency of his mother, whom he physically resembles.

32. THE UNKNOWN CHILD will be born in 1874. What will it be ?

SYNOPSES OF THE PLOTS OF THE ROUGON-MACQUART NOVELS

La Fortune des Rougon.

In the preface to this novel Zola explains his theories of heredity, and the work itself forms the introductory chapter to that great series which deals with the life history of a family and its descendants during the Second Empire.

The common ancestress of the Rougons and the Macquarts was Adélaïde Fouque, a girl who from youth had been subject to nervous seizures. From her father she inherited a small farm, and at the age of eighteen married one of her own labourers, a man named Rougon, who died fifteen months afterwards, leaving her with one son, named Pierre. Shortly after her husband's death she fell completely under the influence of Macquart, a drunken smuggler and poacher, by whom in course of time she had a son named Antoine and a daughter named Ursule. She became more and more subject to cataleptic attacks, until eventually her mind was completely unhinged. Pierre Rougon, her legitimate son, was a man of strong will inherited from his father, and he early saw that his mother's property was being squandered by the Macquarts. By means approximating to fraud he induced his mother, who was then facile, to sell her property and hand over the proceeds to him. Soon after he married Félicité Peuch, a woman of great shrewdness and keen intelligence, by whom he had three sons (Eugène, Aristide, and Pascal) and two daughters (Marthe and Sidonie). Pierre Rougon was not particularly prosperous, but his eldest son, Eugène, went to Paris and became mixed up in the Bonapartist plots which led to the *Coup d'État* of 1851. He was consequently able to give his parents early information as to the probable course of events, and the result of their action was to lay the foundations of the family fortune.

The scene of the book is the Provençal town of Plassans, and the tragic events attending the rising of the populace against the *Coup d'État* are told with accuracy and knowledge. There is a charming love idyll between Silvère Mouret, a son of Ursule Macquart, and a young girl named Miette, both of whom fell as victims in the rising which followed the *Coup d'État*.

Mr. E. A. Vizetelly, in his Introduction to the English translation of *The Conquest of Plassans* (London : Chatto & Windus), points out that almost every incident in *The Fortune of the Rougons* is based upon historical fact. "For instance," he says, "Miette had a counterpart in Madame Ferrier, that being the real name of the young woman who, carrying the insurgents' blood-red banner, was hailed by them as the Goddess of Liberty on their dramatic march. And in like way the tragic death of Silvère, linked to another hapless prisoner, was founded by M. Zola on an incident that followed the rising, as recorded by an eye-witness."

Son Excellence Eugène Rougon.

An account of the career of Eugène Rougon, the eldest son of Pierre Rougon (*La Fortune des Rougon*), who went to Paris from Plassans, becoming involved in the plots which resulted in the *Coup d'État* of 1851 and the return of a Bonaparte to Imperial power. The future career of Rougon was assured ; his services had been too important to be overlooked, and he ultimately became Minister of State and practically Vice-Emperor. He fell for a time under the influence of Clorinde Balbi, the daughter of an Italian adventuress, but, realizing the risk of compromising himself, he shook himself free, and married a lady whose position in society tended to make his own still more secure. The novel gives an excellent account of the political and social life of the Second Empire, and of the cynical corruption which characterized the period.

In a preface to the English translation (*His Excellency*. London : Chatto & Windus), Mr. E. A. Vizetelly states that in his opinion, " with all due allowance for its somewhat limited range of subject, *Son Excellence Eugène Rougon* is the one existing French novel which gives the reader a fair general idea of what occurred in political spheres at an important period of the Empire. But His Excellency Eugène Rougon is not, as many critics and others have supposed, a mere portrait or caricature of His Excellency Eugène Rouher, the famous Vice-Emperor of history. Symbolism is to be found in every one of Zola's novels, and Rougon, in his main lines, is but the symbol of a principle, or, to be accurate, the symbol of a certain form of the principle of authority. His face is Rouher's, like his build and his favourite gesture ; but with Rouher's words, actions, opinions, and experiences are blended those of half a dozen other personages. He is the incarnation of that craving, that lust for power which impelled so many men of ability to throw all principle to the winds and become the instruments of an abominable system of government. And his transformation at the close of the story is in strict accordance with historical facts."

La Curée.

In this novel Aristide Saccard, who followed his brother Eugène to Paris in the hope of sharing the spoils of the Second Empire (*La Fortune des Rougon*), was successful in amassing a vast fortune by speculation in building-sites. His first wife having died, he married Renée Béraud du Châtel, a lady of good family, whose dowry first enabled him to throw himself into the struggle of financial life. In a magnificent mansion which he built in the Parc Monceau a life of inconceivable extravagance began. The mushroom society of Paris was at this period the most corrupt in Europe, and the Saccards soon came to be regarded as leaders in every form of pleasure. Vast though their fortune was, their expenses were greater, and a catastrophe was frequently imminent. Renée, satiated with prodigality of every kind, entered on an infamous *liaison* with her husband's son, a *liaison* which Aristide condoned in order to extract money from his wife. Renée ultimately died, leaving her husband immersed in his feverish speculations.

The novel gives a powerful though unpleasant picture of Parisian society in the period which followed the restoration of the Empire in 1851.

L'Argent.

After a disastrous speculation, Aristide Saccard (*La Fortune des Rougon* and *La Curée*) was forced to sell his mansion in the Parc Monceau and to cast about for means of creating a fresh fortune. Chance made him acquainted with Hamelin, an engineer whose residence in the East had suggested to him financial schemes which at once attracted the attention of Saccard. With a view to financing these schemes the Universal Bank was formed, and by force of advertising became immediately successful. Emboldened by success, Saccard launched into wild speculation, involving the bank, which ultimately became insolvent, and so caused the ruin of thousands of depositors. The scandal was so serious that Saccard was forced to disappear from France and to take refuge in Belgium.

The book was intended to show the terrible effects of speculation and fraudulent company promotion, the culpable negligence of directors, and the impotency of the existing laws. It deals with the shady underwoods of the financial world.

Mr. E. A. Vizetelly, in his preface to the English translation (*Money*. London : Chatto & Windus), suggests that Zola in sketching Saccard, that daring and unscrupulous financier, " must have bethought himself of Mirès, whose name is so closely linked to the history of Second Empire finance. Mirès, however, was a Jew, whereas Saccard was a Jew-hater, and outwardly, at all events, a zealous Roman Catholic. In this respect he reminds one of Bontoux, of Union Général notoriety, just as Hamelin the engineer reminds one of Feder, Bontoux's associate. Indeed, the history of M. Zola's Universal Bank is much the history of the Union Général. The latter was solemnly blessed by the Pope, and in a like way Zola shows us the Universal receiving the Papal benediction. Moreover, the secret object of the Union Général was to undermine the financial power of the Jews, and in the novel we find a similar purpose ascribed to Saccard's Bank. The Union, we know, was eventually crushed by the great Israelite financiers, and this again is the fate which overtakes the institution whose meteor-like career is traced in the pages of *L'Argent*."

Le Rêve.

Written as a "passport to the Academy," this novel stands alone among the Rougon-Macquart series for its pure, idyllic grace. Angelique, a daughter of Sidonie Rougon (*La Curée*), had been deserted by her mother, and was adopted by a maker of ecclesiastical embroideries, who with his wife lived and worked under the shadow of an ancient cathedral. In this atmosphere the child grew to womanhood, and as she fashioned the rich embroideries of the sacred vestments she had a vision of love and happiness which was ultimately realized, though the realization proved too much for her frail strength, and she died in its supreme moment. The vast cathedral with its solemn ritual dominates the book and colours the lives of its characters.

La Conquête de Plassans.

The heroine of this book is Marthe Rougon, the youngest daughter of Pierre and Félicité Rougon (*La Fortune des Rougon*), who had inherited much of the neurasthenic nature of her grandmother Adélaïde Fouque. She married her cousin, François Mouret. Plassans, where the Mourets lived, was becoming a stronghold of the clerical party, when Abbé Faujas, a wily and arrogant priest, was sent to win it back for the Government. This powerful and unscrupulous ecclesiastic ruthlessly set aside every obstacle to his purpose, and in the course of his operations wrecked the home of the Mourets. Marthe having become infatuated with the priest, ruined her family for him and died neglected. François Mouret, her husband, who by the machinations of Faujas was confined in an asylum as a lunatic, became insane in fact, and having escaped, brought about a conflagration in which he perished along with the disturber of his domestic peace.

The book contains a vivid picture of the petty jealousies and intrigues of a country town, and of the political movements which followed the *Coup d'État* of 1851.

Pot-Bouille.

A study of middle-class life in Paris. Octave, the elder son of François Mouret, has come to the city, where he has got a situation in "The Ladies' Paradise," a draper's shop carried on by Madame Hédouin, a lady whom he ultimately marries. The interest of the book centres in a house in Rue de Choiseul which is let in flats to various tenants, the Vabres, Duvreyiers, and Josserands among others. The inner lives of these people, their struggles, their jealousies and their sins, are shown with an unsparing hand. Under the thin skin of an intense respectability there is a seething mass of depravity, and with ruthless art Zola has laid his subjects upon the dissecting-table. Of plot there is little, but as a terrible study in realism the book is a masterpiece.

Au Bonheur des Dames.

Octave Mouret, after his marriage with Madame Hédouin, greatly increased the business of "The Ladies' Paradise," which he hoped would ultimately rival the *Bon Marché* and other great drapery establishments in Paris. While an addition to the shop was in progress Madame Mouret met with an accident which resulted in her death, and her husband remained a widower for a number of years. During this time his business grew to such an extent that his employees numbered many hundreds, among whom was Denise Baudu, a young girl who had come from the provinces. Mouret fell in love with her, and she, after resisting his advances for some time, ultimately married him. The book deals chiefly with life among the assistants in a great drapery establishment, their petty rivalries and their struggles; it contains some pathetic studies of the small shopkeepers of the district, crushed out of existence under the wheels of Mouret's money-making machine.

La Faute de l'Abbé Mouret.

Serge Mouret, the younger son of François Mouret (see *La Conquête de Plassans*), was ordained to the priesthood and appointed curé of Les Artaud, a squalid village in Provence, to whose degenerate inhabitants he ministered with small encouragement. He had inherited the family taint of the Rougon-Macquarts, which in him took the same form as in the case of his mother—a morbid religious enthusiasm bordering on hysteria. Brain fever followed, and bodily recovery left the priest without a mental past. Dr. Pascal Rougon, his uncle, hoping to save his reason, removed him from his accustomed surroundings and left him at the Paradou, the neglected demesne of a ruined mansion-house near Les Artaud, where he was nursed by Albine, niece of the caretaker. The Abbé fell in love with Albine, and, oblivious of his vows, broke them. A meeting with Archangias, a Christian Brother with whom he had been associated, and a chance glimpse of the world beyond the Paradou, served to restore his memory, and, filled with horror at himself, he fled from that enchanted garden. A long mental struggle followed, but in the end the Church was victorious, and the Abbé returned to her service with even more feverish devotion than before. Albine, broken-hearted, died among her loved flowers in the Paradou.

The tale is to some extent an indictment of the celibacy of the priesthood, though it has to be admitted that the issue is not put quite fairly, inasmuch as the Abbé was, at the time of his lapse, in entire forgetfulness of his sacred office. As a whole, the book contains some of Zola's best work, and is both poetical and convincing.

Une Page d'Amour.

A tale of Parisian life, in which the principal character is Hélène Mouret, daughter of Mouret the hatter, and sister of Silvère Mouret (*La Fortune des Rougon*) and François Mouret (*La Conquête de Plassans*). Hélène married M. Grandjean, son of a wealthy sugar-refiner of Marseilles, whose family opposed the marriage on the ground of her poverty. The marriage was a secret one, and some years of hardship had followed, when an uncle of M. Grandjean died, leaving his nephew a substantial income. The couple then moved to Paris with their young daughter Jeanne, but the day after their arrival Grandjean was seized with illness from which he died. Hélène remained in Paris, though she had at first no friends there except Abbé Jouve and his half-brother M. Rambaud. Jeanne had inherited much of the family neurosis, along with a consumptive tendency derived from her father, and one of her sudden illnesses caused her mother to make the acquaintance of Doctor Deberle. An intimacy between the two families followed, which ripened into love between the doctor and Hélène. Events were precipitated by an attempt on the part of Hélène to save Madame Deberle from the consequences of an indiscretion in arranging an assignation with M. Malignon, with the result that she was herself seriously compromised in the eyes of Doctor Deberle and for the first and only time fell from virtue. Jeanne, whose jealous affection for her mother amounted to mania, was so affected by the belief that she was no longer the sole object of her mother's love that she became dangerously ill and died soon afterwards. This bitter punishment for her brief lapse killed Hélène's love for Doctor Deberle, and two years later she married M. Rambaud. As Mr. Andrew Lang has observed, Hélène was a good and pure woman, upon whom the fate of her family fell.

In writing the book Zola announced that his intention was to make all Paris weep, and there is no doubt that, though a study in realism, it contains much that is truly pathetic. The descriptions of Paris under varying atmospheric aspects, with which each section of the book closes, are wholly admirable.

Le Ventre de Paris.

A study of the teeming life which surrounds the great central markets of Paris. The heroine is Lisa Quenu, a daughter of Antoine Macquart (*La Fortune des Rougon*). She has become prosperous, and with prosperity her selfishness has increased. Her brother-in-law Florent had escaped from penal servitude in Cayenne and lived for a time in her house, but she became tired of his presence and ultimately denounced him to the police. The book contains vivid pictures of the markets, bursting with the food of a great city, and of the vast population which lives by handling and distributing it. " But it also embraces a powerful allegory," writes Mr. E. A. Vizetelly in his preface to the English translation (*The Fat and the Thin*. London : Chatto & Windus), " the prose song of the eternal battle between the lean of this world and the fat— a battle in which, as the author shows, the latter always come off successful. M. Zola had a distinct social aim in writing this book."

La Joie de Vivre.

Pauline Quenu (*Le Ventre de Paris*), having been left an orphan, was sent to live with relatives in a village on the Normandy coast. It was a bleak, inhospitable shore, and its inhabitants lived their drab, hopeless lives under the morbid fear of inevitable death. The Chanteaus, Pauline's guardians, took advantage of her in every way, and Lazare Chanteau, her cousin, with whom she fell in love, got from her large sums of money to carry out wild schemes which he devised. The character of Pauline is a fine conception ; basely wronged and treated with heartless ingratitude, her hopes blighted and her heart broken, she found consolation in the complete renunciation of herself for the sake of those who had so greatly injured her.

" The title selected by M. Zola for this book," says Mr. E. A. Vizetelly in his preface to the English translation (*The Joy of Life*. London : Chatto & Windus), " is to be taken in an ironical or sarcastic sense. There is no joy at all in the lives of the characters whom he portrays in it. The story of the hero is one of mental weakness, poisoned by a constantly recurring fear of death ; whilst that of his father is one of intense physical suffering, blended with an eager desire to continue living, even at the cost of yet greater torture. Again, the story of the heroine is one of blighted affections, the wrecking of all which might have made her life worth living."

L'Assommoir.

A terrible study of the effects of drink on the moral and social condition of the working-class in Paris. There is probably no other work of fiction in which the effects of intemperance are shown with such grimness of realism and uncompromising force.

Gervaise Macquart, daughter of Antoine Macquart (*La Fortune des Rougon*), having accompanied her lover Lantier to Paris, taking with her their two children, was deserted by him a few weeks after their arrival in the city. She got employment in the laundry of Madame Fauconnier, and a few months later married Coupeau, a zinc-worker, who, though the son of drunken parents, was himself steady and industrious. For a while everything prospered with the Coupeaus ; by hard work they were able to save a little money, and in time a daughter (Nana) was born to them. Then an accident to Coupeau, who fell from the roof of a house, brought about a change. His recovery was slow, and left him with an unwillingness to work and an inclination to pass his time in neighbouring dram-shops. Meantime Gervaise, with money borrowed from Goujet, a man who loved her with almost idyllic affection, had started a laundry of her own. She was successful for a time, in spite of her husband's growing intemperance and an increasing desire in herself for ease and good living; but deterioration had begun, and with the reappearance of Lantier, her old lover, it became rapid. Coupeau was by this time a confirmed loafer and drunkard, while Gervaise was growing careless and ease-loving. Lantier, having become a lodger with the Coupeaus, ceased doing any work, and as he never paid anything for his board, his presence not unnaturally hastened the downfall of his hosts. Circumstances conspired to renew the old relations between Gervaise and Lantier, and by easy stages she descended that somewhat slippery stair which leads to ruin. The shop was given up, and she again got employment in the laundry of Madame Fauconnier, though she was no longer the capable workwoman of former times. Nana, her daughter, vicious from childhood, had taken to evil courses; her husband had at least one attack of *delirium tremens;* and she herself was fast giving way to intemperance. The end was rapid. Coupeau died in the asylum of Sainte-Anne after an illness the description of which is for pure horror unparalleled in fiction; while Gervaise, after sinking to the lowest depths of degradation and poverty, died miserably in a garret. The tragedy of it all is that Gervaise, despite her early lapse with Lantier, was a good and naturally virtuous woman, whose ruin was wrought by circumstances and by the operation of the relentless laws of heredity.

It may be useful to note here that though Zola states in *L'Assommoir* that Gervaise and Lantier had two sons (Claude, born 1842, and Étienne, born 1846), he makes a third son (Jacques, born 1844), not elsewhere mentioned, the hero of *La Bête Humaine,* a subsequent work in the Rougon-Macquart series.

L'Œuvre.

A novel dealing with artistic life in Paris towards the close of the Second Empire.

Claude Lantier, the eldest son of Auguste Lantier and Gervaise Macquart (*La Fortune des Rougon* and *L'Assommoir*), had been educated at Plassans by an old gentleman who was interested by his childish skill in drawing. His benefactor died, leaving him a sum which yielded an annual income of a thousand francs, and he came to Paris to follow an artistic career. There he met Dubuche, Pierre Sandoz, and others of his former schoolboy friends, and the little band formed a coterie of revolutionary spirits, whose aim was to introduce new ideas and drastic changes into the accepted canons of art. Claude attempted to embody his theories in a picture which he called *Plein Air* (" Open Air "), in which he went direct to nature for inspiration, and threw aside all recognized conventions. The picture was refused by the committee of the *Salon*, and when subsequently shown at a minor exhibition was greeted with derision by the public. The artist was in despair, and left Paris with Christine Hallegrain, a young girl between whom and himself a chance acquaintanceship had ripened into love. They lived happily in a little cottage in the country for several years, a son being born to them, but Claude became restless, and they returned to Paris. Here he gradually became obsessed by an idea for a great picture, which would show the truth of his theories and cover his detractors with confusion. By this time there is no doubt that his mind was becoming affected by repeated disappointments, and that the family virus was beginning to manifest itself in him. Everything was now sacrificed to this picture ; his little fortune was gradually encroached on, and his wife and child (he had married Christine some time after their return to Paris) were frequently without the necessaries of life. Christine was, however, devoted to her husband, and did all she could to induce him to leave the picture, which she saw was increasing his mental disturbance. This was becoming more serious, and in the death of his child he saw only the subject of a picture, *L'Enfant Mort*, which was exhibited at the *Salon* and was received with even more contempt than *Plein Air*. Despite all the efforts of Christine, Claude returned to his intended masterpiece, and one morning, in despair of achieving his aims, hanged himself in front of the fatal picture.

As a study of artistic life the novel is full of interest. There is little doubt that the character of Claude Lantier was suggested by that of Édouard Manet, the founder of the French Impressionist school, with whom Zola was on terms of friendship. It is also certain that Pierre Sandoz, the journalist with an idea for a vast series of novels dealing with the life history of a family, was the prototype of Zola himself.

La Bête Humaine.

A novel dealing with railway life in France towards the close of the Second Empire. The hero is Jacques Lantier, the second son of Gervaise Macquart and Auguste Lantier (*La Fortune des Rougon* and *L'Assommoir*). When his parents went to Paris with his two brothers, he remained at Plassans with his godmother, " Aunt Phasie," who afterwards married Misard, a railway signalman, by whom she was slowly poisoned to secure a small legacy which she had concealed. After Jacques had passed through the School of Arts and Crafts at Plassans he became a railway engine-driver, and entered the service of the Western Railway Company, regularly driving the express train between Paris and Havre. He was a steady man and a competent engineer, but from his early youth he had been affected by a curious form of insanity, the desire to murder any woman of whom he became fond. " It seemed like a sudden outburst of blind rage, an ever-recurring thirst to avenge some very ancient offences, the exact recollection of which escaped him." There was also in the employment of the railway company, as assistant station-master at Havre, a compatriot of Lantier named Roubaud, who had married Séverine Aubry, the godchild of President Grandmorin, a director of the company. A chance word of Séverine's roused the suspicions of Roubaud regarding her former relations with the President, and, driven to frenzy by jealousy, he compelled her to become his accomplice in the murder of Grandmorin in an express train between Paris and Havre.

Though slight suspicion fell upon the Roubauds, they were able to prove an alibi, and as, for political reasons, it was not desired that Grandmorin's character should be publicly discussed, the inquiry into the murder was dropped. By a singular chance, however, Jacques Lantier had been a momentary witness of the crime, and the Roubauds became aware of his suspicions. To secure his silence they invited him constantly to their house, and a *liaison* with Séverine followed. For the first time Lantier's blood lust was not aroused ; the knowledge that this woman had killed seemed to constitute her a being apart and sacred. After the murder of Grandmorin a gradual disintegration of Roubaud's character set in, and he became in time a confirmed gambler. His relations with his wife were ultimately so strained that she induced Lantier to promise to murder him, in order that they might fly together to America with the proceeds of a small legacy she had received from Grandmorin. The arrangements were made, but at the last moment Lantier's frenzy overtook him, and it was Séverine who was struck down by the knife destined for her husband. Lantier escaped without suspicion ; but Roubaud, who was found on the scene of the crime under circumstances considered compromising, was tried, and along with a companion equally innocent, was sentenced to penal servitude for life. But Nemesis was not distant ; Jacques had aroused the jealous fury of his fireman, Pecqueux, who, one night in 1870, attacked him as they were driving a train loaded with soldiers bound for the war. A fierce struggle followed, and in the end the two men fell from the engine and were cut in pieces beneath the wheels of the train, which, no longer under control, rushed on into the darkness with its living freight.

Germinal.

A novel dealing with the labour question in its special relation to coal-mining. The scene of the book is laid in the north of France at a time preceding and during a great strike ; the hero is Étienne

Lantier (*La Fortune des Rougon* and *L'Assommoir*). In a moment of passion Lantier had struck one of his superiors, and having been dismissed from his employment as an engineer, found it difficult to get work, till, after drifting from place to place, he eventually became a coal-miner. The hardships of the life and its miserable remuneration impressed him deeply, and he began to indoctrinate his comrades with a spirit of revolt. His influence grew, and he became the acknowledged leader of the strike which followed. The result was disastrous. After weeks of misery from cold and hunger the infuriated workmen attempted to destroy one of the pits, and were fired upon by soldiers sent to guard it. Many were killed, and the survivors, with their spirits crushed, returned to work. But worse was yet to come. Souvarine, an Anarchist, disgusted with the ineffectual struggle, brought about an inundation of the pit, whereby many of his comrades were entombed. Among them was Lantier, who was, however, eventually rescued.

As a study of the ever-existing struggle between capital and labour the work has no rival in fiction ; the miseries and degradation of the mining class, their tardy revolt against their employers, and their sufferings from hunger during its futile course, these are the theme, and the result is a picture of gloom, horrible and without relief.

Nana.

A novel dealing largely with theatrical life in Paris. Nana, the daughter of Coupeau and Gervaise Macquart his wife (*L'Assommoir*), has been given a part in a play produced at the Théâtre des Variétés, and though she can neither sing nor act, achieves by the sheer force of her beauty an overwhelming success. All Paris is at her feet, and she selects her lovers from among the wealthiest and best born. But her extravagance knows no bounds, and ruin invariably overtakes those who yield to her fascination. After squandering vast sums she goes to the East, and stories spread that she has captivated a viceroy and gained a great fortune in Russia. Her return to Paris is speedily followed by her death from small-pox. In this novel the life of the courtesan class is dealt with by Zola with unhesitating frankness ; there are many vivid studies of theatrical manners ; and the racecourse also comes within its scope. The work was intended to lay bare the canker which was eating into the social life of the Second Empire and ultimately led to the *débâcle* of 1870.

La Terre.

This is a novel which treats of the conditions of agricultural life in France before the war with Prussia, and the subsequent downfall of the Second Empire. It is, in some respects, the most powerful of all Zola's novels, but in dealing with the subject he unfortunately thought it necessary to introduce incidents and expressions which, from their nature, must always render it impossible to submit the book in its entirety to the general English reader.

Its connection with the Rougon-Macquart series is somewhat slight. Jean Macquart, son of Antoine Macquart and brother of Gervaise (*La Fortune des Rougon*), having served his time in the Army, came to the plain of La Beauce, and became an agricultural labourer on the farm of La Borderie, which belonged to Alexandre Hourdequin. He fell in love with Lise Mouche, who, however, married Buteau, and Macquart subsequently married her sister Françoise. Constant quarrels now arose between the two sisters as to the division of their father's property, and in the end Françoise was murdered by her sister. Macquart, tired of the struggle, decided to rejoin the army, which he did immediately after the outbreak of war.

The interest of the book is, however, largely concerned with the life history of the Fouans, a family of peasants, the senior member of which, having grown old, divided his land among his three children. The intense and brutish rapacity of these peasants, their utter lack of any feeling of morality or duty, their perfect selfishness, not stopping short of parricide, form a picture of horror unequalled in fiction. It is only to be regretted that the author, in leaving nothing to the imagination, has produced a work suitable only for the serious student of sociology.

La Débâcle.

In the earlier volumes of the Rougon-Macquart series Zola had dealt with every phase of life under the Second Empire, and in this novel he tells the story of that terrific land-slide which overwhelmed the regime. It is a story of war, grim and terrible ; of a struggle to the death between two great nations. In it the author has put much of his finest work, and the result is one of the masterpieces of literature. The hero is Jean Macquart, son of Antoine Macquart and the brother of Gervaise (*La Fortune des Rougon*). After the terrible death of his wife, as told in *La Terre*, Jean enlisted for the second time in the army, and went through the campaign up to the battle of Sedan. After the capitulation he was made prisoner, and in escaping was wounded. When he returned to active service he took part in crushing the excesses of the Commune in Paris, and by a strange chance it was his hand that killed his dearest friend, Maurice Levasseur, who had joined the Communist ranks. *La Débâcle* has been described as " a prose epic of modern war," and vast though the subject be, it is treated in a manner that is powerful, painful, and pathetic.

In the preface to the English translation (*The Downfall*. London : Chatto & Windus) Mr. E. A. Vizetelly quotes from an interview with Zola regarding his aim in writing the work. A novel, he says, " contains, or may be made to contain, everything ; and it is because that is my creed that I am a novelist. I have, to my thinking, certain contributions to make to the thought of the world on certain subjects, and I have chosen the novel as the best way of communicating these contributions to the world. Thus *La Débâcle*, in the form of a very precise and accurate relation of a series of historical facts—in other words, in the form of a realistic historical novel—is a document on the psychology of France in 1870. This will explain the enormous number of characters which figure in the book. Each character represents one *état d'âme psychologique* of the France of the day. If my work be well done, the reader will be able to understand what was in men's minds and what was the bent of men's minds—what they thought and how they thought at that period."

Le Docteur Pascal.

In this, the concluding novel of the Rougon-Macquart series, Zola gathers together the threads of the preceding volumes and makes a vigorous defence of his theories of heredity. The story in the book is both simple and sad. Doctor Pascal Rougon, a medical man at Plassans and a distinguished student of heredity, had brought up his niece Clotilde (daughter of Aristide Rougon *alias* Saccard) from childhood. Years afterwards they found that they passionately loved one another, but they did not marry, as Pascal, who had lost money, thought that by doing so she would sacrifice her interests. (In this connection it is right to mention that marriage between an uncle and a niece is legal in France, and is not uncommon.) With fine self-sacrifice Pascal persuaded Clotilde to go to Paris to live with her brother, who was wealthy and wanted her to nurse him. Soon after her departure Pascal showed symptoms of a fatal affection of the heart, and after some weeks of great suffering telegraphed for Clotilde to come back. One hour before her return he died. His mother, Madame Félicité Rougon, who feared that his researches on heredity might bring scandal on the family, burned all his papers, and in one hour destroyed the work of a lifetime. A child was born to Clotilde seven months after the death of Doctor Pascal ; a child which he had intensely desired, in the hope that through it might come the regeneration and rejuvenation of his race.

Zola, in an interview quoted by Mr. E. A. Vizetelly in the preface to his translation of *Le Docteur Pascal* (London : Chatto & Windus), states that in this book he has been able to defend himself against all the accusations which have been brought against him. " Pascal's work on the members of his family," says Zola, " is, in small, what I have attempted to do on humanity, *to show all so that all may be cured*. It is not a book which, like *La Débâcle*, will stir the passions of the mob. It is a scientific work, the logical deduction and conclusion of all my preceding novels, and at the same time it is my speech in defence of all that I have done before the court of public opinion."

THE ZOLA DICTIONARY

A

ADÈLE, the girl for whom Auguste Lantier deserted Gervaise Macquart. They lived together for seven years, a life of constant bickerings and quarrels, accompanied, not infrequently, by blows, until the connection was ended by Adèle running away. Her sister was Virginie, with whom Gervaise fought in the public washing-house on the day of her desertion by Lantier. *L'Assommoir*.

ADÈLE, maid - servant to the Josserands, and one of Hector Trublot's friends. *Pot-Bouille*.

ADÈLE, an assistant in the shop of Quenu, the pork-butcher. It was she who took charge of the shop on the sudden death of her master, and subsequently sent Pauline Quenu to Madame Chanteau. *La Joie de Vivre*.

ADOLPHE, an artillery driver in the same battery as Honoré Fouchard. In accordance with a rule of the French artillery, under which a driver and a gunner are coupled, he messed with Louis, the gunner, whom, however, he was inclined to treat as a servant. At the battle of Sedan, before the Calvary d'Illy, where the French were almost exterminated by the Prussian artillery, Adolphe fell, killed by a wound in the chest; in a last convulsion he clasped in his arms Louis, who had fallen at the same moment, killed by the same shot. *La Débâcle*.

ALBINE, niece of Jeanbernat, keeper of the Paradou, a neglected demesne in Provence. Her father had ruined himself and committed suicide when she was nine years old, and she then came to live with her uncle. She grew up in that vast garden of flowers, herself its fairest, almost in ignorance of the world outside, and when Abbé Mouret came to the Paradou forgetful of his past, she loved him unconsciously from the first. As she nursed him towards health, and his mind began again to grow from that fresh starting-point to which it had been thrown

B

back, there developed an idyll as beautiful and as innocent as that which had its place in another and an earlier garden. The awakening of Abbé Mouret to the recollection of his priesthood ended the romance, for the call of his training was too strong for his love. One effort Albine made to bring him back, and it was successful in so much that one day he returned to the Paradou. Again there followed the struggle between the flesh and the Church, and again the Church prevailed. Broken-hearted, Albine passed for the last time through her loved garden, gathering as she went vast heaps of flowers. More and more she gathered, till her room was nearly full ; then, closing the door and windows, she lay down amongst the flowers, and allowed herself to be suffocated by their overpowering perfume. *La Faute de l'Abbé Mouret.*

ALEXANDRE, a porter at the Halles Centrales, where he became a friend of Claude Lantier. He was involved along with Florent and Gavard in the revolutionary meetings at Lebigre's wine-shop, and was sentenced to two years' imprisonment. *Le Ventre de Paris.*

ALEXANDRE, one of the warders at the asylum of Les Tulettes. He was a friend of Antoine Macquart, and at his request allowed François Mouret to escape from the asylum, with disastrous results to Abbé Faujas and his relations. *La Conquête de Plassans.*

ALEXANDRE, a boy employed in the shop known as *Au Bonheur des Dames. Pot-Bouille.*

AMADIEU, a speculator on the Paris Bourse who made a fortune by a rash purchase of mining stock. He went into the affair without calculation or knowledge, but his success made him revered by the entire Bourse. He placed no more orders, however, but seemed to be satisfied with his single victory. *L'Argent.*

AMANDA, one of the singers at a café concert in Boulevard Rochechouart. *L'Assommoir.*

AMÉLIE, a *demi-mondaine* who lodged at the Hotel Vanneau, which was kept by Madame Correur. *Son Excellence Eugène Rougon.*

AMÉLIE, wife of a journeyman carpenter who occupied a little room at the top of Vabre's tenement-house in Rue Choiseul. *Pot-Bouille.*

ANDRÉ (LE PÈRE), an old countryman at Chavanoz, the

village where Miette spent her childhood. *La Fortune des Rougon.*

ANGÈLE (SISTER), a nun attached to the infirmary of the college of Plassans. Her Madonna-like face turned the heads of all the older pupils, and one morning she disappeared with Hermeline, a student of rhetoric. *L'Œuvre.*

ANGELIQUE MARIE, born 1851, was the daughter of Sidonie Rougon, by an unknown father. Soon after her birth she was taken to the Foundling Hospital by a nurse, Madame Foucart, and no further inquiries were ever made about her. She was at first boarded with Françoise Hamelin, by whom she was not unkindly treated, and subsequently went to Paris with Louis Franchomme and his wife, who wished to teach her the trade of artificial-flower making. Franchomme having died three months later, his widow went to reside at Beaumont with her brother Rabier, taking Angelique with her. Unfortunately, Madame Franchomme died a few months afterwards, leaving Angelique to the care of the Rabiers, who used her badly, not even giving her enough to eat. In conse-

quence of their treatment, she ran away on Christmas Day, 1860, and the following morning was found in a fainting condition by Hubert, the chasuble-maker, who noticed her lying in the snow within the porch of the cathedral of Beaumont. Hubert and his wife took the child into their house, and, becoming attached to her, ultimately adopted her as their daughter, teaching her the art of embroidering vestments, in which she became very skilful. Angelique, though an amiable girl, was at first liable to violent attacks of temper, and it was only by the exercise of much patience and tact on the part of Madame Hubert that this tendency was overcome. The girl was always a dreamer, and her cloistered life with the Huberts, along with constant reading of the lives of the saints, brought out all that was mystic in her nature. A chance meeting between Angelique and a young man named Félicien led to their falling in love, she being in entire ignorance of the fact that he was the son of Monseigneur d'Hautecœur, and a member of one of the oldest and proudest families in France. Félicien's father having refused his consent to a marriage, and a personal appeal to him by Angelique having failed, the lovers were separated for a time. The girl gradually fell into ill-health, and seemed at the point of death when Monseigneur himself came to administer the last rites of the Church. Having been miraculously restored to a measure of health, Angelique was married to Félicien d'Hautecœur in the great cathedral of Beaumont. She was very feeble, and as she was leaving the church on the arm of her husband she sank to the ground. In the midst of her happiness she died ; quietly and gently as she had lived. *Le Rêve.*

ANGLARS (IRMA D'), a *demimondaine* of former times who had been celebrated under the First Empire. In her later years she retired to a house which she owned at Chamont, where she lived a simple yet stately life, treated with the greatest respect by all the neighbourhood. *Nana.*

ANNOUCHKA, mistress of Souvarine, and implicated with him in a political plot. Disguised as a countryman, she assisted in the undermining of a railway over which an imperial train was to pass,

and it was she who eventually lit the fuse. She was captured along with others, and Souvarine, who had escaped, was present at her trial during six long days. When she came to be executed, she looked in vain among the crowd for her lover, till Souvarine mounted on a stone, and, their eyes having met, remained fixed in one long gaze till the end. *Germinal.*

ANTONIA, waiting-maid to Clorinde Balbi, with whom she was on familiar terms. *Son Excellence Eugène Rougon.*

ARCHANGIAS (BROTHER), a Christian Brother, who lived at Les Artaud, and taught the children there. He was a coarse-minded man of violent temper, whose hatred of women led him to make the gravest charges against them. He constituted himself a spy on the actions of Abbé Mouret, and was partly the means of calling back the priest's memory of his sacred calling. He insulted Jeanbernat and Albine so grossly, that after the girl's death the old man attacked him and cut off his right ear with a pocket-knife. *La Faute de l'Abbé Mouret.*

AUBERTOT (MADAME ELIZABETH), sister of M. Béraud du Châtel, and aunt of Renée and

Christine. She gave a large sum of money to Saccard on his marriage to Renée. *La Curée.*

AUBRY (SÉVERINE), youngest daughter of a gardener in the employment of Grandmorin. Her mother died when she was in infancy, and she was only thirteen when she lost her father also. President Grandmorin, who was her godfather, took charge of her, and brought her up with his daughter Berthe. The two girls were sent to the same school at Rouen, and spent their holidays together at Doinville. Ignorant and facile, Séverine yielded to the designs of the old President, who subsequently arranged a marriage for her with Roubaud, an employé of the Western Railway Company. For three years the couple lived happily, but a moment of forgetfulness, a trifling lie which she neglected to sustain, revealed everything to Roubaud. In an accession of jealous fury he forced his wife to become his accomplice in the murder of Grandmorin, and it was she who threw herself across the limbs of the President while her husband struck the fatal blow. Suspicions fell upon the Roubauds, and indeed the truth was known to M. Camy-Lamotte, but political considerations made it desirable that the character of President Grandmorin should not be publicly discussed, and the inquiry into the murder was dropped. The domestic relations between the Roubauds were becoming more and more strained, and Séverine became entirely enamoured of Jacques Lantier. In order to free herself from her husband, she persuaded Lantier to murder Roubaud and fly with her to America. The arrangements were completed when Lantier was seized with one of the homicidal frenzies to which he was subject, and it was Séverine herself who fell under his knife instead of their intended victim. *La Bête Humaine.*

AUGUSTE, keeper of an eating-house known as *Le Moulin d'Argent* on Boulevard de la Chapelle. The wedding party of Coupeau and Gervaise was given there. *L'Assommoir.*

AUGUSTE, a waiter at the Café des Variétés. *Nana.*

AUGUSTE, a young swine-herd at La Borderie. He assisted Soulas, the old shepherd, to look after the sheep. *La Terre.*

AUGUSTINE, a young girl who assisted Gervaise Coupeau in her laundry. She was squint-eyed and mischievous, and was always making trouble with the other employées. As she was the least qualified and therefore the worst-paid assistant in the laundry, she was kept on after decreasing business caused the others to leave. *L'Assommoir.*

AUGUSTINE, an artificial-flower maker who was employed by Madame Titreville. *L'Assommoir.*

AURÉLIE (MADEMOISELLE), an elderly friend of Madame Deberle, at whose house she was a frequent visitor. She was in straitened circumstances. *Une Page d'Amour.*

AURÉLIE (MADAME). *See* Madame Aurélie Lhomme. *Au Bonheur des Dames.*

AURIGNY (LAURE D'), a celebrated *demi-mondaine* of the Second Empire. At a sale of her effects, Aristide Saccard bought a diamond necklace and aigrette for his second wife. *La Curée.*

B

BABET, one of the peasant girls of Les Artaud, who came to decorate the church for the festival of the Virgin. She was a hunchback. *La Faute de l'Abbé Mouret.*

BACHELARD (PÈRE), brother of Narcisse Bachelard and uncle of Madame Josserand. He conducted for forty years a boarding-school known as the Institution-Bachelard. *Pot-Bouille.*

BACHELARD (ÉLÉONORE). *See* Madame Josserand. *Pot-Bouille.*

BACHELARD (NARCISSE), a commission agent, whose keen business instincts were not blunted by his intemperate habits. He was a brother of Madame Josserand, and had at one time promised to give a dowry to her daughter Berthe ; this promise he was unwilling to implement, and when spoken to on the subject usually feigned intoxication ; eventually he suggested the somewhat dishonest plan by which Berthe's intended husband was hoodwinked into the belief that the dowry would be duly forthcoming. His *protégée*, Fifi, having compromised herself with Gueulin, his nephew, he insisted on their marriage, and presented the girl with a dowry. *Pot-Bouille.*

BADEUIL (CHARLES) married Laure Fouan, and went to

live at Chartres. He tried commerce without much success, and, haunted by a desire for rapid fortune, acquired a *maison publique* which had fallen into bad repute through mismanagement. Thanks to the firm control of Badeuil, and the extraordinary activity of his wife, the establishment prospered, and in less than twenty-five years the couple had saved three hundred thousand francs. They were then able to realize the dream of their life, and to retire to the country, where they purchased a property named Roseblanche, near Madame Badeuil's native place. M. Badeuil was a handsome man, sixty-five years of age, with a solemn face, and the air of a retired magistrate. He was respected by his neighbours, and held the strictest views on morality. The old couple lived in complete happiness, their only worry being that Vaucogne, who had married their daughter Éstelle and taken over the property in Chartres, was not managing it properly. *La Terre.*

BADEUIL (MADAME LAURE), wife of the preceding, was the youngest daughter of Joseph Casimir Fouan. She was the sister of La Grande, of Père Fouan, and of Michel Fouan, known as Mouche. When her father's estate was divided, she got no land, but received an indemnity in money instead. After she and her husband acquired the establishment in Chartres, she assisted ably in its management. At the time of their retirement to the country, she was a woman of sixty-two years of age, of respectable appearance and an air of religious seclusion. She set a good example by going regularly to Mass, and paid great attention to the education of her granddaughter, Élodie, whom she endeavoured to bring up in entire ignorance of life. She had, however, still a passion for active life, and in busy seasons frequently returned to Chartres to assist her daughter, who had taken over the establishment there. Madame Badeuil received the greatest surprise of her life when she found that her granddaughter, whom she had brought up in the innocence of ignorance, was quite aware of the source of the family fortune, and was ready to take up the work begun by her grandparents. *La Terre.*

BADEUIL (ÉSTELLE), daughter of the preceding, was educated by the Sisters of the Visitation at Châteaudun, and at eighteen was married to Hector Vaucogne, by whom she had one daughter, Élodie. She was thirty years of age before she had any suspicion of the calling of her parents, and at that time she took over the management of their establishment. She proved a capable manager, and in spite of the laziness of her husband, was able to keep up the reputation of the house, though in a few years she killed herself with hard work. *La Terre.*

BADINGUET, a popular nickname for Napoleon III. It was the name of the workman whose clothes he wore when he escaped from the fortress of Ham. *Son Excellence Eugène Rougon.*

BAILLEHACHE, a notary at Cloyes, was born in 1805, and succeeded to several generations of lawyers. He had a large business amongst the peasantry, in whose quarrels he mediated with professional calmness. He arranged the division of Fouan's property between the various members of the old man's family. *La Terre.*

BAILLEHACHE (MADEMOISELLE), eldest sister of the preceding, was born in 1799. She was plain-looking, but good-natured, and at thirty-two married Alexandre Hourdequin, to whom she brought a considerable dowry. She had two children, a son and a daughter, and died in 1855. *La Terre.*

BALBI (CLORINDE), daughter of Comtesse Balbi, was a lady of great beauty, but of eccentric habits. Her position in society being precarious, she determined to establish it by a good marriage, and used every endeavour to induce Eugène Rougon to make her his wife. Having become fascinated by her beauty and charm, he made overtures which she resisted in the belief that he would be the more certain to marry her. He practically decided to do so, but reflection convinced him that marriage with Clorinde Balbi could only injure his prospects of political success. He suggested to her that she should marry his friend Delestang, who was a man of wealth and position, and had expressed admiration for her. Though naturally piqued at such a suggestion coming from Rougon, she consented, and soon after was married. She remained on outwardly friendly terms with Rougon, who was still infatuated by her, but was determined to make him regret the slight he had put upon her. After Rougon's return to office, Delestang, her husband, was, at her request, appointed Minister of Commerce and Agriculture. She had not, however, forgiven Rougon, and privately took a leading part in the agitation against his administration. Having become on somewhat equivocal terms with the Emperor, she was able to secure the acceptance of Rougon's second resignation, and the office of Minister of the Interior for her husband. *Son Excellence Eugène Rougon.*

BALBI (COMTESSE LENORA), an Italian lady who lived in Paris with her daughter Clorinde. Little was known of her past, and it was generally believed that she was in the employment of the Sardinian Government. After her daughter's marriage to Delestang, she left Paris for some time, the eccentricity of her habits having begun to excite remark. M. de Plouguern, who had originally met her in Italy, remained her lover for thirty years. *Son Excellence Eugène Rougon.*

BALTHAZAR, the old horse driven by Madame François between Nanterre and Paris. *Le Ventre de Paris.*

BAMBOUSSE, mayor of the commune of Les Artaud, was more prosperous than the others of his class, as he owned several fields of corn, olives, and vines. His daughter Rosalie having become compromised with Fortuné Brichet, Abbé Mouret strongly urged him to consent to a marriage between them, but this he at first refused, as he would lose the services of his daughter, and Fortuné was too poor to make him any return. He ultimately consented, and the marriage was solemnized by Abbé Mouret. *La Faute de l'Abbé Mouret.*

BAMBOUSSE (CATHERINE), younger daughter of the preceding, was always in disgrace with Brother Archangias on account of her idle habits and her friendship for Vincent Brichet. *La Faute de l'Abbé Mouret.*

BAMBOUSSE (ROSALIE), elder daughter of the preceding. As she had become compromised by Fortuné Brichet, Abbé Mouret urged her father to consent to their marriage, but this he refused to do, though he ultimately consented and the wedding took place. Her child died, and was buried on the same day as Albine. *La Faute de l'Abbé Mouret.*

BAPTISTE, Aristide Saccard's footman. *La Curée.*

BAPTISTIN, a clerk in the employment of Larsonneau, who made him play the part of principal in a scheme whereby he intended to blackmail Aristide Saccard. *La Curée.*

BAQUET (LA MÈRE), a wine dealer who sold the wines of Orléans at a cheap rate. *L'Assommoir.*

BARILLOT, " call-boy " at the Théâtre des Variétés, where he had been for thirty years. He was a little, sallow man, with a shrill voice. *Nana.*

BASTIAN, a drummer in the 106th regiment of the line, commanded by Colonel de Vineuil. During the retreat on Sedan, after the battle was over, he had the misfortune to be struck by a stray bullet. He was removed to an ambulance at the house of M. Delaherche, where he died during the division of treasure of the Seventh Army Corps. The gold coins which the sergeant put into his dying hands rolled on to the ground, and were picked up by a wounded companion. *La Débâcle.*

BATAILLE, an old white horse, which had been for six years in the coal-pit at Voreux. It was killed by the flooding of the mine. *Germinal.*

BAUDEQUIN, a draughtsman who lived on the first floor of the house in which lived the Coupeaus and the Lorilleux. He was a confirmed sponger who was in debt all round, but spent his time in smoking and talking with his friends. *L'Assommoir.*

BAUDEQUIN, the proprietor of a café in the Boulevard des Batignolles, which was the resort on Sunday evenings during many years of Claude Lantier, Pierre Sandoz, Dubuche, Mahoudeau, and their friends, a band of youths devoted to art and determined to conquer Paris. Gradually, however, the little company became submerged by a flood of newcomers, and in time the meetings ceased. The café changed hands three times, and when, after some years, Claude and Sandoz chanced to return, they found everything completely altered. *L'Œuvre.*

BAUDU (M.), proprietor of a drapery shop opposite " The Ladies' Paradise." The business had been in existence for many years and M. Baudu conducted it on such old-fashioned lines that in competition with Mouret's great establishment it was rapidly disappearing. He had acquired it from his father-in-law, and in turn he proposed to hand it to Colomban, his shopman, who was engaged to be married to Geneviève, his only daughter. Baudu postponed the marriage, however, from time to time, as he did not wish to hand over the business in a worse state than that in which he himself got it. Meanwhile Colomban had become infatuated with Clara Prunaire, who ultimately induced him to run off. Geneviève, who was in bad health, died soon afterwards, and before long her mother died also. The business had gone from bad to worse, and, in the end, Baudu lost everything, only avoiding bankruptcy by a complete surrender. Like many of his neighbours, he was crushed out of existence by Octave Mouret's triumphant success. *Au Bonheur des Dames.*

BAUDU (MADAME ELIZABETH), wife of the preceding, was the daughter of a draper whose business she brought to her husband. Her health was broken down by worry, and by anxiety regarding her daughter Geneviève, whose death she did not long survive. *Au Bonheur des Dames.*

BAUDU (CAPTAIN), son of Baudu, the draper. He went to Mexico. *Au Bonheur des Dames.*

BAUDU (DENISE) was the daughter of a dyer at Valognes. The death of her father left her with two young brothers dependent on her, and, the elder having got a situation in Paris, she determined to accompany him. M. Baudu, her uncle, had formerly promised assistance, but when Denise arrived she found that his business was rapidly being ruined by the steady extension of " The Ladies' Paradise," an enormous drapery establishment belonging to Octave Mouret. In these circumstances she could not be dependent on her uncle, and, to his annoyance, she applied for and got a situation in the rival business. On account of petty jealousies, her life there was not happy, and, having incurred the enmity of Jouve, one of the inspectors, she was dismissed on a false accusation. A time of great hardship followed, only lightened by the kindness of old Bourras, in whose house she had rented a room for herself and her young brother Pépé. She next got a situation with Robineau, who had bought a silk merchant's business, and she remained there for some time. While Denise was at "The Ladies' Paradise" she had attracted the attention of Octave Mouret, and, chancing to meet her one day, he asked her to return. As she found that Robineau's business was not prospering, she consented, and from that time her position in "The Ladies' Paradise" was assured. Mouret had fallen in love with her, and she with him, but she had sufficient strength of mind to refuse his proposals. Ultimately he asked her to marry him, and to this she agreed. *Au Bonheur des Dames.*

Madame Denise Mouret had two children, the elder being a girl and the younger a boy. These resembled their mother, and grew magnificently. *Le Docteur Pascal.*

BAUDU (GENEVIÈVE), daughter of Baudu, the draper. She was engaged for a number of years to Colomban, her father's shopman, but in consequence of the state of trade the marriage was put off from time to time. Geneviève ultimately learned that her fiancé

had become infatuated with Clara Prunaire, one of the shop-girls in "The Ladies' Paradise." Her health, never good, suffered greatly, and soon after Colomban's disappearance she died. *Au Bonheur des Dames.*

BAUDU (JACQUELINE). *See* Blanche de Sivry.

BAUDU (JEAN), the elder brother of Denise. He worked for a time with a cabinet-maker in Valognes, but earned nothing, though he learned to carve so well that a gentleman promised to find a place for him with an ivory-carver in Paris. He accepted the offer, and came to the city with his sister and young brother. At first he earned only his board and lodging, and, as he was good-looking and a favourite with women, he made heavy inroads on his sister's small purse. Ultimately, when he did get a wage, he took the earliest opportunity of getting married, inducing his sister, as usual, to give him what little money she had been able to save. *Au Bonheur des Dames.*

BAUDU (PÉPÉ), the youngest brother of Denise. He was a mere child when the family came to Paris, and it was only by the greatest self-sacrifice that Denise was able to support him. When she went to "The Ladies' Paradise" he was boarded with Madame Gras, and after his sister's dismissal he went with her to the room rented from old Bourras, who showed great kindness to both of them. After Denise returned to "The Ladies' Paradise," Pépé again went to live with Madame Gras for a time. *Au Bonheur des Dames*.

BAUDU (THÉRÈSE), wife of Jean Baudu. *Au Bonheur des Dames*.

BAUGÉ, who was the younger son of a grocer at Dunkerque, came to Paris and got a situation in the linen department of the "Bon Marché," where he was able to make a fairly good income. He became the lover of Pauline Cugnot, whom he afterwards married, and, in order to be near her, left the "Bon Marché" and took an appointment in "The Ladies' Paradise." *Au Bonheur des Dames*.

BAUGÉ (MADAME), wife of the preceding. *See* Pauline Cugnot. *Au Bonheur des Dames*.

BAVOUX, a salesman in Octave Mouret's shop. *Au Bonheur des Dames*.

BAZOUGE, an undertaker's assistant who lived in an attic of the same tenement-house as the Coupeaus and the Lorilleux. He was generally drunk and made ribald jests about his dismal calling. It was he who buried Gervaise Coupeau after she was found dead in an attic adjoining his own. *L'Assommoir*.

BEAUCHAMP (FLORE), an artist's model, who lived in Rue de Laval. She was fresh in colouring, but too thin. *L'Œuvre*.

BEAUDOIN, a friend of the Hamelins whom they had known at Beyrout, where he lived. He promised to marry Caroline Hamelin after the death of her husband, but instead of waiting for that event he obtained the hand of a young and rich girl, the daughter of an English Consul. *L'Argent*.

BEAUDOIN, Captain in the 106th regiment of the line, commanded by Colonel de Vineuil. He was educated at Saint-Cyr, and having a fine tenor voice and good manners, along with Bonapartist principles, he was early marked for advancement. With his men he was unpopular, and, not caring for his profession, he did not readily adapt himself to the necessities of war. In the march to the Meuse he lost his baggage, and arrived at Sedan in a pitiable condition, his uniform soiled, his face and hands dirty. In former days at Charleville he had been on intimate terms with Gilberte Maginot, whom he now found at Sedan, married to Jules Delaherche. Their former relations were renewed for the moment, and next day Beaudoin rejoined his company, astonishing every one by the neatness of his attire. At the attack on the Calvary d'Illy he was severely wounded, and having been removed to the ambulance at Delaherche's house, his arm was amputated ; but the hæmorrhage had been too great, and he did not survive. *La Débâcle.*

BEAU-FRANÇOIS (LE), chief of a band of brigands, whose terrible exploits were still recounted in La Beauce. *La Terre.*

BEAURIVAGE (DUC DE), a character in *La Petite Duchesse*, a piece staged by Fauchery at the Théâtre des Variétés. The part was taken by Bosc. *Nana.*

BEAUVILLIERS (COMTE CHARLES DE), a man of dissipated habits, who succeeded to the immense fortune of the Beauvilliers, which he completely squandered in a few years. He was killed in an accident of the chase, some said by the vengeance of a keeper. They found later a document signed by him in 1854 undertaking to pay ten thousand francs to a girl named Léonie Cron. *L'Argent.*

BEAUVILLIERS (COMTESSE DE), an old lady who lived with her daughter Alice in a house in the Rue Saint-Lazare, adjoining the Orviedo mansion. The family had at one time possessed large estates, but these had all gone, and the Comtesse and her daughter had barely sufficient to live upon, though they endeavoured to keep up before their neighbours as much as possible of their ancient state. Having made the acquaintance of Saccard, the Comtesse invested a small sum in the Universal Bank, increasing it from time to time until her whole means were involved. By the failure of the bank she was entirely ruined, and, to complete the catastrophe, Busch, who had become possessor of some papers compromising the honour of her dead husband, took the opportunity of blackmailing her. When she had handed over her jewels to him, she was left penniless. *L'Argent.*

BEAUVILLIERS (ALICE), daughter of Comtesse de Beauvilliers. The extravagance of her father had dissipated the family estates, and she and her mother were left with barely sufficient to keep up appearances. She was plain-looking, and had reached the age of twenty-five years without any offers of marriage. It was, however, in the hope of providing a suitable dowry for her, that the Comtesse invested her money in the Universal Bank, with disastrous results. Alice, who had few amusements, interested herself in charities, and frequently visited the institutions founded by Princess d'Orviedo. On a visit to *L'Œuvre du Travail* she was attacked and robbed of a small sum by Victor Saccard, who was at that time an inmate. Her injuries were severe, and a serious illness followed. The failure of the Universal Bank left her and her mother in poverty. *L'Argent.*

BEAUVILLIERS (FERDINANDE DE), son of Comte Beauvilliers. He was for a time a cause of anxiety to his mother on account of some youthful extravagances, but early settled down, and having received a commission in the Papal troops, served with distinction. He was delicate, however, and died of fever in Rome. *L'Argent.*

BECKER, a jeweller in Paris. He supplied a set of sapphires for the mistress of Comte de Muffat. *Nana.*

BÉCOT, a grocer in Rue Montorgueil. Having become a widower, he took to dissolute courses, and his shop was gradually swallowed up, with its dried vegetables, jars, and drawers of sweetstuff. Eventually the place was sold up, and Bécot died of apoplexy soon afterwards. *L'Œuvre.*

BÉCOT (IRMA), daughter of the preceding. After her father's death she went to live with an aunt, but soon afterwards ran off with a young fellow who lived across the street. She did not remain long with him, but, having a passion for artists, experienced in turn a caprice for Fagerolles, Gagnière, and many others. A young and foolish Marquis furnished a flat for her, and later she occupied a house in Rue de Moscou, the rent of which was twenty thousand francs. In the end she realized her dream of a princely house in the Avenue de Villiers ; the site was bought by one lover, the house built by another, and the furniture provided by a third. But fortune did not alter her tastes ; behind the backs of her serious lovers she still retained her fancy for Art, in the person of Henri Fagerolles, one of her early admirers. *L'Œuvre.*

BEC-SALÉ, *alias* BOIT-SANS-SOIF, a rivet-maker employed in the same factory as Goujet. He drank enormous quantities of brandy, and was a boon companion of Coupeau. On the occasion of Gervaise Coupeau's first visit to the factory to see her son Étienne, Bec-Salé entered into a contest of strength with Goujet in which he was beaten. *L'Assommoir.*

BÉCU, gamekeeper and bell-ringer at Rognes, was a man of fifty years of age who had at one time been in the army. He was an intense Bonapartist, and pretended that he had met the Emperor. Himself a confirmed drunkard, he was on friendly terms with Hyacinthe Fouan, whose poaching expeditions he overlooked. *La Terre.*

BÉCU (LA), wife of the preceding, was on intimate terms with Hyacinthe Fouan. Her chief amusement was to throw Céline Macqueron and Flore Lengaigne against one another under the pretext of reconciling them. Though she was not devout, she made ardent intercessions to Heaven to reserve for her son a lucky number in the drawing for the conscription, but, after the event, turned her anger against the Deity because her prayers had not been answered. *La Terre.*

BÉCU (DELPHIN), son of the preceding, was a strong lad who, on leaving school, went to work as a farm labourer. He was much averse to leaving home, and, having drawn an unlucky number for the conscription, he chopped off with a cleaver the first finger of his right hand, in order that he might be unfit for service. *La Terre.*

BÉCU (MICHEL), uncle of Delphin. He died at Orléans. *La Terre.*

BÉDORÉ, a hosier in Rue Gaillon, whose business was ruined by the extension of " The Ladies' Paradise." *Au Bonheur des Dames.*

BÉJUIN (LÉON), a Member of the Corps Législatif, and a supporter of Eugène Rougon. He was proprietor of the Saint - Florent Cut - Glass Works. " A very worthy fellow, votes straight, never speaks, is very patient and waits contentedly till you think of him, but he is always on the spot to take care that you don't forget him." He received the Cross of the Legion of Honour after Rougon's return to office, and an appointment as Inspector. *Son Excellence Eugène Rougon.*

BÉJUIN (MADAME), wife of the preceding. *Son Excellence Eugène Rougon.*

BELLOMBRE, a neighbour of Doctor Pascal at La Souleiade. He was a retired Professor, sixty-six years of age, who lived in his little house with no other company than his gardener, a man as old and crabbed as himself. His interests were solely centred in himself, and his egotism was a constant subject of irritation with Doctor Pascal. *Le Docteur Pascal.*

BELLOQUE (LE PÈRE), the first art-master of Claude Lantier. A retired infantry captain, with one arm, he had for a quarter of a century taught drawing to the youths of Plassans, in one of the galleries of the Museum. *L'Œuvre.*

BÉNARD, one of the tenants of the house in which Madame Coupeau carried on her laundry business. Bénard and

his wife were of intemperate habits, and few days passed without their fighting with one another. *L'Assommoir.*

BÉRAUD DU CHÂTEL (M.) was the last representative of an old middle-class family. A staunch Republican, he had grown old in the Magistracy, which he resigned at the time of the *Coup d'État.* Since then he lived in retirement in his house on the Île Saint-Louis with his sister Madame Aubertot and his young daughter Christine. His elder daughter Renée, who was educated at a convent, was married to Aristide Saccard, and the circumstances which led to her marriage came as a severe blow to the stern old man. Though on nominally friendly terms with his daughter after her marriage, he never visited her, but when she died he paid her debts. *La Curée.*

BÉRAUD DU CHÂTEL (CHRISTINE), the second daughter of M. Béraud du Châtel, and sister of Madame Renée Saccard. *La Curée.*

BÉRAUD DU CHÂTEL (RENÉE). *See* Madame Renée Rougon, *alias* Saccard.

BERGASSE, a second-hand dealer in Plassans. He supplied the old furniture bought by

Madame Faujas. *La Conquête de Plassans*.

BERGERET (MADAME), *concierge* of the house at Plassy occupied by Hélène Grandjean. *Une Page d'Amour*.

BERLINGOT, a horse which belonged to M. Méchain, and gained the Prix d'Ispahan. *Nana*.

BERLOQUE, *alias* CHICOT, a miner who was killed by a landslip in the pit at Voreux. *Germinal*.

BERNHEIM (LES FRÈRES), proprietors of the glass-works of Saint-Joseph where Josserand was employed as cashier. *Pot-Bouille*.

BERTHIER (MADAME) was a friend of Madame Deberle, and took part in the amateur theatricals arranged by that lady. *Une Page d'Amour*.

BERTHIER, authorized clerk to Mazaud, the stockbroker. *L'Argent*.

BERTHOU, the celebrated painter of *Nero in the Arena*. Claude Lantier took lessons from him for six months, but their ideas were not in sympathy, and repeatedly the master told Claude that he would never do anything good. *L'Œuvre*.

BERTRAND, a large dog which belonged to Sandoz. It barked furiously at visitors, until it recognized a friend of its master, whom it would greet with joyous welcome. *L'Œuvre*.

BESNUS (CLARISSE), an actress at the Théâtre des Variétés, where she played the parts of Iris in the *Blonde Venus*, and Geraldine in the *Petite Duchesse*. She was the mistress of Hector de la Faloise for a time. *Nana*.

BESSIÈRE, station-master at Barentin. He saw the Roubauds in the Havre express on the evening of the murder of President Grandmorin, and his evidence confirmed their *alibi*. *La Bête Humaine*.

BEULIN-D'ORCHÈRE (M.) was a member of a legal family. After being public prosecutor at Orléans and advocate-general at Rouen, he came to Paris as counsellor at the Appeal Court, of which he afterwards became president. His sister Véronique married Eugène Rougon. He was appointed first president of the Court of Paris after Rougon's return to office. *Son Excellence Eugène Rougon*.

BEULIN - D'ORCHÈRE (VÉRONIQUE), a quiet, subdued woman about thirty-six years of age, who lived with her brother and seldom went out except to attend Low Mass at Saint-Sulpice. She married Eugène Rougon, to whom she brought a considerable fortune. *Son Excellence Eugène Rougon.*

BIBI-LA-GRILLADE, the sobriquet of one of Coupeau's fellow-workmen, with whom he was on intimate terms. He was one of the party at Coupeau's wedding with Gervaise Macquart. *L'Assommoir.*

BIJARD, a drunken locksmith, who killed his wife by systematic ill-usage. On the rare occasions when he worked, he always had a bottle of alcohol beside him, from which he took large draughts every half-hour. After the death of his wife, he transferred his cruelty to his little daughter Lalie, who did not long survive. *L'Assommoir.*

BIJARD (MADAME) lived with her husband and their children in the same tenement as the Coupeaus and Lorilleux. She was a hard-working woman who did washing for Gervaise Coupeau's laundry, but her husband, a drunken brute, abused her to such an extent that she ultimately died of injuries received at his hands, or, more accurately, feet. The poor woman, in order to save her husband from the scaffold, said before she died that she had hurt herself by falling on the edge of a tub. *L'Assommoir.*

BIJARD (LALIE), daughter of the preceding, a child of eight when her mother died, had acted as the little mother of the family. "Without a word said, quite of her own accord, she took the dead woman's place, to such an extent that her foolish brute of a father, to make the likeness complete, battered about the daughter now as he had battered the mother before. When he came in drunk, he felt the need of a woman to attack. He did not even notice what a tiny little thing Lalie was; he hit her as he would have hit a grown woman. He beat her shamelessly, he kicked her for a yes or no; and she took it all with a resigned look in her beautiful eyes, without a murmur. Then when her father was tired of kicking her from corner to corner of the room, she waited until she had the strength to pick herself up, and then went back to her work. It was part of her daily task to be beaten." As the result of this infamous treatment the child died, but again the man unfortunately escaped punishment. *L'Assommoir*.

BIJARD (HENRIETTE), second daughter of Bijard. She was five years old at the time of her mother's death. *L'Assommoir*.

BIJARD (JULES), third child of Bijard. When his mother died he was three years old. *L'Assommoir*.

BIJOU, the pet dog of Nana. He excited the jealousy of Comte de Muffat. *Nana*.

BILLECOQ (HERMINIE), a *protégée* of Madame Correur, who induced Eugène Rougon to provide a dowry, in order that she might marry an officer who had compromised her. The officer did not, however, fulfil his promise, but went off with the dowry, of which he had obtained possession. *Son Excellence Eugène Rougon*.

BLACHET, a deputy. He desired leave of absence. *Son Excellence Eugène Rougon*.

BLAISOT, a banker at Paris. *L'Argent*.

BLANCHETTE, a cow which belonged to Lise and Françoise Fouan. *La Terre*.

BLÉRIOT (M. DE), prefect of the department in which Plassans is situated. He accompanied Colonel Masson and the troops which crushed the Republican rising in 1851. *La Fortune des Rougon*.

BLEUZE, a rope-walk at Montsou which was ruined by the miners' strike. *Germinal*.

BLOND (MARIA), a young girl of fifteen who had grown up on the pavements of Paris. She frequented the restaurant kept by Laure Piédefer. *Nana*.

BOCHE (M.), the *concierge* of the large tenement-house in which resided the Coupeaus, Lorilleux, and others. He and his wife were friendly with the various tenants in turn, sometimes siding with one and sometimes with another in the quarrels which so frequently arose. In the presence of the landlord, of whom they were afraid, they assumed an air of great importance, and affected not to know the tenants. They were present at Gervaise Coupeau's birthday party. *L'Assommoir*.

BOCHE (MADAME), wife of the preceding. *L'Assommoir*.

Nana informed Satin that Madame Boche is dead. *Nana*.

BOCHE (PAULINE), daughter of the preceding, was a girl of about the same age as Nana Coupeau, whose companion she was in all kinds of mischief. *L'Assommoir.*

BOCQUET (MADAME), mother of Clarisse. *Pot-Bouille.*

BOCQUET (CLARISSE), a woman on whom Duveyrier squandered large sums of money. She ultimately gained such complete influence over him, and made him so unhappy, that he attempted to commit suicide. *Pot-Bouille.*

BODIN (DOCTOR) was the regular medical attendant of Madame Hélène Grandjean and her daughter Jeanne. A sudden illness of Jeanne made it necessary to call in Doctor Deberle, who subsequently met the older man in consultation from time to time. *Une Page d'Amour.*

BOHAIN (MARQUIS DE), an elderly nobleman whose presence and manners were of a kind to adorn a board of directors, and whose illustrious name was of value on a prospectus. He was in consequence always in demand by new companies. Since he began living by speculation, he and his wife had been legally separated, so far as estate went, and he lived with her only as a lodger, with nothing of his own except his clothes. " On two occasions already he had refused to pay up what he owed ; he pocketed as long as he won, but as soon as he lost he did not pay." At the request of Saccard, the Marquis became a director of the Universal Bank. When the great gamble in the shares of the bank began, the Marquis followed his usual plan ; having played through Mazaud for a rise, he refused to pay his losses, though he had gained two million francs through Jacoby, through whom he had played for a fall. *L'Argent.*

BONGRAND, a great artist, painter of the *Village Wedding.* He was a stout man, forty-five years old, with an expressive face and long grey hair ; recently he had become a member of the Institute and an officer of the Legion of Honour. The grandson of a farmer in the Beauce country, the son of a man risen to the middle classes, with peasant blood in his veins, owing his culture to a mother of very artistic tastes, he was rich, had no need to sell his pictures, and retained many tastes and opinions of Bohemian life. His masterpiece, the *Village Wedding,* had brought about a revolution in art only parallel with

Courbet, and he was acknowledged as Master by all the
artists of the young school.
The picture remained, however, his greatest work,
though he objected to have it
so designated, in the fear that
it might be thought his
powers were failing. A later
picture called the *Village
Funeral* was intended to sur-
pass it, but failed to arrest
attention, and was indeed
only an echo of the earlier
work. He was one of the few
mourners at the funeral of
Claude Lantier. *L'Œuvre.*

BONHOMME, the horse which for
a quarter of a century had
carried Doctor Pascal on his
visits to his patients. Lat-
terly the old Bonhomme became blind, and was no longer
driven, but being much loved
by his master, was tenderly
cared for until his death. *Le
Docteur Pascal.*

BONNAUD, formerly head of
the counting-house of a railway company. *Pot-Bouille.*

BONNEHON (MADAME), sister of
President Grandmorin. She
was married to a wealthy
manufacturer, who left her a
widow at the age of thirty.
In the mansion-house of Doinville, which belonged to her,
she led a pleasant life, not
without occasional affairs of
the heart, but so correct in
every way that she remained
a leader of society in Rouen.
She was a handsome woman,
and in spite of her fifty years
still retained much of her
former charm. Among her
friends she included Chaumette and Desbazeilles, both
officials of the court at Rouen.
Madame Bonnehon had a
good opinion of the Roubauds,
and did not approve of the
position taken up by her niece
Berthe regarding the legacy
left to them by President
Grandmorin. For the honour
of her family she desired
that the inquiry as to the
murder of the President
should not be continued. *La
Bête Humaine.*

BONNEMORT, the sobriquet of
Vincent Maheu. His family
had been miners for generations, and he himself had
worked in the pit since he was
eight years old. After forty-
five years of work under-
ground he was given a post as
fireman, and for five years
worked each night at the
Voreux pit for a wage of
forty sous. He suffered
greatly from rheumatism,
which eventually turned into
a form of dropsy, while his
mind became affected to some
extent by the sufferings

occasioned by the great strike which took place at Voreux and other neighbouring pits. After the terrible scenes at Montsou, he could only sit in his chair before the fireless grate, with fixed and unseeing eyes, but in a sudden accession of madness he found strength to strangle Cécile Grégoire, who chanced to be left alone with him for a few moments. *Germinal.*

BONNET. *See* De Mareuil.

BORDENAVE, manager of the Théâtre des Variétés. He was a coarse man, with cynical views as to the stage, and cared nothing as to the means by which a popular success might be secured. Though he was well aware that Nana could neither sing nor act, he saw that her beauty was of a type likely to attract the Parisian public, and accordingly gave her the chief part in the *Blonde Venus*. It was he who showed H.R.H. The Prince of Scots the honours of "behind the scenes." *Nana.*

BORGNE-DE-JOUY, one of the band of brigands which was led by Beau-François. He betrayed his companions. *La Terre.*

BOSC, an old actor at the Théâtre des Variétés, where he played the part of Jupiter in the *Blonde Venus*, and the Duc de Beaurivage in the *Petite Duchesse.* He had a good-natured but somewhat drunken appearance. He treated women with disdain, and the idea that any man should trouble himself about them raised in him the only indignation of which he was capable. *Nana.*

BOUCHARD (M.), head-clerk in the office of the Minister of Interior. His house was the first thrown open to Eugène Rougon on his arrival in Paris. Later on, Bouchard inherited his father's property, and at fifty-four years of age married Adèle Desvignes. He was appointed head of a department after Rougon's return to office. *Son Excellence Eugène Rougon.*

BOUCHARD (MADAME), wife of the preceding, was the daughter of a respectable family at Rambouillet. M. Bouchard "had been anxious to marry a young lady from the provinces, because he made a point of having a steady wife. However, the fair and adorable little Adèle, with her innocent blue eyes, had in less than four years proved to be a great deal more than a mere flirt." *Son Excellence Eugène Rougon.*

BOULAND (MADAME), the nurse who attended Madame Lazare Chanteau. *La Joie de Vivre.*

BOUM, a horse which belonged to M. Gasc and ran in the Grand Prix de Paris. *Nana.*

BOURDELAIS, an upper clerk in the office of the Minister of Finance. *Au Bonheur des Dames.*

BOURDELAIS (MADAME) was a short, fair woman of thirty, with a delicate nose and sparkling eyes, who had married a chief clerk in the Treasury. She was an old schoolfellow of Madame Desforges. Belonging to a good middle - class family, she managed her household and three children with an excellent knowledge of practical life. *Au Bonheur des Dames.*

BOURDEU (M.), formerly Prefect of the Drome, but turned out of office by the Revolution of 1848. Politically he was a Legitimist, and he was a friend of M. Rastoil, at whose house the party was in the habit of meeting. At one time he was suggested as a likely candidate for the representation of Plassans, but he retired after Delangre had been brought forward through the machinations of Abbé Faujas. Madame de Condamin promised him, however, that through her influence he would be rewarded with a prefecture. *La Conquête de Plassans.*

BOURDONCLE, the son of a poor farmer near Limoges, started at "The Ladies' Paradise" at the same time as Octave Mouret. He was very active and intelligent, but he lacked that touch of genius possessed by his companion, before whom he had bowed from the first. Acting on Mouret's advice, he put all his savings into the business, and, after passing through the various grades, he became in time one of the six persons who assisted Mouret to govern "The Ladies' Paradise," exercising a general control of the whole staff. *Au Bonheur des Dames.*

BOURGAIN-DESFEUILLES (GENERAL). During the war of 1870 he was at the head of a brigade of infantry, of which the 106th regiment of the line, commanded by Colonel de Vineuil, formed part. Like so many other officers he proved himself incompetent, and after the capitulation he, alone among the generals, took advantage of the pretext of illness to sign an undertaking to the Germans not to take any further part in the war. *La Débâcle.*

BOURGUIGNON, a master zinc-worker from whom Coupeau got employment. *L'Assommoir*.

BOUROCHE (SURGEON-MAJOR), of the 106th regiment of the line, commanded by Colonel Vineuil. During the battle of Sedan he installed an ambulance in a factory belonging to Jules Delaherche, where he was soon overwhelmed with work. With untiring energy he performed one operation after another until the place became like a slaughter-house. Behind a clump of trees were thrown the bodies of the dead, and the limbs amputated from the living. Depressed for a moment by the vastness of his task, Bouroche nearly lost heart, exclaiming, " What is the use ? " but his instincts of discipline recalled him to work, and he continued to operate even after the supply of chloroform was exhausted. During the insurrection at Paris he served with the army of Versailles, but consented to treat one of his old soldiers, Maurice Levasseur, who had been mortally wounded in the ranks of the Commune. *La Débâcle*.

BOURRAS, an old man who sold umbrellas and walking-sticks in a tumble-down house which adjoined " The Ladies' Paradise." His business was ruined by the growth of that concern, and he expressed bitter hatred towards Octave Mouret, its proprietor. Denise Baudu rented a room from him after her dismissal from " The Ladies' Paradise," and he showed much kindness to her and Pépé, her young brother. He refused several offers by Mouret, who wished to purchase his lease in order to extend his own shop, and ultimately, having become bankrupt, was forced to leave without a penny. *Au Bonheur des Dames*.

BOURRETTE (ABBÉ), one of the clergy of the church of Saint-Saturnin at Plassans. He did duty as vicar during the illness of Abbé Compan, and had been led to expect the reversion of the appointment. Pressure brought to bear on Bishop Rousselot led to the selection of Abbé Faujas, and Bourrette was put off with vague promises for the future. He was a simple-minded, amiable man, who accepted his disappointment without murmuring, and continued on friendly terms with Faujas. *La Conquête de Plassans*.

BOUTAREL, a doctor who attended Nana. He was a

handsome man, still young, who had a large practice in the *demi-monde*. Always gay and laughing, he was popular with his patients, but took care not to compromise himself with any of them. *Nana.*

BOUTAREL (MADAME), a lady who lived in the country and economized for months at a time, only coming to Paris occasionally. When she came, she made straight for "The Ladies' Paradise" and spent all her savings in an afternoon. *Au Bonheur des Dames.*

BOUTELOUP (LOUIS), a workman at the Voreux pit. He lodged with Madame Levaque, whose lover he became. *Germinal.*

BOUTEROUE (HILARION), second child of Vincent Bouteroue, and grandson of Marianne Fouan (La Grande). The latter had never forgiven the marriage of her daughter, and would do nothing to assist the two children after the death of their parents. Hilarion, who was of weak intellect, was looked after from childhood by his sister Palmyre, who wore herself out in his service. After Palmyre's death his grandmother gave him shelter, but took advantage of his great strength by employing him at work of the hardest kind.

Ultimately Hilarion committed a serious assault on the old woman, and in defending herself she struck him on the head with a bill-hook, inflicting a wound from which he died. *La Terre.*

BOUTEROUE (PALMYRE), sister of the preceding, worked like a slave to support her brother, and died completely worn out by toil and hardship at the age of thirty-five. *La Terre.*

BOUTEROUE (VINCENT), a poor peasant, whom the daughter of the Pechards insisted on marrying despite the opposition of her mother. They both died of want, leaving two children, Palmyre and Hilarion. *La Terre.*

BOUTEROUE (MADAME VINCENT). *See* Mademoiselle Péchard.

BOUTHEMENT PÈRE, a shopkeeper at Montpellier, who sent his son to Paris to learn business. He was disgusted to find that a simple salesman in Paris could earn three times as much as he himself could make, and he was stupefied on seeing the vast emporium in which his son served. *Au Bonheur des Dames.*

BOUTHEMONT, manager of the silk department at "The Ladies' Paradise." Noisy and too fond of company, he was not much good for the sales, but for buying he had not his equal. Nearly every month he went to Lyons, living at the best hotels, with authority to treat the manufacturers with open purse. He had, moreover, liberty to buy what he liked, provided he increased the sales of his department in a certain proportion settled beforehand ; and it was on this proportion that his commission was based. Eventually, however, his position was undermined, and Madame Desforges, having become jealous of Mouret, and wishing to injure him, introduced Bouthemont to Baron Hartmann, who lent him money to start an opposition establishment called " The Four Seasons." This was burned down three weeks after its opening, but the enormous loss was covered by insurance. *Au Bonheur des Dames.*

BOUTIGNY, Lazare Chanteau's partner in the chemical business, into which he put thirty thousand francs. After the failure of the venture, he took over the whole concern, and began to manufacture potash from seaweed by the old methods. He was very successful in this, and by degrees began to employ on a small scale the scientific systems which had before proved disastrous. In a few years he amassed a considerable fortune. *La Joie de Vivre.*

BOUTIN, a retired artist's-model who kept a studio in Rue de la Huchette, which was frequented by Claude Lantier, who went there for purposes of study. A subscription of twenty francs enabled young artists to have the free use of models. *L'Œuvre.*

BOUTIN, an old epileptic attended by Doctor Pascal at Plassans. He died in one of his fits. *Le Docteur Pascal.*

BOVES (COMTE DE), Inspector-General of the Imperial Stud, a tall, handsome man who had married his wife for her great beauty. Notwithstanding this, he carried on a *liaison* with Madame Guibal, whose demands upon his purse were so heavy that he was obliged to economize in his own establishment. *Au Bonheur des Dames.*

BOVES (COMTESSE DE), wife of the preceding, was a beautiful woman of about forty years of age. She was a constant customer at " The Ladies' Paradise," but as her husband kept her very short of money, was seldom able to buy anything. Eventually temptation proved too strong for her, and she was caught in the act of stealing some valuable lace. The matter was, however, kept quiet, and a scandal avoided. *Au Bonheur des Dames.*

BOVES (BLANCHE DE), daughter of the preceding. She usually accompanied her mother on her shopping expeditions to " The Ladies' Paradise," and, it is to be feared, was not unaware of the theft of lace by her. She married Paul de Vallagnosc. *Au Bonheur des Dames.*

BRAMAH, an English horse which won the Grand Prix de Paris. It belonged to Lord Reading. *Nana.*

BRAMBILLA (SIGNOR), a Venetian political refugee, and a friend of Comtesse Balbi. *Son Excellence Eugène Rougon.*

BRÉTIGNY (COMTESSE DE). Auguste Lantier, reading the news from a journal to his friends Coupeau and Mes - Bottes, announced that the eldest daughter of the Comtesse de Brétigny was to be married to Baron de Valençay, aide-decamp to His Majesty the Emperor. *L'Assommoir.*

BRETON - LE - CUL - SEC, one of the band of brigands led by Beau-François. *La Terre.*

BRICHET, the father of Fortuné, Rosalie Bambousse's lover. He was a little man, withered by age, and with a cringing manner. He tilled a small piece of stony land near Les Artaud, and was very poor. *La Faute de l'Abbé Mouret.*

BRICHET (MADAME), wife of the preceding, a tall, lachrymose woman, was the one solitary devotee of the village of Les Artaud. Whenever she had been to communion, she hung about the parsonage, knowing that the priest's servant always kept a couple of loaves for her from the last baking. *La Faute de l'Abbé Mouret.*

BRICHET (FORTUNÉ), son of the preceding, was a largely built, bold-looking young fellow of about twenty-five years of age, who had been the lover of Rosalie Bambousse for some time before Abbé Mouret was able to induce the girl's parents to consent to her marriage. *La Faute de l'Abbé Mouret.*

BRICHET (VINCENT), brother of Fortuné, was the boy who assisted Abbé Mouret in serving Mass. He was an idle young scamp, and constantly incurred the chastisement of Brother Archangias, who predicted a bad end for him on account of his friendship for

Catherine Bambousse. *La Faute de l'Abbé Mouret.*

BRIQUET, a peasant of Rognes. His son drew the number 13 for the conscription. *La Terre.*

BRON (MADAME), *concierge* at the Théâtre des Variétés. She sold liquor to the employés at the theatre. *Nana.*

BRU, an old house-painter who lived in a garret in the same tenement-house as the Coupeaus, where he starved with cold and hunger. He had lost three sons in the Crimea, and he lived on what he could pick up, now that for two years past he could hold a brush no longer. Gervaise Coupeau showed him some kindness and asked him to her famous birthday party. Things having gone from bad to worse with him, he was found one morning lying dead in his garret. *L'Assommoir.*

BRÛLÉ (LA), mother of La Pierronne. She was the widow of a miner who had been killed in the pit, and lived with her daughter at the settlement known as the Deux-Cent-Quarante. A terrible old woman, frantic to revenge on the masters the death of her husband, she was the leader in the outrages perpetrated

by the strikers in the Montsou district. It was she who gave the signal for the attack on the troops, but at the first volley fired by the soldiers she fell back stiff and crackling like a bundle of dry faggots, stammering one last oath in the gurgling of blood. *Germinal.*

BRUNET (LES), a bourgeois family in the new quarter of Plassans, of whom Madame Félicité Rougon was jealous. *La Fortune des Rougon.*

BUDIN (LES), peasants of Rognes, whose daughter was said to have been cured of a fever by Sourdeau, who cut a live pigeon in two, and applied the halves to her head. *La Terre.*

BUQUIN-LECOMTE, a deputy at the Corps Législatif. He desired leave of absence. *Son Excellence Eugène Rougon.*

BURGAT, a blacksmith, one of the band of insurgents which entered Plassans in December, 1851. *La Fortune des Rougon.*

BURNE, an English jockey who rode a horse called Spirit in the Grand Prix de Paris. *Nana.*

BUSCH, a man of German origin who came to Paris, and engaged in business of a shady character on the fringe of the Bourse. " In addition to usury and a secret traffic in jewels and precious stones, he particularly occupied himself with the purchase of ' bad debts.' " 'In pursuit of creditors he was unsparing, and his methods were not infrequently of the nature of blackmail. Jordon, Madame de Beauvilliers, and Saccard himself fell into his power, though Saccard refused to submit to extortion. Another of Busch's lines of business was the purchase of depreciated shares and debentures, thousands of which he collected together, selling them to bankrupts who found difficulty in accounting for real or imaginary losses. His one redeeming feature was his extraordinary love for his brother Sigismond, whom he nursed with the greatest care until his death. *L'Argent.*

BUSCH (SIGISMOND), brother of Busch, the money-lender, was an able man, educated at a German University, and speaking several languages. He had met Carl Marx at Cologne in 1849, and became a contributor to the *New Rhenish Gazette.* " From that time he professed Socialism with an ardent faith, giving his entire being to the idea of an approaching social renovation, which would assure the happiness of the poor and humble." After his master was banished from Germany, Sigismond, engrossed in his dreams, was so careless of his material affairs that he would have perished of hunger had his brother not taken him to live with him. From this time the elder Busch, ferocious as a wolf towards a debtor, looked after his brother with almost maternal care, and was heartbroken when Sigismond died of consumption a few years later. *L'Argent.*

BUTEAU, second son of Père Fouan ; brother of Hyacinthe and of Fanny Delhomme ; cousin and husband of Lise Mouche ; father of Jules and Laure. From early youth he was of violent temper, and having drawn a lucky number in the conscription, he went away from home, and got work, first at the farm of La Borderie and later at La Chamade. He was a true son of the soil, knowing nothing of the world beyond the narrow district in which he was born, and possessing that fierce passion for the land which is the characteristic of so many peasants. When Père Fouan made a division of his property among his family, Buteau was dissatisfied with the lot which he drew, and refused to take possession of it. In this attitude he persisted for two years, until the formation of a new road gave a greatly increased value to his share. In the same way he refused to marry his cousin Lise Mouche, by whom he already had a son, until, after her father's death, she had inherited a share of his property. Buteau's chief anxiety then became to prevent a division of this land between his wife and her sister Françoise, and when, after the girl's marriage to Jean Macquart, this became imminent, he and his wife eventually murdered her. His father had been a witness of the crime, and as his silence was essential, he too was cruelly done to death. After these terrible events Buteau was able to sleep calmly, for the land, his overwhelming passion in life, was his beyond possibility of dispute. *La Terre.*

BUTEAU (MADAME), wife of the preceding. *See* Lise Mouche. *La Terre.*

BUTEAU (JULES), the eldest child of the preceding, who were not married till three years after his birth. At nine years old he was the sole friend of old Fouan, but he soon came to neglect the old man. *La Terre.*

BUTEAU (LAURE), the second child of the Buteaus. At four years old she had already the hard eyes of her family, and was hostile to her grandfather, old Fouan. By jealousy she detached from him her brother Jules. *La Terre.*

C

CABASSE, a franc-tireur of the woods of Dieulet. He was the favourite companion of Ducat, and along with Guillaume Sambuc formed part of the band which so greatly embarrassed the Prussians in the neighbourhood of Sedan. He took part in the execution of Goliath Steinberg, the German spy. *La Débâcle.*

CABIN (MADAME), the woman who looked after the bedrooms occupied by the saleswomen in "The Ladies' Paradise." In consideration of small bribes, she allowed numerous breaches of the strict rules of the establishment. *Au Bonheur des Dames.*

CABIROCHE (SIMONNE), an actress at the Théâtre des Variétés. She was the daughter of a furniture dealer in the Faubourg Saint-Antoine, and had been educated at a boarding-school in order that she might become a governess. She played the part of Isabelle in the *Petite Duchesse*. *Nana*.

CABUCHE, a quarryman at Bécourt, who lived alone in a hut in the middle of the forest. He was condemned to five years' imprisonment for having killed a man in a tavern brawl, but on account of his good conduct was liberated at the end of four years. From that time he was avoided by every one, and lived like a savage in the woods. Louisette, the younger daughter of Madame Misard, who was then fourteen years old, met him one day in the forest, and a strange friendship was formed between them, the rough man almost adoring this child, who alone was not afraid to speak to him. The girl afterwards went as a servant to Madame Bonnehon, but one evening Cabuche found her at his door, half mad with fright and on the verge of brain fever. He nursed her tenderly, but she died a few days later. The conduct of President Grandmorin was believed to be the cause of Louisette's flight from Doinville, and Cabuche was overheard to say in ungovernable rage that he would " bleed the pig." This remark led Denizet, the examining magistrate, to attribute to him the murder of the President, which was committed soon afterwards by the Roubauds, and still later he had the misfortune to be found beside the body of Séverine Roubaud, who had been murdered by Jacques Lantier. He was found guilty of the two crimes, neither of which he committed, and was sentenced to imprisonment for life. It was Cabuche's wagon, loaded with huge blocks of stone, that Flore stopped in front of an express train in order to cause an accident. *La Bête Humaine*.

CADET-CASSIS, the sobriquet of Coupeau. *L'Assommoir*.

CADINE, a young girl who when only two years old was found by Madame Chantemesse and adopted by her. She was brought up along with Marjolin, and the two became inseparable companions and lovers. When she was eleven years old she set up as a dealer in birds' food, but in a year or two became a flowerseller. After the accident to Marjolin by which his intellect was affected, Cadine looked after him, and the two were seldom found apart. *Le Ventre de Paris.*

CAFFIN (ABBÉ), the predecessor of Abbé Mouret as *curé* at Les Artaud. He was originally from Normandy, and had a large face which always seemed laughing. His history was bad, and he had been sent in disgrace to this hot and dusty corner of Provençe. *La Faute de l'Abbé Mouret.*

CAMPARDON (ACHILLE), an architect, in whose house Octave Mouret boarded when he first came to Paris. His views on religion were somewhat free, but having been appointed diocesan architect he gradually became orthodox, though this did not prevent him from carrying on an intrigue with Gasparine, his wife's cousin, who ultimately came to live with the family. *Pot-Bouille.*

CAMPARDON (MADAME), wife of the preceding, *née* Rose Domergue. Born at Plassans, she was an old friend of Madame Mouret, and when Octave Mouret came to Paris he boarded with the Campardons. After the birth of her child, Madame Campardon was an invalid, and was obliged to spend much of her

D

time in bed, amusing herself by reading the works of Dickens. She tacitly accepted the *liaison* between her husband and Gasparine her cousin, whom she ultimately asked to live with the family and manage the household affairs. *Pot-Bouille.*

CAMPARDON (ANGÈLE), daughter of the preceding. She was brought up at home by her parents, in order that she might remain ignorant of the realities of life, but intercourse with the servants in a large tenement - house early developed her unnatural precocity. *Pot Bouille.*

CAMPENON, an incapable person to whom M. de Marsy gave a post as prefect, which Eugène Rougon had promised to Du Poizat. *Son Excellence Eugène Rougon.*

CAMY-LAMOTTE, secretary to the Minister of Justice, an office of great influence. It was his duty to prepare the list of promotions, and he was in constant communication with the Tuileries. He was a handsome man, who started his career as a substitute ; but through his connections and his wife he had been elected deputy and made grand officer of the Legion of Honour. In examining the papers of President Grandmorin, he discovered the identity of the murderers, but knowing the probability of serious scandal arising in the event of public inquiry, he said nothing, and later, struck by the courage and charm of Séverine Roubaud, who threw herself on his protection, he gave instructions that all proceedings were to be stopped. He rewarded Denizet, the examining magistrate, with a decoration and the promise of early promotion. *La Bête Humaine.*

CANIVET, an old peasant, of whom Zéphyrin Lacour announced the death to Rosalie Pichon. *Une Page d'Amour.*

CARNAVANT (MARQUIS DE), a nobleman of Plassans. Said to have been intimate with the mother of Félicité Puech during the early period of her married life. He visited Pierre Rougon and his wife occasionally, and after their retirement from business he interested them in politics. *La Fortune des Rougon.*

CAROLINE, an artificial-flower maker employed by Madame Titreville. She was very unhappy at home. *L'Assommoir.*

CAROLINE (MADAME). *See* Caroline Hamelin.

CAROUBLE, a baker at Montsou. His business was threatened by the competition of Maigrat. *Germinal.*

CASIMIR, a liquor-dealer on the road to Montsou. *Germinal.*

CASSOUTE, an inhabitant of Plassans, who formed one of the group of insurgents which accompanied Antoine Macquart to the Rougon's house. He was left there to signal the return of Pierre Rougon, but not being very intelligent, allowed himself to be sent by Rougon to the Town Hall, where he was arrested. *La Fortune des Rougon.*

CATHERINE, servant to Granoux. She talked for a long time before letting in Pierre Rougon and Roudier, who came to seek her master to save Plassans. *La Fortune des Rougon.*

CAUCHE, the commissary of police attached to the railway station at Havre. He was a former officer who considered his present occupation as practically a sinecure, spending much of his time at the café. He was a confirmed gambler, who could lose or win without change of expression. A room on the first floor of the Café du Commerce was his usual haunt, and there Roubaud frequently spent half the night playing cards with him. Later, it fell to him to arrest Roubaud on the charge of murdering President Grandmorin. *La Bête Humaine.*

CAZENOVE (DOCTOR), a man of fifty-four years of age, of a vigorous and lean habit, who after thirty years' service in the navy settled down at Arromanches, where an uncle of his had left him a house. He affected scepticism of the power of medicine, but was unremitting in the care of his patients. Among the earliest of these was Madame Chanteau, and he became on intimate terms with the family, for some time acting as trustee to Pauline Quenu. *La Joie de Vivre.*

CÉCILE (MADEMOISELLE), daughter of a butcher in the neighbourhood of the *Halles Centrales. Le Ventre de Paris.*

CELESTE, lady's maid and confidante of Madame Renée Saccard. *La Curée.*

CÉLESTINE, a friend of Clemence. She was neurotic, and had a horror of the hair of cats, seeing it everywhere, and even turning her tongue in the belief that some of it had got into her mouth. *L'Assommoir.*

CESAR, a bull at the farm of La Borderie. *La Terre.*

CHADEUIL (MADAME), a milliner in the Rue Sainte-Anne. Octave Mouret's shop, *Au Bonheur des Dames,* ruined her within two years. *Au Bonheur des Dames.*

CHAÎNE, the companion of Mahoudeau, the sculptor. He was born at Saint-Firmin, a village about six miles from Plassans, where he served as a cowboy until he was drawn in the conscription. Unfortunately for him, a gentleman of the district who admired the walking-stick handles which he carved out of roots with his knife, persuaded Chaîne that he was a rustic genius, and with extreme foolishness persuaded him to go in for painting. Having got from his father a sum of forty pounds, he went to Paris, where his small fortune lasted him for a year. Then, as he had only twenty francs left, he took up his quarters with his friend Mahoudeau. He had no talent, but had a certain skill in copying pictures with extreme exactness. The relations of Chaîne and Mahoudeau with Mathilde Jabouille led to a coldness between the two friends, and ultimately they ceased to be on speaking terms, though they continued to live together, and even to sleep in the same bed. Some time afterwards Chaîne gave up art, and started a booth at country fairs, in which he ran a wheel-of-fortune for trifling prizes. The booth was decorated with some of his alleged master-pieces. *L'Œuvre.*

CHAMBOUVARD, a celebrated sculptor. He was said to be the son of a veterinary surgeon of Amiens, and at forty-five had already produced twenty masterpieces. He had, however, a complete lack of critical acumen, and was unable to distinguish between the most glorious offspring of his hands and the detestably grotesque figures which he happened to put together now and then. At one *Salon* he exhibited a *Sower*, admirable in every way, while at another he showed an execrable *Reaping Woman*, so bad that it seemed like a hoax ; but he was no less pleased with the later work, feeling sure that he had turned out yet another masterpiece. *L'Œuvre.*

CHAMPION, a master hatter at Montrouge. Auguste Lantier pretended to have left his employment because they had

not the same political views. *L'Assommoir.*

CHAMPION, a retired sergeant, who was afterwards delivery manager at "The Ladies' Paradise." *Au Bonheur des Dames.*

CHANTEAU PÈRE came originally from the south of France, beginning his life as a journeyman carpenter. He created a considerable timber business at Caen, but being somewhat daring in his speculation, he left it rather embarrassed at the time of his death. *La Joie de Vivre.*

CHANTEAU (M.), a cousin of M. Quenu, by whom he was nominated guardian of his daughter Pauline Quenu. On the death of his father, he succeeded to a timber business at Caen. Being an inactive man, unaspiring and careful, he contented himself with putting his affairs on a safe basis, and living on a moderate but sure profit. He married Eugénie de la Vignière, who was an ambitious woman and hoped to rouse his indolent nature. Her schemes were, however, frustrated by the ill-health of her husband, who suffered from gout to such a degree that he ultimately sold his business to Devoine, and retired to Bonneville, where he had a house. His sufferings from gout gradually became more and more severe until he was a complete invalid. His ward Pauline Quenu showed him much kindness, and the Abbé Horteur played draughts with him regularly. *La Joie de Vivre.*

Until the end of his life he was taken care of by Pauline. *Le Docteur Pascal.*

CHANTEAU (MADAME), wife of the preceding, *née* Eugénie de la Vignière, was the orphan daughter of one of the ruined squireens of the Cotentin. An ambitious woman, she hoped to induce her husband to overcome his indolent nature, but her plans were upset by the ill-health into which he fell, and she transferred to her son her hopes for the family's rise in life. From this source she had nothing but disappointment, as one after another of Lazare's schemes failed. To enable him to get money to start his chemical works, she encouraged the idea of marriage between him and Pauline Quenu, her husband's ward, who thereupon lent him thirty thousand francs. Little by little, Madame Chanteau got possession for the family use of nearly all Pauline's fortune,

but with each fresh loan her feelings towards the girl became more embittered until her affection for her had turned to hate. From this time, she discouraged her son's marriage with Pauline, and endeavoured to turn his thoughts towards Louise Thibaudier, who had a considerable fortune. She died of dropsy after a short illness. *La Joie de Vivre.*

CHANTEAU (LAZARE), born 1844, son of M. Chanteau, was educated at the college of Caen, where he took his bachelor's degree. He was undecided as to what profession he would adopt, and for some time his inclination turned towards music. Under the influence of Pauline Quenu he decided on medicine, and went to Paris, where at first he made good progress in his studies. Unfortunately he tired of this, and led a life of extravagance and dissipation, failing to pass his examinations. Having chanced to make the acquaintance of Herbelin, a celebrated chemist, Lazare entered his laboratory as an assistant. From him he got the idea of turning seaweed to profitable account by the extraction of chemicals by a new method. With a view to the commercial employment of this process he borrowed thirty thousand francs from Pauline Quenu, and entered into partnership with an old college friend named Boutigny who invested a similar sum in the business. Lazare was quite carried away by his enthusiasm, and the works were built on much too large a scale, the cost greatly exceeding the original estimates. More money was required, and a marriage having already been arranged between Lazare and Pauline Quenu, she at once lent him another ten thousand francs. Some slight success was at first attained, but this only led to fresh extravagances in the way of apparatus, and before long a hundred thousand francs of Pauline's money had been expended. By this time it was evident that the process could not be worked on a commercial scale, and Lazare, utterly discouraged, handed over his share to Boutigny for a trifling sum. A scheme for the protection of Bonneville against the inroads of the sea was the next subject to attract him, and he entered into it with his usual enthusiasm. More money was, of course, required, and, as before, this was found by Pauline. Failure again met his efforts ; the barricade was washed away by the first high sea. All along Lazare had been subject to fits of morbid depression, accompanied by a frenzied fear of death, and after the death of his mother this mental disturbance became even more acute. The marriage with Pauline had been put off on one excuse or another, and ultimately she saw that his affections had been transferred to Louise Thibaudier. With noble self-sacrifice, she released him from his engagement, and his marriage to Louise followed. He went to Paris as manager of an insurance company, but soon tiring of business, he returned to Bonneville, where he lived so tormented by the fear of death that life itself had little charm for him. *La Joie de Vivre.*

Having become a widower, he left his son with Pauline Quenu, and went to America to seek his fortune. *Le Docteur Pascal.*

CHANTEAU (MADAME LAZARE), wife of the preceding. *See* Louise Thibaudier. *La Joie de Vivre.*

CHANTEAU (PAUL), the infant

son of Lazare Chanteau. *La Joie de Vivre.*

CHANTECAILLE (i.e. SINGSMALL), an usher at the college of Plassans. He was so good-natured that he allowed the pupils to smoke when out walking. *L'Œuvre.*

CHANTEGREIL, a poacher, who was sent to the galleys for shooting a gendarme. He was the father of Miette. *La Fortune des Rougon.*

CHANTEGREIL (MARIE), known as Miette, born 1838, daughter of Chantegreil, the poacher, who was sentenced to the galleys for murder. She went to live with her aunt, the wife of Rebufat, farmer at Plassans. Here she met Silvère Mouret, and an idyllic love affair followed. When Silvère joined the Republican Insurrection in 1851, Miette, fired by his enthusiasm, accompanied him, and carried the banner of revolt. In the attack by the regular troops, which soon followed, she fell mortally wounded. *La Fortune des Rougon.*

CHANTEGREIL (EULALIE). *See* Madame Eulalie Rebufat.

CHANTEMESSE (MADAME), a customer of Madame François, the market-gardener. It was she who brought up the two foundling children, Marjolin and Cadine. *Le Ventre de Paris.*

CHANTEREAU (MADAME), wife of an ironmaster. She was a cousin of the Fougerays, and a friend of the Muffats. With Madame du Joncquoy and Madame Hugon she gave an air of severe respectability to the drawing-room of Comtesse Sabine de Muffat. Her husband owned a foundry in Alsace, where war with Germany was feared, and she caused much amusement to her friends by expressing the opinion that Bismarck would make war with France and would conquer. *Nana.*

CHARBONNEL (M.), a retired oil-merchant of Plassans. His cousin Chevassu, a lawyer, died leaving his fortune of five hundred thousand francs to the Sisters of the Holy Family. Charbonnel, being next heir, contested the will on the ground of undue influence; and the Sisterhood having petitioned the Council of State to authorize the payment of the bequest to them, he went to Paris, accompanied by his wife, in order to secure the influence of Eugène Rougon. The matter dragged on for some months, and was then indefinitely delayed by Rougon's resignation of the Presidency of the Council of State. After Rougon's appointment as Minister of the Interior, he induced the Council of State to refuse the petition of the Sisterhood, and M. Charbonnel accordingly succeeded to the estate. Subsequently the Charbonnels accused the Sisters of having removed some of Chevassu's silver plate, and Rougon ordered the police to make a search in the convent. This caused a scandal in the town, and brought the Charbonnels, as well as Rougon, into popular disfavour. *Son Excellence Eugène Rougon.*

CHARBONNEL (MADAME), wife of the preceding. She accompanied her husband to Paris to assist him in looking after their interests in the estate of his cousin Chevassu. *Son Excellence Eugène Rougon.*

CHARDON (ABBÉ), the candidate favoured by Abbé Fenil for the vacancy in the church of Saint-Saturnin at Plassans. *La Conquête de Plassans.*

CHARDON (MADAME), a *protégée* of Madame Mélanie Correur. The State having refused to accept some furnishings supplied by her, Eugène Rougon, the Minister, arranged the

matter. *Son Excellence Eugène Rougon.*

CHARLES, a waiter at the Café Riche. It was he who served supper to Maxime Saccard and Renée in the White Salon. *La Curée.*

CHARLES, the attendant at the public washing-house where Gervaise Macquart had her great fight with Virginie. *L'Assommoir.*

CHARLES, a butcher whose shop was in Rue Polonceau. The Coupeaus dealt with him. *L'Assommoir.*

CHARLES, coachman in the service of Nana. He left her after a violent scene, in the course of which he called her a slut. *Nana.*

CHARLES, a cousin of the little soldier Jules from Plogof. *Germinal.*

CHARLES, coachman to Aristide Saccard. He was discovered stealing oats, and was dismissed. In revenge, he disclosed to Madame Caroline the relations between his master and the Baroness Sandorff. *L'Argent.*

CHARLES (MONSIEUR AND MADAME). *See* Badeuil.

CHARPIER, a grain merchant at Vendôme. He became bankrupt, and his papers having been purchased by Fayeux on behalf of Busch, the latter found among them a document signed by Comte de Beauvilliers, undertaking payment of a large sum to Léonie Cron. *L'Argent.*

CHARRIER, a bricklayer who amassed a fortune by speculations in building-sites during the early days of the Second Empire. Along with Mignon, his partner, he had many business dealings with Aristide Saccard. *La Curée.*

CHARVET, one of the party which met at Lebigre's wineshop to discuss revolutionary subjects. He was the best educated of the coterie, and his flood of bitter words generally crushed his adversaries. *Le Ventre de Paris.*

CHASSAGNE (DOCTEUR), director of the asylum at Moulineaux, where Saturnin Josserand was confined for a time. *Pot-Bouille.*

CHAUMETTE, counsellor at the court of Rouen. At the trial of Roubaud he acted as assessor to the assizes. *La Bête Humaine.*

CHAUMETTE FILS, son of the preceding, was a substitute at Rouen. He was the latest fancy of Madame Bonnehon, who did all she could to secure his advancement. *La Bête Humaine.*

CHAVAILLE (ROSALIE), cousin of La Méchain, and mother of Victor Saccard. She fell into a life of vice and poverty, and died at the age of twenty-six. *L'Argent.*

CHAVAL, a miner employed at the Voreux pit. From the first he had an instinctive hatred towards Étienne Lantier, caused partly by jealousy regarding Catherine Maheu, whose lover he became. He treated the girl very badly, and she ultimately left him. During the strike he took up a position antagonistic to Lantier, who was one of the leaders, and even undertook the direction of a party of Belgians brought in by the mine-owners to work the pits. By a strange chance, Chaval met Lantier and Catherine in a gallery of the pit after a terrible accident, which resulted in its being flooded ; a struggle followed, and Chaval was killed, his body being thrown into the water. But the rise of the flood brought him back time after time to the feet of the others, as if his jealousy continued even after death. *Germinal.*

CHAVE (CAPTAIN), brother of Madame Maugendre, and

uncle of Madame Jordan. He was a petty gambler of a class who frequent the Bourse daily, in order to make an almost certain profit of fifteen or twenty francs, which must be realized before the day's operations are over. He said he was forced to speculate, as the pension which he received from the Government was not sufficient to keep him from starvation. *L'Argent.*

CHAVIGNAT, an employé at the Ministry of Public Education. *Pot-Bouille.*

CHÉDEVILLE (DE), deputy for Eure-et-Loir under the Empire. He was an old beau who had flourished in the reign of Louis Philippe, and was still supposed to have Orléanist sympathies, though his reputed friendship with the Emperor was sufficient to secure his success at the polls. He had gone through all his money, and had now only the farm of La Chamade left. His political career was cut short by a scandal which gave offence at the Tuileries, and he was defeated by Rochefontaine, who was nominated by Government as the official candidate. *La Terre.*

CHERMETTE (MADAME DE), a friend of Madame Deberle. *Une Page d'Amour.*

CHEVASSU, a lawyer at Faverolles, who died leaving his fortune to the Sisters of the Holy Family. His cousin, M. Charbonnel, got the will reduced on the ground of undue influence. *Son Excellence Eugène Rougon.*

CHEZELLES (MADAME LÉONIDE DE), a school friend of Comtesse Muffat, who was five years her senior. She was the wife of a magistrate. " It was rumoured that she deceived him quite openly, but people pardoned her offence, and received her just the same, because, said they, ' She's not answerable for her actions.' " *Nana.*

CHIBRAY (COMTE DE), aide-de-camp to the Emperor. He was for a time the lover of Renée Saccard. *La Curée.*

CHOUARD (MARQUIS DE), father of Comtesse Sabine Muffat de Beuville. He was a Councillor of State and Chamberlain to the Empress, but, notwithstanding this, had kept up his relations with the Legitimist party ; he was known for his piety, and expressed the belief that his class should show an example in morals to the lower orders. In secret, however, his life was vicious, and many damaging stories were known of him.

He was one of Nana's admirers, and after a visit to her he was struck by sudden imbecility and semi-paralysis, the result of sixty years of debauchery. *Nana.*

CHOUARD (SABINE DE), daughter of the preceding and wife of Comte Muffat de Beuville. She was married at seventeen, and ever since had led a cloistered existence with a pious husband and a dictatorial stepmother. The death of her stepmother made little difference, and the family continued to live in an atmosphere of frigid respectability. At thirty-four Sabine looked little older than her own daughter, and would not have been taken for more than twenty-eight. About this time Comte Muffat fell entirely under the influence of Nana, and a change came over the household. Sabine accepted the attentions of Fauchery, whose mistress she became, and soon after launched into a course of extravagance which in the end went far to complete the ruin to which her husband was himself contributing. Other lovers followed Fauchery, and in the end she ran off with the manager of a large drapery store. Ulti-

mately she returned, and was pardoned by her husband, who had lost his own self-respect as a result of his intrigue with Nana. *Nana.*

CHOUTEAU, an old man of over ninety years of age, who with his wife lived in a little hut in Beaumont, furnished for them by Angelique with articles taken from the attic of her adopted parents. She, as well as Félicien d'Hautecœur, showed them much kindness. *Le Rêve.*

CHOUTEAU, a soldier in the 106th regiment of the line, commanded by Colonel de Vineuil. He belonged to the squad of Corporal Jean Macquart. Originally a housepainter of Montmartre, his time was almost expired when the outbreak of war prevented his leaving the army. A revolutionary in his ideas, he was the leader in every breach of discipline among his companions, suggesting to them that they should throw away their knapsacks and guns ; on the plateau of Floing, in front of the enemy, he declared that as he had not eaten he would not fight. Sergeant Sapin having been severely wounded, Chouteau offered, along with Loubet, to remove him to the ambulance, and the two men disappeared from the battlefield. After the defeat of the French Army he was made prisoner at Iges, where he continued to advise his companions in committing all kinds of excesses, going the length of handing a knife to Lapoulle in order that he might kill Pache, who had hidden some provisions from him. Along with Loubet he made an attempt to escape from the Germans, and in this he attained success by treacherously sacrificing his comrade. During the Commune he took an active part in the excesses which were then committed; but during the sanguinary repression which followed he was seen in the blouse of an honest workman applauding the massacre which ensued. *La Débâcle.*

CHRISTINE. *See* Christine Hallegrain.

CHUCHU (MADEMOISELLE), an actress at the Variétés. A *liaison* between her and Flory led to the ruin of the latter on the Stock Exchange. *L'Argent.*

CLARISSE, waiting-maid in the service of Baroness Sandorff. She betrayed to Delcambre the confidences of her mistress. *L'Argent.*

CLÉMENCE, a clerk at the fish auction. She attended the meetings in Lebigre's wineshop along with Charvet, with whom she lived. *Le Ventre de Paris.*

CLÉMENCE (MADEMOISELLE) occupied a room in the same tenement-house as the Coupeaus and Lorilleux, where she took in ironing, as well as added to her income by less reputable means. When Gervaise Coupeau's laundry was at the height of its success Clémence got regular employment there, but when business began to go she had to leave. *L'Assommoir.*

CLÉMENCE, lady's maid to Madame Duveyrier. *Pot-Bouille.*

CLORINDE. *See* Clorinde Balbi.

CLOU, Municipal Councillor at Rognes. He played the trombone at choral services in church. *La Terre.*

CŒUR (GERMAINE), a *demi-mondaine* who was on intimate terms with many members of the Paris Bourse. *L'Argent.*

COGNET, a roadman at Rognes. He was an old drunkard, who beat his daughter unmercifully. *La Terre.*

COGNET (JACQUELINE), *alias* LA COGNETTE, daughter of the preceding. She went to La Borderie at the age of twelve years, and before long had several lovers. She made her fortune, however, by resisting her master, Alexandre Hourdequin, for six months, and when she ultimately became his mistress she had made her position so secure that he was afterwards unable to part with her. Notwithstanding her relations with Hourdequin, she had other lovers, and the old shepherd Soulas, from motives of revenge, informed Hourdequin of her intimacy with one of them, a man named Tron. The latter, having been dismissed, killed Hourdequin and burned down the farm, so that Jacqueline was compelled to leave La Borderie no richer than she had come. *La Terre.*

COLICHE (LA), a fine cow which belonged to the Mouche family and was a great favourite with them. *La Terre.*

COLIN, a notary at Havre. It was in his presence that the Roubauds made a mutual will, leaving everything to the last survivor. *La Bête Humaine.*

COLOMBAN PÈRE, a veterinary surgeon known to all in the district of Seine-et-Oise. He was of dissolute habits. *Au Bonheur des Dames.*

COLOMBAN, a shopman who had been for many years in the employment of M. Baudu. He was engaged to his master's daughter Geneviève, but the marriage was put off from time to time as Baudu's business was not prosperous. Meantime, Columban had become infatuated by Clara Prunaire, a girl employed in "The Ladies' Paradise," and his affection for Geneviève rapidly cooled. Ultimately he went off with Clara, thereby hastening the death of Geneviève, who had been in bad health for some time. *Au Bonheur des Dames.*

COLOMBE. *See* Père Colombe.

COMBELOT (M. DE), an Imperial Chamberlain whom the Department of the Landes had chosen as deputy upon the formally expressed desire of the Emperor. He was a tall, handsome man, with a very white skin, and an inky black beard, which had been the means of winning him great favour among the ladies. He was married to a sister of Delestang. *Son Excellence Eugène Rougon.*

COMBELOT (MADAME DE). *See* Henriette Delestang.

COMBETTE, a chemist at Chêne-Populeux. He was assessor to the mayor, and the information which he received on the night of 27th August, 1870, satisfied him of the unhappy state of the Army of Châlons, which was then on its way to the front. *La Débâcle.*

COMBETTE (MADAME), wife of the preceding. It was she who on the evening of 27th August, 1870, offered hospitality to the soldier Maurice Levasseur, who was worn out with fatigue and with the pain of his foot, which had been injured by the long march. *La Débâcle.*

COMBEVILLE (DUCHESSE DE), mother of Princess d'Orviedo. *L'Argent.*

COMBOREL ET CIE, a firm of ship-owners who entered into the great transport syndicate founded by Aristide Saccard. *L'Argent.*

COMPAN (ABBÉ), vicar of the church of Saint-Saturnin at Plassans. He was on bad terms with Abbé Fenil, and consequently the other priests were afraid to have any intercourse with him, Abbé Bourrette alone visiting him during his last illness. *La Conquête de Plassans.*

CONDAMIN (M. DE), commissioner of woods and rivers for the district of Plassans. He was an elderly man, whose morality was looked upon with some suspicion by the respectable inhabitants of Plassans. He married a young wife, whom he brought from no one knew where, but who had evidently influential friends at Paris, as it was she who got her husband and Dr. Porquier decorated. *La Conquête de Plassans.*

CONDAMIN (MADAME DE), wife of the preceding. She was at first received with some suspicion at Plassans, nothing being known of her past history, but by the charm of her manner she soon overcame prejudice. Madame Mouret having asked her assistance in connection with the Home for Girls proposed by Abbé Faujas, she entered heartily into the scheme and used her influence on its behalf. Acting on advice from her influential friends at Paris, she assisted Faujas in the schemes which resulted in the election of M. Delangre as deputy for Plassans. *La Conquête de Plassans.*

CONIN, a stationer at the corner of Rue Feydeau, who supplied note-books to most members of the Bourse. He was assisted in the business by his wife, and seldom came out of the back shop. *L'Argent.*

CONIN (MADAME), wife of the preceding. She was on too friendly terms with many of her customers, but was so discreet that no scandal arose. *L'Argent.*

COQUART (LES), proprietors of the farm of Saint-Juste, which, however, they were forced by bad times to sell. The family consisted of the father, mother, three sons, and two daughters. *La Terre.*

COQUETS, neighbours of the Lorilleux in Rue de la Goutte-d'Or. They took a fancy to light their cooking-stove on the stair-landing, and, as they also owed their term's rent, they were given notice to quit. *L'Assommoir.*

CORBIÈRE (COMTE DE), proprietor of the Paradou, an estate near Artaud. When he died, the care of the property was confided to Jeanbernat, a foster-brother of the Comte. *La Faute de l'Abbé Mouret.*

CORBREUSE (DUC DE), proprietor of a racing-stable. *Nana.*

CORNAILLE, the principal draper in Valognes. Denise Baudu served her apprenticeship to him. *Au Bonheur des Dames.*

CORNEMUSE, a racehorse which won the prize of the City of Paris. *Nana.*

CORNILLE, a member of the firm of Cornille and Jenard, who held in the eighteenth century the mineral concession of Joiselle, which was joined in 1760 to two neighbouring concessions, those of Comte de Cougny and of Baron Desrumaux, in order to form the Company of the Mines of Montsou. *Germinal.*

CORNILLE (ABBÉ), one of the clergy of the cathedral of Beaumont. He accompanied Monseigneur d'Hautecœur when the latter came to administer the last rites of the Church to Angelique. *Le Rêve.*

CORREUR (MADAME MÉLANIE) was the daughter of a notary of Coulonges, a town in the district of Niort. When she was twenty-four years old she eloped with a journeyman butcher, and thereafter lived in Paris, ignored by her family. For some time she kept a boarding-house at the Hôtel Vanneau in the Rue Vanneau, where among her lodgers were Eugène Rougon, Du Poizet, and Théodore Gilquin. She established a claim on Rougon's gratitude, and he assisted a number of her friends in obtaining pensions and appointments. Having ascertained that her brother, M. Martineau, had made a will by which she would benefit, she, knowing him to be in bad health, denounced him to Rougon as a dangerous Republican. His arrest and sudden death followed. *Son Excellence Eugène Rougon.*

COSINUS, a racehorse which ran in the Grand Prix de Paris. *Nana.*

COSSARD (LE PÈRE), prompter at the Théâtre des Variétés. He was a little hunchback. *Nana.*

COUDELOUP (MADAME), a baker in Rue des Poissonniers. She supplied the Coupeaus until Lantier decided that they must have finer bread from a Viennese bakery. *L'Assommoir.*

COUGNY (COMTE DE), owner in the eighteenth century of the mining concession of Cougny, which in 1760 was joined to two neighbouring concessions to form the Company of the Mines of Montsou. *Germinal.*

COUILLOT (LES), peasants at Rognes. Their son got the number 206 in the drawing for the conscription. *La Terre.*

COUPEAU, a zinc-worker, who married Gervaise Macquart after her desertion by Lantier. He was the son of a drunken father, but was himself steady and industrious until a serious accident caused by a fall from a roof brought about a change. After that he became unwilling to work and began to spend his time in public-houses; his days of work became fewer and fewer, until, a confirmed drunkard, he lived entirely on his wife's earnings. Attacks of delirium tremens followed, and in the end he died in the Asylum of Sainte-Anne after an attack of more than usual violence. *L'Assommoir.*

COUPEAU (MADAME GERVAISE), wife of the preceding. *See* Gervaise Macquart. *L'Assommoir.*

COUPEAU (ANNA, known as NANA), born 1852, was the only child of Coupeau and Gervaise Macquart, his wife. Almost from infancy she was allowed to run wild in the gutters of Paris, and even in childhood her instincts were vicious. At thirteen years of age she was sent to learn artificial-flower making in the establishment of Madame Titreville, whose forewoman was Madame Lerat, Nana's aunt. She had been there some time when she began to receive attentions from an elderly gentleman who had noticed her going to work.

Meantime her father and mother had taken to drink so seriously that home life had become intolerable, and, after one of innumerable quarrels, Nana ran away to her venerable admirer. After a few months she tired of him and left, to spend her time amongst the low-class dancing-halls, in one of which she was found by her father, who brought her home, where she remained for a fortnight, and then ran off again. From time to time she returned, but her visits gradually became less frequent till they ceased. *L'Assommoir.*

At sixteen years of age she had a child to an unknown father, and two years later was installed in a flat in Boulevard Haussmann by a rich merchant of Moscow, who had come to pass the winter in Paris. Bordenave, the director of the Théâtre des Variétés, gave her a part in a play called *La Blonde Venus*, and though her voice was poor and she was ignorant of acting, she was by the sheer force of her beauty an immediate and overwhelming success. All Paris was at her feet ; Comte Muffat, Steiner, the Prince of Scots himself, came in turn to offer homage. It seemed as if this girl, born

of four or five generations of drunkards and brought up on the pavements of Paris, was to revenge her race upon the idle rich by the wild extravagances into which she dragged them. Muffat and Steiner were her lovers, and ruined themselves by the vast sums which she squandered ; Georges Hugon killed himself from jealousy of his brother Philippe, who embezzled for her sake, and brought himself to imprisonment and disgrace ; Vandeuvres too, after courting dishonour, met death at his own hand ; and Foucarmont, stripped bare and cast off, went to perish in the China seas. The procession was unending ; more money was always required. After a successful appearance in a play called *Melusine*, Nana suddenly left Paris and went to the East. Strange stories were told of her—the conquest of a viceroy, a colossal fortune acquired in Russia—but nothing definite was known. When she returned to Paris in 1870 she found that her son Louiset had been attacked by small-pox, and she herself contracted the disease from him. A few days later she died in a room in the Grand Hotel, nursed only by Rose Mignon, who had come

E

to her in her trouble. The war with Germany had just broken out, and as she lay dying the passing crowds were shouting ceaselessly, " A Berlin, A Berlin." *Nana.*

COUPEAU (LOUIS). *See* Louiset.

COUPEAU (MADAME), mother of Coupeau the zinc-worker. She was an old woman, and, her sight having given way, was unable to support herself. Her daughter, Madame Lorilleux, refused anything but the most trifling assistance, and ultimately Gervaise Coupeau took the old woman into her own house and supported her till her death, which occurred some years later. *L'Assommoir.*

COURAJOD, a great landscape painter, whose masterpiece, the *Pool at Gagny,* is in the Luxembourg. Long before his death he disappeared from the world of art, and lived in a little house at Montmartre surrounded by his hens, ducks, rabbits, and dogs. He refused to speak of his former fame, and when Claude Lantier called on him the old man seemed to be entering into a second childhood, forgetful of his past. *L'Œuvre.*

COUTARD, a soldier of infantry who belonged to the Second Division of the First Army Corps, which was defeated at Wissembourg on 4th August, 1870. He and his companion Picot were slightly wounded, and were left behind, not being able to rejoin their regiments for three weeks, most of which they spent tramping the country through wet and mud, endeavouring to overtake the vanquished army of France. *La Débâcle.*

CRASSE (LA), i.e. " The Dirty." Sobriquet of a professor at the college of Plassans, so called by the pupils as he marked by the constant rubbing of his head the back of every chair he occupied. *L'Œuvre.*

CREVECŒUR, a lace merchant in Rue Mail. Henri Deloche left his employment, and entered Octave Mouret's shop on the same day as Denise Baudu. *Au Bonheur des Dames.*

CRON, a carter at Vendôme. He was the father of Léonie Cron. *L'Argent.*

CRON (LÉONIE), the girl to whom the Comte de Beauvilliers gave the document which afterwards came into the hands of Busch, and was used by him as a means of blackmailing the widow of the Comte. *L'Argent.*

CUCHE, a family of fisher people who resided at Bonneville. They were ruined by their house being washed away by the sea. The father and mother lived extremely dissolute lives, and their son grew up little better than a savage. Pauline Quenu made great efforts to reform him, but he refused to work and resisted all attempts to make him settle down. *La Joie de Vivre.*

CUDORGE (MADAME), a seller of umbrellas in the Rue Neuve de la Goutte d'Or, where she was a neighbour of Gervaise Lantier. *L'Assommoir.*

CUGNOT (PAULINE), daughter of a miller at Chartres who was ruined by a lawsuit. She came to Paris, and eventually got a situation at "The Ladies' Paradise," where she showed much kindness to Denise Baudu, who was at first badly treated by the other employées there. Later on she married Baugé, her lover, but was allowed to retain her situation. *Au Bonheur des Dames.*

D

DABADIE, chief station-master at Havre. He was a handsome man, with the bearing of a commercial magnate engrossed in business. Indeed, he willingly left the passenger department of the station to his assistants, in order that he might give particular attention to the enormous transit of merchandise at the docks. It was said that he was on friendly terms with Mademoiselle Guichon, the office-keeper at the station. *La Bête Humaine.*

DAGUENET (PAUL), the favoured lover of Nana. His father, who was highly esteemed by Louis Philippe, occupied a prefecture up to the time of his death. As for himself, he had gone through three hundred thousand francs in eighteen months in the pursuit of pleasure, and was only able to keep going by small speculations on the Stock Exchange. Attracted by the fortune of Éstelle Muffat, he decided to marry her, and with the assistance of Nana obtained the consent of Count Muffat. Become serious after marriage, Daguenet came under the influence of Théophile Venot, and was ruled with a rod of iron by his wife, who now exhibited a character entirely unsuspected before. He now went to Mass, and was furious with his father-in-law, who was ruining the family on account of Nana. *Nana.*

DAGUENET (MADAME). *See* Éstelle Muffat de Beuville.

DAIGREMONT, a Paris financier
who was possessed of an
enormous fortune. It was
said that his fidelity was not
quite reliable, and that on
one occasion at least he played
his allies false and swept away
the profits. He was ap-
proached by Saccard before
the foundation of the Universal Bank, and being assured
that Eugène Rougon was to
back up his brother, he agreed
to become one of the directors.
He supported Saccard during
the great gamble in the shares
of the bank, and even on the
day of the collapse had
promised to come on the
market and buy so heavily
as to put up the price of
the shares. Having received
information through Jacoby
that Gundermann was determined at any cost to break
the market, Daigremont deserted Saccard, and instead
of buying, sold all the shares
he had, thereby bringing
about the final collapse. *L'Argent.*

DAIGREMONT (MADAME), wife of
the preceding. She was celebrated for her beauty and
for her fine singing. *L'Argent.*

DALICHAMP, a doctor at Raucourt, six kilometres from
Remilly. He was a man of
brusque manner, but of excellent heart, who showed
much kindness to his patients.
In the middle of August,
1870, he established an ambulance at Raucourt, and
after Jean Macquart, severely
wounded, had arrived at the
house of Père Fouchard, Dalichamp attended him secretly
till his recovery. It was
through him that Henriette
Weiss and Jean gained their
knowledge of the disasters
which were everywhere over-
taking the French army. *La
Débâcle.*

DAMBREVILLE, a Government
official who married in order
to secure promotion through
the influence of his wife.
Pot-Bouille.

DAMBREVILLE (MADAME), wife
of the preceding. An elderly
woman with a passion for
Léon Josserand, whose ap-
pointment as Maître des Requêtes she procured by her
influence. She promised to
secure a wealthy wife for him,
but delayed to do so until
he insisted on a match being
arranged between him and
her niece Raymonde. Her
friendly relations with him
continued to subsist even
after his marriage. *Pot-
Bouille.*

DAMBREVILLE (RAYMONDE), niece of Dambreville. *See* Madame Léon Josserand.

DANSAERT, a head captain in the Voreux pit. He was brutal and overbearing with the workmen, but humble in the presence of his superiors. Though it was well known that he was the lover of La Pierronne, he was friendly with her husband, and got information from him regarding the progress of the strike. On the day of the accident in the pit he became mad with fear, and leaped into one of the cages, leaving his men at the bottom. This action, together with the scandals regarding him, caused the company to decide on his dismissal. *Germinal.*

DASTE (MADAME), a friend of the Saccards and of Madame de Lauwerens. *La Curée.*

DAUVERGNE, deputy station-master for the main lines at the Gare Saint-Lazare. He occupied with his family, Claire, Henri, and Sophie, a house belonging to the railway company in the Impasse d'Amsterdam. *La Bête Humaine.*

DAUVERGNE (CLAIRE), daughter of the preceding and sister of Sophie. The two sisters were both charming blondes, one eighteen and the other twenty, who, amidst a constant stream of gaiety, looked after the housekeeping with the six thousand francs earned by the two men. The elder one would be heard laughing, while the younger sang, and a cage full of exotic birds rivalled one another in roulades. *La Bête Humaine.*

DAUVERGNE (HENRI), a chief guard in the service of the Western Railway Company. He was in love with Séverine Roubaud, but was aware of her *liaison* with Jacques Lantier. He was injured in the railway accident at Croix-de-Maufras, and having been removed to a house which belonged to Séverine, he was nursed by her there. In a hallucination of illness, he believed that he heard, outside his window, Roubaud arranging with Cabuche for the murder of Séverine : his mistaken evidence was greatly instrumental in leading to the conviction of the two men. *La Bête Humaine.*

DAUVERGNE (SOPHIE), the elder of the two sisters. *La Bête Humaine.*

DAVOINE, the purchaser of Chanteau's timber business at Caen. When Chanteau became incapacitated by gout, he sold his business to Davoine for a hundred thousand francs, of which one-half was to be paid in cash and the balance to remain in the business. Davoine was, however, constantly launching into speculations, and the consequence was that the profits were drained away, and the balance sheet generally showed a loss. He ultimately became bankrupt, and Chanteau lost all the money he had left in the business. *La Joie de Vivre.*

DEBERLE (DOCTOR HENRI), a medical man of Passy who inherited from his father a large fortune and an excellent practice. A chance call to attend Jeanne Grandjean led to an intimacy with her mother, which resulted in the fleeting love episode which forms the subject of the novel. Deberle, deceived by the circumstances under which Hélène Grandjean prevented an assignation between his wife and M. Malignon, believed that Hélène had arranged an assignation with himself, and she found it impossible to enlighten him without compromising his wife. The brief *liaison* was terminated by the illness and death of Jeanne. *Une Page d'Amour.*

DEBERLE (MADAME JULIETTE), wife of the preceding, was the elder daughter of M. Letellier, a wealthy silk merchant of Paris. Empty-headed and fond of gaiety, she was carried away by the attentions of M. Malignon, an idle young man who went everywhere in Paris society, and to whom she was foolish enough on one occasion to grant an assignation. Madame Hélène Grandjean, who was on intimate terms with the family, warned Madame Deberle that her husband's suspicions had been aroused, and that lady, seeing in time the folly of her action, broke off the intrigue. *Une Page d'Amour.*

DEBERLE (LUCIEN), the young son of Doctor Deberle. He was a playmate of Jeanne Grandjean. *Une Page d'Amour.*

DECKER (BARONNE), a friend of the Marquis de Chouard, who occasionally visited her at Viroflay. *Nana.*

DEJOIE, a man who was appointed by Saccard to be attendant at the offices of the newspaper purchased in the interest of the Universal Bank. He had a small sum of money, intended for the dowry of his daughter, and to increase this he invested it in shares of the bank. On the rise of the shares he gained a large sum, but, refusing to sell, he lost everything in the final catastrophe. *L'Argent.*

DEJOIE (JOSÉPHINE), wife of Dejoie, who first knew her when she was cook with Madame Lévêque, sister-in-law of Durieu, the brewer. She was afterwards with Dr. Renaudin, and then in a shop in Rue Rambuteau. The husband and wife were never fortunate enough to get employment in one place. Joséphine died when her daughter was fourteen years old. *L'Argent.*

DEJOIE (NATHALIE), daughter of the preceding. In order to provide a dowry for her, her father invested all his savings in shares of the Universal Bank, losing everything after its failure. She was a pretty girl, but absolutely heartless, and after the downfall of the bank she ran away from home, leaving her old father in his poverty. *L'Argent.*

DELAHERCHE (MADAME), mother of Jules Delaherche. Her husband's gay life rendered her unhappy, and after she became a widow she trembled lest her son should take to the same courses as his father; so, after marrying him to a woman who was devout and of simple tastes, she sought to keep him in a dependent state as though he were a mere youth. At fifty years of age, his wife having died, Delaherche determined to marry a young widow about whom there had been much gossip, and did so in spite of all the remonstrances of his mother. After that she only lived on in silent remonstrance, spending most of her time shut up in her own room. The miseries of war told severely on the old woman, and to these were added domestic troubles, for she became aware of her daughter-in-law's relations with Captain Baudoin and Edmond Lagarde. After the occupation of Sedan by the Prussians she devoted herself to nursing her old friend Colonel Vineuil, who had been brought to the house severely wounded. She remained with him till his death, shut up from the world, and refusing to hear of the defeats daily accumulating against their unhappy country. *La Débâcle.*

DELAHERCHE (JULES), one of the principal cloth manufacturers of Sedan. He owned a large factory in Rue Maqua, which had been the property of the family for a hundred and sixty years; in the rear of the building was a palatial courtyard shaded with old trees, gigantic elms dating from the foundation of the establishment. Jules, married to a woman dull and plain-looking, had been kept by his mother in the dependent position of a mere boy, but at fifty years of age, his wife being dead, he became enamoured of Gilberte Magi-not, a pretty young widow of Charleville, and married her in spite of the determined opposition of his mother. An ardent Bonapartist, he was much excited by a chance meeting with Napoleon III, but after the repeated defeats of the army in the war with Prussia his loyalty cooled, and he ultimately charged the Emperor with all the miseries which ensued. After the battle of Sedan an am-bulance was established in the courtyard of his factory, and the wounded Colonel Vineuil was removed to his house. *La Débâcle.*

DELAHERCHE (MADAME JULES). *See* Gilberte Vineuil. *La Dé-bâcle.*

DELANGRE (M.), mayor of Plas-sans. He was the son of a bricklayer, and when he passed as a lawyer had to be content with petty suits that no one else would take up. It was said that he became the lover of Madame Rastoil, and it was certainly through her influence that he won his first cases. He was shrewd enough to show no particular political proclivities ; so after the *Coup d'État* of 1851, when they were looking out for a mayor, his name was at once thought of. He was elected, and from that time everything prospered with him. As a result of much scheming by Abbé Faujas, Delangre was adopted as can-didate for the representation of Plassans, and was elected by a triumphant majority over Maurin, the Republican candidate. After his election, he voted steadily with the Government, thus accom-plishing the object for which Faujas was sent to the town. *La Conquête de Plassans.*

DELANGRE (MADAME), wife of the preceding. " She was a tame little woman of a ser-vant-like meekness, whose dis-soluteness had remained a matter of legend in Plassans." She was consulted by Madame Mouret regarding the Home for Girls proposed by Abbé Faujas, and agreed to act on the Committee. *La Con-quête de Plassans.*

DELANGRE (LUCIEN), son of M. Delangre, mayor of Plassans. He was a young barrister of four-and-twenty, short and sharp-eyed, with a crafty brain, and pleaded with all the coolness of an old practitioner. On the suggestion of Abbé Faujas he took a leading part in starting the Club for Young Men at Plassans. *La Conquête de Plassans.*

DELAROCQUE, a stockbroker who was married to the sister of Jacoby. *L'Argent.*

DELCAMBRE, Public Prosecutor, afterwards Minister of Justice. Having been for some time the lover of Baroness Sandorff, he was much annoyed at her subsequent intimacy with Saccard, and after the failure of the Universal Bank he instigated the proceedings which led to the conviction of its officials. *L'Argent.*

DELESTANG (M.), son of a wine merchant at Bercy, was himself a retired attorney and owner of a model farm. He was a man of great wealth, but of foolish and shallow character. Having got into political trouble at the time of the *Coup d'État* of 1851, he was helped out of an awkward position by Eugène Rougon. Acting on the sug-

gestion of Rougon, he married Clorinde Balbi, and soon after was appointed Minister of Commerce and Agriculture. After Rougon's second retirement from office Delestang was appointed to succeed him as Minister of the Interior. *Son Excellence Eugène Rougon.*

DELESTANG (MADAME), wife of the preceding. *See* Clorinde Balbi.

DELESTANG (HENRIETTE), sister of Delestang, the Minister, and wife of M. de Combelot, Chamberlain to Napoleon III. She had a passion for the Emperor, who, however, would not look at her. *Son Excellence Eugène Rougon.*

DELEZUE founded, along with his brother, in 1822, the drapers' shop in Paris known as *Au Bonheur des Dames.* When he died, his daughter Caroline, who was married to Hedouin, succeeded to his share in the business. *Pot-Bouille.*

The beginning of the business was exceedingly modest; there was only one window in the shop, and the stock was a small one. At that time the principal shop in the neighbourhood was the *Vieil Elbeuf,* of which Baudu afterwards became proprietor. *Au Bonheur des Dames.*

DELEUZE (UNCLE), one of the founders of the shop known as *Au Bonheur des Dames.* After the death of his elder brother he continued the business along with his niece Madame Hedouin. He became much affected by rheumatism, and left the management in the hands of Hedouin. *Pot-Bouille.*

Madame Hedouin, having become a widow, married Octave Mouret. Three months afterwards her uncle died, leaving her his share in the business. *Au Bonheur des Dames.*

DELEUZE (CAROLINE). *See* Caroline Hedouin.

DELHOMME was the son-in-law of Père Fouan, whose daughter Fanny he married. He was the owner of a small farm, which he managed so well that he became one of the richest of the peasant proprietors at Rognes. He was a man of calm, upright nature, and was frequently selected as arbiter in petty disputes. In his own affairs, however, he allowed himself to be much influenced by his wife. He was a municipal councillor, and ultimately became mayor. *La Terre.*

DELHOMME (MADAME), *née* Fanny Fouan, wife of the preceding. At first a not unamiable woman, she became hardened, and eventually the cleanliness of her house became a mania with her. She was unkind to her father, with whose little weaknesses she had no patience, and her persecution of him was carried to such an extent that he ceased to live with her and her husband. She was so annoyed at this that she refused to speak to him again, and her ill-will was not even terminated by his death. When her husband became mayor her conceit knew no bounds. *La Terre.*

DELHOMME (ERNEST), known as Nenesse, son of the preceding. From childhood he had a fancy for dressing himself up and aping the city lads, and as he had always a horror of the land he went to Chartres to assist in a restaurant, with which was connected a public dancing-hall. His parents effected an insurance against him being drawn in the conscription; but he drew a lucky number, and the loss of the money caused his mother considerable annoyance. He proposed to take over the *maison de tolerance* at Chartres which belonged to his grand-aunt Madame Badeuil and her husband, and he eventually did so by marrying their grand-daughter Élodie Vaucogne. *La Terre.*

DELOCHE, a bailiff in needy circumstances who resided at Briquebec. He treated his son Henri very badly. *Au Bonheur des Dames.*

DELOCHE (HENRI), a young man who got employment at "The Ladies' Paradise" at the same time as Denise Baudu. He fell in love with Denise, but though she refused to marry him, they remained on friendly terms, and on one occasion he threw a glass of wine at Favier, a fellow-shopman, who repeated a slander about her. *Au Bonheur des Dames.*

DELORME, a relation of the Quenus. On the suggestion of Madame Chanteau he was nominated a member of the family council of Pauline Quenu. He consented to her emancipation. *La Joie de Vivre.*

DENEULIN, a cousin of the Grégoires. Like his cousin, he inherited a denier in the Montsou mines, but being an enterprising engineer, tor-

mented by the desire for a royal fortune, he had hastened to sell out when the value of the denier reached a million francs. His wife possessed through an uncle the little concession of Vandame, on which were two abandoned pits—Jean-Bart and Gaston-Marie—and he invested all his money in the reopening of these pits. He was a bad manager, however, and after his wife's death he was pillaged by every one. The great strike at Montsou completed his ruin, and he was ultimately compelled to sell his pits to the great company which had already acquired all the neighbouring mines, himself receiving a situation as divisional engineer. *Germinal.*

DENEULIN (JEANNE), second daughter of the preceding. Having lost their mother when very young, she and her sister were brought up alone, somewhat badly, being spoiled by their father. Jeanne was fond of painting, and had already had three landscapes refused by the *Salon*. Her sister and she remained cheerful in the midst of their father's loss of fortune, and proved themselves excellent managers. *Germinal.*

DENEULIN (LUCIE), elder daughter of Deneulin. She was fond of music, and at one time talked of going on the stage. Like her sister, she showed an admirable spirit at the time of her father's downfall. *Germinal.*

DENIZET, examining magistrate (*juge d'instruction*) at Rouen. The son of a Normandy cattle-breeder, he studied law at Caen, but had entered the judicial department of the Government late in life ; and his peasant origin, aggravated by his father's bankruptcy, made his promotion slow. After being substitute in various places he was sent to Rouen, where he acted as examining magistrate. He was fond of his profession, and at the beginning of the inquiry into the murder of President Grandmorin allowed himself to be carried away by his desire to elicit the facts of the case. He received, however, a hint from Camy-Lamotte, the secretary to the Minister of Justice, that caution must be exercised, and his desire to be decorated and removed to Paris was so great that he sacrificed the interests of justice, and caused the case to be hushed up. Later, the murder of Séverine Roubaud reopened the Grand-morin inquiry, and Denizet was allowed a free hand in dealing with the affair. By a masterpiece of logical deduction he set out to prove the complicity of Cabuche and Roubaud, a complicity, however, which had no existence in fact, and the demonstration of which by Denizet produced a gross error of justice. *La Bête Humaine.*

DEQUERSONNIÈRE, an architect with whom Louis Dubuche served his apprenticeship. He was a former winner of the Grand Prize, and was architect of the Civil Branch of Public Works, an officer of the Legion of Honour, and a member of the Institute. His principal production was the church of Saint-Mathieu, a building which shared the characteristics of a pastry-cook's mould and a clock in the style of the First Empire. *L'Œuvre.*

DESBAZEILLES, President of the Assize Court at Rouen on the occasion of the trial of Roubaud. He was a bachelor, and an old friend of Madame Bonnehon ; a friendship which still continued, notwithstanding his sixty years. He was the literary glory of the Court, and his cleverly turned sonnets were well known. *La Bête Humaine.*

DESFORGES, a stock-broker. The friendship of his wife with Hartmann, the great financier, had been very useful to him. He died leaving a fortune, the amount of which was minimized by some and exaggerated by others. *Au Bonheur des Dames.*

DESFORGES (MADAME HENRIETTE),daughter of a Councillor of State and widow of a stock-broker, who left her a small fortune. " Even during her husband's lifetime, people said she had shown herself grateful towards Baron Hartmann, whose financial tips had proved very useful to them ; and later on, after her husband's death, the acquaintance had probably continued, but always discreetly." Octave Mouret, having met her at the house of a mutual friend, made love to her, chiefly with a view to gaining Baron Hartmann's assistance through her influence. Madame Desforges was extremely jealous when she learned of Mouret's affection for Denise Baudu and the probability of his marrying her. In order to injure him, she introduced Bouthemont to Baron Hartmann, who lent him money to start an opposition establishment called " The Four Seasons." *Au Bonheur des Dames.*

DÉSIR (VEUVE), an elderly woman who kept a ball-room known as Bon-Joyeux. She called all the miners her children, and grew tender at the thought of the flood of beer which she had poured out for them during the last thirty years. She gave her ball-room to the miners to hold a meeting during the strike, and when the police arrived to break it up she held the door long enough to allow those present to escape. *Germinal.*

DESLIGNIÈRES, a toy-seller in Rue Saint-Roch. *Au Bonheur des Dames.*

DESMARQUAY, a money-changer in Rue Saint-Lazare. Trublot was employed in his office. *Pot-Bouille.*

DESROCHES, a notary at Chêne-Populeux. His house there was requisitioned for the Emperor on 27th August, 1870, during the march of the army of MacMahon. *La Débâcle.*

DESROCHES (MADAME), mother of the preceding. Their house adjoined the early home of Maurice Levasseur, and she had been good to him when he was a child. When the house was requisitioned for the Emperor, she had to give up her room to him and take refuge in the garret. *La Débâcle.*

DESRUMAUX (BARON), one of the founders of the coal industry in the north of France. For forty years he struggled without yielding, in the midst of continual obstacles, and when at last his pits began to yield a small profit, two neighbouring concessions, that of Cougny, belonging to the Comte de Cougny, and that of Joiselle, belonging to the Cornille and Jenard Company, nearly overwhelmed him with their competition. Happily, on 25th August, 1760, a treaty was made between the three concessions, uniting them into a single one known as the Montsou Mining Company. *Germinal.*

DESVIGNES (ADÈLE). *See* Madame Bouchard.

DIDE (AUNT). *See* Adélaïde Fouque.

DIEUDONNÉ (MADAME), wife of a small farmer at Séguiranne. She brought up her niece Sophie, who was cured of phthisis by Doctor Pascal. *Le Docteur Pascal.*

DOMERGUE was formerly Director of Roads and Bridges at Plassans. He was the father of Madame Campardon. *Pot-Bouille.*

DOMERGUE (MADAME), wife of the preceding, lived a retired life at Plassans with her husband. She introduced Octave Mouret to her daughter, Madame Campardon, when he came to Paris. *Pot-Bouille.*

DOMERGUE (ROSE). *See* Madame Achille Campardon.

DROUARD (MADAME), an old actress at the Théâtre des Variétés. She played the part of Juno in the *Blonde Venus. Nana.*

DUBREUIL, a cousin of the Levasseurs. He was sub-manager of the sugar refinery at Chêne-Populeux at the time Weiss was employed there; then, in 1868, he retired to a little property near Sedan which had come to his wife as a legacy. On the evening before the battle, foreseeing the disaster, he removed his wife and children to Bouillon, and next day the house was completely destroyed during the struggle. *La Débâcle.*

DUBRUEL, a pork-butcher at Plassans who took part in the attack on the Town Hall. Three days later he was killed in the ambush arranged by Pierre Rougon against the Republicans. *La Fortune des Rougon.*

DUBUCHE (ALICE), daughter of Louis Dubuche and of Régine Margaillan, his wife. She was so delicate that at six years old she was still unable to walk. Her father endeavoured to strengthen her muscles by occasionally making her hold on to the bar of a trapeze for a few moments, but the exercise only seemed to produce extreme terror in the unfortunate child. *L'Œuvre.*

DUBUCHE (GASTON), the elder child of Louis Dubuche and of Régine Margaillan, his wife. At the age of ten he had the feeble limbs of a little child, and though he regularly exercised on a trapeze, he was unable to raise himself on his wrists, the least exertion producing profuse perspiration. *L'Œuvre.*

DUBUCHE (LOUIS), eldest son of a baker of Plassans, and companion from childhood of Claude Lantier and Pierre Sandoz. His mother, who was very ambitious, sent him to Paris, where he studied architecture at the School of Art. His reverence for established formulas caused him to be out of sympathy with the advanced school of painting advocated by Claude Lantier and his friends, though he expressed large ideals regarding his own profession. In time he became a first-class pupil at the school, and with infinite trouble gained the regulation "honourable mention." But his parents no longer sent him any money; it became necessary for him to gain his living, and he was already tired of earning a few francs by assisting an architect incapable of drawing his own plans. By the aid of his master, Dequersonnière, he gained a medal for a plan of a villa, and this brought him prominently under the notice of Margaillan, a wealthy building contractor, whose daughter Régine he married soon afterwards. The marriage was not a success; his wife was always ailing, and the two children which were born to them were so delicate as to cause constant anxiety. His business relations with his father-in-law were a failure, some of his ventures resulting in heavy loss, and Margaillan soon thrust him aside, treating him with insolence and neglect. His only satisfaction was that he had been able to repay to his parents the money they advanced for his education in Paris. *L'Œuvre.*

DUBUCHE (MADAME LOUIS), wife of the preceding. *See* Régine Margaillan. *L'Œuvre.*

DUCAT, a franc-tireur of the woods at Dieulet. He was formerly a bailiff at Blainville, but had to leave on account of a criminal charge against him. He was a friend of Cabasse and of Guillaume Sambuc, and took part in the murder of Goliath Steinberg. *La Débâcle.*

DUCHESNE (GEORGES), a lover of Madame Bouchard, for whom she asked the patronage of Eugène Rougon, which he refused on the ground of his respect for her husband. *Son Excellence Eugène Rougon.*

DUCLOUX (LA), an old woman who lived in the neighbourhood of Croix de Maufras, having formerly been servant in an inn. Misard was authorized to employ her as gatekeeper on the railway after the death of Flore. She was anxious to marry Misard, and seeing him constantly searching for the little hoard of money which had been hidden by his deceased wife, La Ducloux cleverly led him to believe that she knew where the money was hidden. After she became the second Madame Misard she became infected with the feverish anxiety of her husband, and joined with him in his untiring search. *La Bête Humaine.*

DUMONTEIL, a rich silk manufacturer at Lyons. He supplied to Octave Mouret a special make of silk with which he achieved great success. *Au Bonheur des Dames.*

DU POIZAT PÈRE, an old bailiff at Coulonges. He was an old miser who refused any money to his son Léopold, and even threatened him with a pistol when he tried to borrow from him. He lived alone in an old ruinous house with a loaded gun behind the door. His son, having become a prefect, and wishing to dazzle the old man with his fine position, attempted to force the door; then followed a drama mysterious and without witness, at the end of which the old man was found lying at the foot of his staircase, with his head split open. *Son Excellence Eugène Rougon.*

DU POIZAT (LÉOPOLD), son of a process-server at Coulonges, a little town in the district of Niort. His father, who had amassed a considerable fortune by usury, sent him to study law in Paris, giving him an allowance of only a hundred francs a month. Some months before the revolution of February, 1848, he became acquainted with Eugène Rougon, who, like himself, was boarding at that time with Madame Correur at the Hôtel Vanneau. During the Bonapartist intrigues he assisted Rougon in some risky undertakings, and later on worked energetically to secure his election to the Legislative Assembly as member for Deux-Sèvres. After the *Coup d'État* Rougon used his influence on behalf of Du Poizat, and got him appointed subprefect at Bressuire. He resigned this appointment on the advice of Rougon after the resignation of the latter as President of the State Council. After Rougon's return to office he was appointed prefect at Niort. His extreme harshness and overbearing conduct produced a public scandal, and the sudden death of his father, under peculiar circumstances, still further increased his unpopularity. He was at his own request transferred to another prefecture by Delestang, who succeeded Rougon as Minister of the Interior. *Son Excellence Eugène Rougon.*

DURIEU, a wealthy brewer who, carried away by the charm of

Caroline Hamelin, married her. He became an alcoholic maniac, and on one occasion pursued his wife with a knife. A separation was arranged, and Durieu ultimately died in an asylum. *L'Argent.*

DURIEU (MADAME). *See* Caroline Hamelin.

DURIEU (LE PÈRE), a messenger at Plassans. He was a taciturn old Provençal. *Le Docteur Pascal.*

DUTILLEUL. A flour-miller at Montsou whose mills were stopped by the strike. *Germinal.*

DUVEYRIER (ALPHONSE), a counsellor at the Court of Appeal ; married Clotilde, daughter of M. Vabre. He was a man of dissolute habits, to whom his wife's cold nature and love of music were repugnant, and he spent much of his time away from home. He squandered large sums of money on a woman named Clarisse Bocquet, who afterwards left him. Having found her again, he fell under her influence so completely as to allow her to treat him abominably. So unhappy did he become, that he attempted to commit suicide by shooting himself ; the wound was, however, not a serious one,

F

and he recovered. *Pot-Bouille.*

DUVEYRIER (MADAME CLO-TILDE), wife of the preceding, was the only daughter of M. Vabre, a notary of Versailles. She did not get on well with her husband, who found her cold nature irksome, and, perhaps even more so, her love of piano-playing. Her musical evenings were attended by Octave Mouret, the Josserands, and others of the same circle. *Pot-Bouille.*

DUVEYRIER (GUSTAVE), son of the preceding, a thin, precocious boy of sixteen, who was being educated at the Lycée Bonaparte. *Pot-Bouille.*

DUVILLARD, the owner of a large house bought by Octave Mouret for the enlargement of his shop. *Au Bonheur des Dames.*

E

ÉCOSSE (S.A.R. LE PRINCE D'), the son of a queen and heir to a throne. He was tall and strong, with a fair beard and a fresh complexion. He was an habitué of the Théâtre des Variétés, and an admirer of Nana, whom he wished to bring to London as a singer. Later, Nana spoke of him with little respect. *Nana.*

ECREVISSE (L'), a celebrated *demi-mondaine* of the Second Empire. *La Curée.*

EMPEREUR, one of the dogs of the shepherd Soulas. He was a fierce animal, and, like his master, hated Jacqueline Cognet. *La Terre.*

ERNESTINE, a woman who once occupied a room in Bourras's house, and had written her name in candle-smoke on the ceiling. *Au Bonheur des Dames.*

ESCORAILLES (MARQUIS D'), father of Jules d'Escorailles. " The Escorailles family was one of the oldest in Plassans, where it was treated with the utmost respect ; and Rougon, who in former days had often dragged his worn-down boots past the old Marquis's house, took a pride in protecting and assisting the young man. The family retained an enthusiastic devotion for Henri V, though it allowed its heir to serve the Empire." The Marquis and his wife visited Paris specially to ask the assistance of Rougon in furthering the interests of their son. After Rougon's proceedings against the Sisters of the Holy Family, in the interest of the Charbonnels, they again visited Paris to insist on their son retiring from the administration, as they said they could not allow him to be mixed up in any persecution of the Church. *Son Excellence Eugène Rougon.*

ESCORAILLES (MARQUISE D'), wife of the preceding. *Son Excellence Eugène Rougon.*

ESCORAILLES (JULES D'), son of the Marquis d'Escorailles, a nobleman of Plassans, at whose request Rougon got Jules an appointment as auditor at the Council of State. After Rougon's return to office he appointed M. Escorailles his private secretary. He carried on an intrigue with Madame Bouchard. *Son Excellence Eugène Rougon.*

ESPANET (MARQUIS D'), husband of the Marquise Adeline. He was made aide-de-camp to the Emperor, but by his riotous conduct scandalized the older nobility. He never appeared in society with his wife. *La Curée.*

ESPANET (MARQUISE D'), one of the most prominent leaders of society of the Second Empire, was the inseparable companion of Madame Haffner, whose name was always associated with hers by the public. They were both schoolfellows and friends of Madame Renée Saccard. *La Curée.*

EUGÉNIE, cook for a short time to Madame Théophile Vabre. *Pot-Bouille.*

EUGÉNIE, a child buried in the cemetery of Cayenne at Saint-Ouen, where Bongard and Sandoz read the inscription on a poor cross, without railing, set up slantingly across a path, " *Eugénie, three days.*" *L'Œuvre.*

EUGÉNIE (EMPRESS), referred to in *Son Excellence Eugène Rougon*, and *La Débâcle.*

EULALIE, a laundress who lived in Rue Montmartre. Gilquin, when visiting her, chanced to overhear in an adjoining room a conversation between some Italians who had come to Paris to assassinate the Emperor. *Son Excellence Eugène Rougon.*

EULALIE, a fish-seller, mistress of Bec-Salé, *alias* Boit-sans-soif. *L'Assommoir.*

EULALIE (LA MÈRE), a vegetable seller at Montmartre. She lodged with Madame Méchain. *L'Argent.*

EUSÈBE, a choir-boy in the church of Saint-Saturnin at Plassans. He accompanied Abbé Bourrette to the death-bed of Abbé Compan. *La Conquête de Plassans.*

F

FAGEROLLES PÈRE, a manufacturer of zinc objects of art who lived in a gloomy old house in Rue Vieille-du-Temple. His workshop was on the ground floor, above it was a warehouse, and still higher, facing a courtyard, were the rooms in which he lived with his son Henri. He intended to bring up Henri as a designer of ornaments for his own trade, and when the boy showed higher ambitions, taking to painting proper and talking about the School of Art, there were quarrels, blows, a series of falling-outs and reconciliations. Even when the young man had achieved some success, the manufacturer of artistic zincwork, while resigned to letting him have his will, treated him harshly, like a lad who was spoiling his career. Later, in the desire of a decoration for himself, the merchant forgot his former opposition ; he held out his son, who had now arrived at notoriety, as an additional claim for his own distinction. *L'Œuvre.*

FAGEROLLES (HENRI), son of the preceding. In the gloomy house of his father he grew up like a true child of the Paris pavements. Though his father desired him to become a designer of ornaments for use in his trade, the lad had higher ambitions, and desiring to study painting, became a student at the School of Art. Notwithstanding this orthodox training, he was a disciple of Claude Lantier and his somewhat revolutionary band, whom he delighted by sly attacks upon his professors and praise of themselves. He paid particular court to Claude, under whose artistic influence he had come, and though he continued to paint with tricky skill, he no longer talked in anything but the jargon of the new open-air school. This did not prevent him, however, from elsewhere making fun of the adepts of that school, whom he accused of doing their work with a kitchen ladle. He made a success with a picture of an actress before her glass, which caught the popular taste, and afterwards appeared as an engraving. Taken up by Naudet, the picture-dealer, he began to receive large prices for his work, and by doing everything in his power to make his way in society his position soon became secure. He was elected a member of the Hanging

Committee of the *Salon*, and secured the admission of Claude Lantier's picture *L'Enfant Mort*. He made large sums of money, in the spending of which he was assisted by Irma Bécot. *L'Œuvre.*

FANNY (MADEMOISELLE), a workgirl in the neighbourhood of Octave Mouret's shop, who was sent there by her employer to match some merinos. *Au Bonheur des Dames.*

FAUCHERY (LÉON), a journalist and dramatic author, who wrote a piece for the Théâtre des Variétés called *La Petite Duchesse*. After numerous *liaisons* he became for a time the lover of Comtesse Sabine Muffat, and under the pressure of Comte Muffat was forced to give to Nana a leading part in *La Petite Duchesse*. Fauchery's *liaison* with the Comtesse Muffat merely interrupted for a time one of older standing with Rose Mignon, whose husband appeared to be content with the position of major-domo in a *ménage à trois*. *Nana.*

FAUCHEUR (LE PÈRE) kept at Bennecourt a small country inn much frequented by artists. In connection with the tavern he carried on a small business in groceries. After the death of the Fau-

cheurs the inn was carried on by their niece Mélie. *L'Œuvre.*

FAUCHEUR (LA MÈRE), wife of the preceding. She was a daughter of old Poirette. *L'Œuvre.*

FAUCONNIER (MADAME) carried on a laundry business in Paris, and gave employment to Gervaise Macquart after her desertion by Lantier. She continued on friendly terms with Gervaise after the latter's marriage to Coupeau, at which she was present. When drink had brought about the Coupeaus' ruin, Madame Fauconnier again took Gervaise into her employment, giving her work until her increasing carelessness and intemperance made her dismissal necessary. *L'Assommoir.*

FAUCONNIER (VICTOR), the young son of Madame Fauconnier. He was an idle scamp about four years older than Nana Coupeau, and was her constant playfellow and companion in all kinds of mischief. *L'Assommoir.*

Nana, in talking over with Satin the events of her childhood, referred to Victor as a youth who had always shown vicious tendencies. *Nana.*

FAUJAS (ABBÉ), a priest of Besançon who, having got

into some trouble there, was sent to Plassans by the Government with the view of undermining the political influence of the clergy, who were strongly Legitimist in their views. At Plassans he took up his residence, along with his mother, in the house of François Mouret. At first he kept entirely in the background, but assisted by Madame Mouret, who had fallen in love with him, and by Madame Félicité Rougon, acting under instructions from her son Eugène, the Minister of State, Faujas soon began to make himself felt in Plassans. He appeared to take no interest in politics, but little by little he gained power, until "the conquest of Plassans" was accomplished and a supporter of the Government was elected as deputy. Meantime his influence over Madame Mouret had become complete, and he had practically taken possession of the Mourets' house, his sister and her husband, as well as his mother, living there with him. Thrust aside and neglected, François Mouret was wrongfully removed to the asylum at Les Tulettes, where confinement soon unhinged his not over-strong intellect. The Abbé now became even more arrogant, and Madame Mouret was barely tolerated in her own house. Ultimately François Mouret escaped from the asylum, and returning by night to his home, set fire to it ; along with him, the Abbé Faujas and all his relations perished in the flames. *La Conquête de Plassans.*

FAUJAS (MADAME), mother of the preceding. She accompanied the Abbé to Plassans and took up house with him there. Absolutely devoted to her son, she made herself his slave, and sacrificed everything and every one to his interests. It was largely through her that the gradual ousting of the Mourets from their own home became possible ; and to accomplish her ends she stopped short at nothing ; seldom speaking, but always watching, she was ready to grasp each opportunity as it arose. Retribution came with the escape of François Mouret from the asylum, and Madame Faujas perished along with the other members of her family in the conflagration raised by him. *La Conquête de Plassans.*

FAUJAS (OLYMPE). *See* Madame Olympe Trouche.

FAUQUENOIX, an associate of Baron Desrumaux in the development of the mines of Montsou. *Germinal.*

FAUVELLE, a sugar-refinery at Montsou, which suffered on account of the strike of miners. *Germinal.*

FAVIER, a salesman in the silk department of "The Ladies' Paradise." He had for some reason an ill-will towards Denise Baudu and spread scandalous stories about her. Henri Deloche, her friend, hearing him do so on one occasion, threw a glass of wine in his face. *Au Bonheur des Dames.*

FAYEUX, a collector of rents at Vendôme. He did business in connection with Busch, and also with La Méchain, whose cousin he was said to be. He speculated on the Bourse through Mazaud, and after the downfall of the Universal Bank it was found that he had embezzled large sums from persons employing him. *L'Argent.*

FENIL (ABBÉ), head of the theological seminary at Plassans. He was a keen ecclesiastic, with strong Legitimist principles, and from the first took up a position antagonistic to Abbé Faujas. Having great influence with the Bishop of Plassans, he was for some time able to prevent Faujas from receiving preferment ; a hint from Government, however, caused the Bishop to change his views, and Abbé Fenil was for the time routed. It was suspected that he ultimately induced Antoine Macquart to plan the escape of François Mouret from the asylum at Les Tulettes ; an escape which led to the death of Abbé Faujas. *La Conquête de Plassans.*

FÉRAUD-GIRAUD FRÈRES, a firm of ship-owners who joined the great transport syndicate formed by Aristide Saccard. *L'Argent.*

FERNAND, a student of chemistry with Combette at Chêne Populeux. He was a cowardly lad, whom fear of the Prussians drove into a fever. *La Débâcle.*

FERNANDE, a chorus-girl at the Théâtre des Variétés. *Nana.*

FÉTU (MÈRE), an old woman whom Hélène Grandjean visited at the request of Abbé Jouve. At her house Hélène frequently met Dr. Deberle, who was attending her professionally at the same time. Below this house was the flat taken by M. Malignon, who had appointed Mère Fétu caretaker, and it was through her that Hélène came to know of the assignation between

Malignon and Madame Deberle. *Une Page d'Amour.*

FIFI, the sobriquet of Fanny Menu, *q.v. Pot-Bouille.*

FINE, the sobriquet of Joséphine Gavaudan. *La Fortune des Rougon.*

FINET (ARISTIDE), the founder of the drapery business known as the *Vieil Elbeuf*, in Paris. He was the father-in-law and predecessor of Hauchecorne. *Au Bonheur des Dames.*

FINET (DÉSIRÉE), daughter of the preceding. She married Hauchecorne, her father's principal salesman, who carried on the business. *Au Bonheur des Dames.*

FINET, a doctor of medicine who resided at Cloyes. He was disgusted by the brutality of his patients, whom he accused of always sending for him when it was too late. His indifference became such that he did not make any inquiries about the death of Rose Fouan, whose end was hastened by her son Buteau, or that of Père Fouan, who was burned alive. *La Terre.*

FIRMIN, chief huntsman to Napoleon III at Compiègne. *Son Excellence Eugène Rougon.*

FLAMINIO, the Comtesse Balbi's man-servant, "with a face like a brigand's, and a long black beard." *Son Excellence Eugène Rougon.*

FLEUR D'ÉPINE, a celebrated chief of brigands who preceded Beau-François. *La Terre.*

FLEURANCE, a putter in the Voreux pit who worked along with the Maheus. She was found dead in her bed, and the vacancy created in the pit was filled by Étienne Lantier. *Germinal.*

FLORE, the elder daughter of Madame Misard (Aunt Phasie). After illness rendered her mother unfit for work, Flore replaced her as gatekeeper at the railway crossing at Croix-de-Maufras. She was a tall and strong girl of eighteen, with a magnificent head of fair hair; disdainful of the male, she had thrashed at least one would-be lover. When she was quite little she had loved Jacques Lantier, and now it was to him alone she would have given herself. Jacques did not care for her, however, and she came to know that he had a mistress, Séverine Roubaud. Convinced of her own right to be loved, for she was stronger and handsomer than the other, the girl was tortured by jealousy; and each Friday, as she saw the express rush past, bearing the two lovers to Paris, was seized with an imperious desire to end everything, and by causing their death prevent them from passing any more. She accordingly brought about a terrible railway accident, in which a large number of persons were killed ; but the crime was useless, for Séverine and Jacques escaped with trifling injuries. The thought that Jacques knew her guilt, and must in future regard her as a monster, rendered life hateful to Flore, and to meet death she set out on a walk of heroic determination through the tunnel of Malaunay, allowing herself to be cut in pieces by an express train. *La Bête Humaine.*

FLORENCE, an actress at the variety theatres. Marsy offered her a valuable house. *Son Excellence Eugène Rougon.*

Pauline Letellier met her one day on the boulevards accompanied by Malignon. Juliette Deberle, who was a little jealous, assured her that Florence was at least forty and very plain-looking. *Une Page d'Amour.*

FLORENT, elder son of a widow who took as her second husband M. Quenu, who, however, died three years later,

leaving a son. Florent was a gentle, studious youth, and his mother lavished all her affection on him, dying in the end from hardships endured in her struggle to keep him at college in Paris. After her death Florent took young Quenu, his half-brother, to live with him in Paris, giving up all thought of continuing to attend the Law School, and taking pupils in order to find means of sustenance. Years of hardship followed, and Florent became imbued with Republican ideas. Two days after the *Coup d'État* of 1851, while the military were firing on the mob in the Boulevard Montmartre, he was knocked down and stunned. When he recovered, he found that he was lying beside the body of a young woman, whose blood had oozed from her wounds on to his hands. He was horrified at the sight, and rushed away to join a party of men who were throwing up barricades in an adjoining street. Worn out with fatigue, he fell asleep, and on awakening found himself in the hands of the police. His hands were still stained with the blood of the young woman, and the authorities assumed that he was a dangerous character. The semblance of a trial followed ; he was condemned and transported to Cayenne. After incredible hardships and sufferings, he escaped and returned to France. Famished and exhausted, he tramped towards Paris, and had fallen in a faint on the road when he was overtaken by Madame François, who took him the rest of the journey on her cart. During his long absence his brother Quenu had at first been taken in by Gradelle, a brother of his mother, to whose business of pork-butcher he ultimately succeeded. Florent on his return from exile was warmly received by his brother and Madame Quenu, who told him that Gradelle, his uncle, had died, leaving a considerable sum, and that as there was no will he was entitled to a half-share. He refused to accept this, but agreed to live with the Quenus. This arrangement answered well at first, but Madame Quenu got tired of seeing him always about the house, and let him see that he must secure employment. After some time he got an appointment as deputy inspector at the Fish Market. He was introduced by Gavard to a small revolutionary circle which met nightly in a café kept by M. Lebigre, and of which he soon became the leader. Meantime Mlle. Saget, who from a chance word of Pauline, the little daughter of Quenu, had learned Florent's past history, spread the story in the markets, and a strong feeling was awakened against him. His sister-in-law, Lisa, alarmed lest her husband should be compromised by the revolutionary conspiracy, thought it her duty to inform the police. She learned, however, that Florent's history had all along been known, Lebigre being a police spy, and that only a favourable opportunity was being awaited to arrest the whole gang of conspirators. The blow fell soon afterwards, and Florent was again sentenced to transportation to Cayenne. *Le Ventre de Paris.*

FLORY was born at Saintes, his father being employed in the local registry office. He came to Paris and entered the office of Mazaud, the stockbroker. At first he did his duties well, but was soon led astray and got into debt. Having started speculation on his own account, he became deeply involved in the Universal Bank, and on the failure of that concern was left with a liability of a hundred thousand francs, to meet which he had not a single sou. Subsequently he was arrested and imprisoned for embezzling a large sum from Mazaud, his employer. *L'Argent.*

FONTAN (ACHILLE), an actor at the Théâtre des Variétés who played parts in *La Blonde Venus* and *La Petite Duchesse.* He became for a time the lover of Nana, but treated her so abominably that she left him. *Nana.*

FONTENAILLES (MLLE. DE) was descended from an aristocratic family, but was in great poverty when a situation was found for her in " The Ladies' Paradise " through the influence of Madame Desforges. She proved incapable of anything but the most menial work, and ultimately married Joseph, one of the porters in the establishment. *Au Bonheur des Dames.*

FOUAN, *alias* BUTEAU. *See* Buteau.

FOUAN (FANNY). *See* Madame Delhomme.

FOUAN (HYACINTHE), the elder son of Père Fouan and Rose Maliverne, his wife. He was an idler and drunkard, who, when he had left the army, after having seen service in

Africa, had taken to tramp the fields, refusing to do any regular work, but living by theft and poaching, as though he were still looting a trembling nation of Bedouins. Withal there looked out of his fine, sunken eyes a merriment that was not altogether evil, the open heart of good-humoured drunkenness. He lived with his daughter in a ruined hut amongst some rocks near Rognes. After the division of land by his father, Hyacinthe soon mortgaged his share and drank the proceeds, never paying to his parents any part of the rent which had been agreed upon. For a time he sheltered his father, but frightened the old man by searching for some bonds which he had concealed. He had, however, neither the cold rapacity of his sister Fanny nor the murderous instincts of his brother Buteau. *La Terre.*

FOUAN (JOSEPH CASIMIR), the father of Marianne, Louis, Michel, and Laure. Born in 1766, he belonged to a family of peasant proprietors which for centuries had owned land, in varying quantities, in the neighbourhood of Rognes. They were originally serfs of the Roques-Bouqueval family. Bit by bit they acquired their land, until, when the Revolution of 1789 arrived, the Fouan of that day, Joseph Casimir, was the owner of twenty-one acres— the conquest of four centuries from the seigneurial territory. When, in 1793, the rest of the estate was declared national property and sold in lots by auction, he was too timid to purchase any, and had the mortification to see La Borderie sold to Isidore Hourdequin, a citizen of Châteaudun, for a fifth of its value. When he became old he divided his twenty-one acres between three of his family, Marianne, Louis, and Michel, and gave a corresponding sum of money to his younger daughter Laure, who had been brought up as a sempstress and was in service at Châteaudun. *La Terre.*

FOUAN (LAURE), younger daughter of the preceding. *See* Madame Charles Badeuil.

FOUAN (LOUIS), known as Père Fouan. He was the son of Joseph Casimir Fouan, and married Rose Maliverne, by whom he had three children, Hyacinthe, Buteau, and Fanny. He received seven acres of land from his father, and his wife brought him twelve acres more. This land he cultivated well, and with a passion for the soil, as such, which amounted to frenzy. It alone had his love, and his wife and children trembled before him under a rude despotism. At seventy years of age he was still healthy, but his limbs were failing, and he reluctantly decided to divide his land between his children. He retained his house and garden, which had come to him with his wife, and his family undertook to pay him a rent for the land handed over to them. Upon this, along with a nest-egg of three hundred francs per annum, known to no one, the old people would be able to live comfortably. The division made, the family soon became rapacious ; Hyacinthe never paid anything, Buteau only a part, and Delhomme, Fanny's husband, alone fulfilled his obligation. Mère Fouan died, and the old man lived alone for a year ; after that he went to his daughter Fanny Delhomme, but her unkindness made his life miserable, and he accepted in turn the hospitality of his two sons, Buteau and Hyacinthe, both of whom had come to suspect the existence of his nest - egg and were anxious to secure it. In this sordid aim Buteau was eventually successful, and his subsequent treatment of the old man was even more infamous than it had been before. From this time Père Fouan lived in isolation ; he spoke to none and looked at none ; as far as appearances went, he might have been blind and dumb. But even worse was to follow. He had seen the assault on Françoise Mouche which resulted in her death, and to ensure his silence he was murdered by Buteau and Lise, his son and daughter-in-law, who attempted to suffocate him, and subsequently burned him alive in his bed. *La Terre.*

FOUAN (MADAME ROSE), wife of the preceding, *née* Maliverne. She worked on the farm like a man, rising first and going to bed last, her only reward being that she had lived. Stupid, and reduced by labour to the level of an animal, she had always trembled before the despotic authority of her husband. She brought up her family without love, and as if she resented their requiring even the simple necessaries of life. She did not long survive the division of land by her husband. Her favouritism for Hyacinthe, her elder son, excited the jealousy of Buteau, who in the course of a quarrel threw her to the ground, when she received such injuries that she died a few hours afterwards. *La Terre.*

FOUAN (MARIANNE). *See* La Grande.

FOUAN (MICHEL). *See* Père Mouche.

FOUAN (OLYMPE), daughter of Hyacinthe. Her mother, who was a tramp, ran off when the child was three years old, leaving her to grow up as best she could. She was passionately fond of geese, of which she had a large flock. When little more than a child, she had as her lovers Delphin Bécu and Nenesse Delhomme. *La Terre.*

FOUCARMONT, a naval officer who in ten years saved some money which he proposed to invest in the United States. He fell into the hands of Nana, however, and was soon completely ruined. When she turned him out of doors penniless, she merely advised him to go back to his ship. He was drowned later in the China seas. *Nana.*

FOUCART, the owner of a cheap restaurant frequented by

Jory, Mahoudeau, and their band. *L'Œuvre.*

FOUCART (MADAME), the nurse who attended Sidonie Rougon at the birth of Angelique and left the child at the foundling hospital. She assisted Sidonie both by taking her into her house and lending her money, but when Madame Foucart herself fell into difficulties Sidonie did nothing for her, not even paying back what she owed. It was from Madame Foucart that Hubert subsequently got information regarding the parentage of Angelique. *Le Rêve.*

FOUCHARD, father of Honoré Fouchard, and uncle, on the mother's side, of Henriette and Maurice Levasseur. He was a small farmer at Remilly, who to make money more quickly took up the trade of butcher also. Avaricious to the last degree, and with a nature of unpitying hardness, he opposed the marriage of Honoré with his servant Silvine Morange. At the end of two years of waiting Honoré went off, after a terrible scene with his father, though the old man still kept the girl, with whom he was well pleased. When the French troops were marching to

Sedan, Fouchard concealed all the animals on his farm, burying even his supply of bread and wine, in the hope of being able to sell to better advantage later on. The death of his son, who was killed in the battle, cost him a few tears, but he was quickly consoled by some good purchases of horses stolen from the battlefield. He took Prosper Sambuc as farm-worker, because the soldier, being liable to imprisonment by the Prussians, could not ask him for any wages. He began to do a considerable trade in butcher-meat with the conquering army, selling them all the diseased animals that he could secure. A suspicion of being concerned in the death of Goliath Steinberg led to his arrest, but he was released soon afterwards, thanks to the intervention of Captain von Gartlauben, a friend of the Delaherches. *La Débâcle.*

FOUCHARD (HONORÉ), only son of the preceding. At twenty years of age, in 1867, he drew a good number for the conscription, but on account of the opposition of his father to his marriage with Silvine Morange, he enlisted, and was sent to Africa, in the artillery. When he heard that Silvine had become the mistress of Goliath Steinberg he became so ill that he had to remain in hospital for three months. He afterwards received a letter from Silvine saying that she had never loved any one but him, and when passing through Remilly on his way to the front, he saw her and forgave everything. His battery was among those which on 1st September, 1870, defended the Calvary d'Illy, but was cut in pieces by the terrible fire of the Prussians. Honoré was killed, and fell across his gun, firmly grasping the letter from Silvine, which in his death-struggle he had drawn from his bosom. *La Débâcle.*

FOUGERAY (MADEMOISELLE DE), eldest daughter of the Baronne de Fougeray. She entered a convent, because, it was said, a young man with whom she was in love had died. The event created much talk in all classes of society in Paris. *Nana.*

FOUQUE (ADÉLAÏDE), generally known as Aunt Dide, the common ancestress of the Rougon-Macquarts, born at Plassans in 1768, was the last representative of a family who had owned a market-garden there for several generations. " This girl, whose father died insane, was a long, lank, pale creature, with a scared look and strange gait." In 1786, six months after the death of her father, she married one of her own workmen, named Rougon, " a rough-hewn peasant from the Basses Alpes." Rougon died fifteen months after his marriage, leaving a son named Pierre. Scarcely a year had elapsed before the widow took as her lover a man named Macquart, who lived in a hovel adjoining her own property, and two children were born. The legitimate son, Pierre Rougon, was brought up along with his half brother and sister, Antoine and Ursule, with whom, however, he was not on good terms. From her eighteenth year Adélaïde was subject to nervous fits, which brought on convulsions, and though she was not yet insane, these repeated shocks produced cerebral disorders. " She lived from day to day like a child ; like a fawning animal yielding to its instincts." These conditions continued for about twenty years, till the death of Macquart, and the children grew up as best they could. By this time Pierre realized the situation, and playing upon his mother's mental weakness, he brought her completely under his sway. On the death of Macquart, Adélaïde went to live in the hovel bequeathed to her by him, and Pierre sold the family property, appropriating the price. Living at first entirely alone, her intellect became more and more affected by the recurring convulsive fits. Subsequently her grandson Silvère Mouret lived with her, but after his execution, of which she was a witness, she became quite insane. *La Fortune des Rougon.*

She was always under restraint, and remained a living sore to the family. The little property which belonged to her son Antoine Macquart was close to the asylum where she was confined, and Pierre Rougon seemed to have placed him there to look after her. Adélaïde seldom spoke, and for twelve years had never moved from her chair. *La Conquête de Plassans.*

At 104 years old she was still living in the asylum at Les Tulettes. She was little better than a skeleton, and in her long, thin face it was only in the eyes that there was any sign of life. Immovable in her chair, she remained from year to year like a spectre, calling up the horrors of her family history. A sudden accident, the death of little Charles Saccard from nasal hæmorrhage, wakened in her sleeping brain recollections of years before ; she saw again the murder of Silvère, killed by a pistol-shot, and she saw also her lover Macquart, the smuggler, killed like a dog by the gendarmes. The shock proved too much for her feeble strength, and she died the following day (in 1873), aged 105 years, three months, and seven days. *Le Docteur Pascal.*

FOUSSET (LE PÈRE), tenant of the farm of Millouard, in the Canton of Orgères. He was a victim of the band of brigands commanded by Beau-François. *La Terre.*

FRANCHOMME (LOUIS), a cousin of Françoise Hamelin and her brother, with whom he went to reside for a time when recovering from a fever. His wife having become fond of Angelique Marie, who lived at that time with Françoise Hamelin, he obtained permission to take her to Paris, where she could be taught the trade of making flowers. Unfortunately, however, he died three months later. *Le Rêve.*

FRANCHOMME (THÉRÈSE), wife of the preceding. After the death of her husband, she, being in delicate health, was obliged to leave the city and go to live with her brother Rabier, a tanner, who was settled at Beaumont. She died a few months afterwards, leaving to the care of the Rabiers the child Angelique, whom she had brought with her from Paris. *Le Rêve.*

FRANCIS, the hairdresser of Nana. He was in the habit of lending money to his customers, and on one occasion he found, with the assistance of Labordette, a hundred thousand francs for Comte Muffat, who required the money for Nana. . *Nana.*

FRANCIS, coachman to the Grégoires. He also did the heavy work of the household. *Germinal.*

FRANÇOIS, a wine-merchant whose shop was situated at the corner of Rue des Poissonniers and of Rue de la Goutte d'Or. Coupeau frequently spent whole days there. *L'Assommoir.*

FRANÇOIS, *concierge* and footman in Nana's establishment. He was the husband of Victorine, the cook. He received visitors in the hall, wearing a gorgeous livery. *Nana.*

FRANÇOIS (MADAME), a market-gardener of Nanterre. She drove regularly to Paris in the early morning with her vegetables, and on one occasion found Florent lying on the road, faint from want and exhaustion. She took him to town in her cart, and subsequently showed kindness to him and Claude Lantier. *Le Ventre de Paris.*

FRANÇOISE, housemaid to Madame Théophile Vabre. *Pot-Bouille.*

FRANÇOISE, the servant of M. and Madame Sandoz in their little house in Rue Nollet. *L'Œuvre.*

FRANGIPANE, a horse which belonged to Baron Verdier and ran in the Grand Prix de Paris. *Nana.*

FREDERIC (MADAME), a widow who held the position of "second hand" in the dress department of "The Ladies' Paradise." *Au Bonheur des Dames.*

FIRMAT, an old peasant of Rognes who was a neighbour of Mouche. He became paralysed. *La Terre.*

FIRMAT (LA), wife of the preceding. She was well known

G

in the village for her knowledge of animals, and was
frequently consulted when it
would otherwise have been
necessary to call in a veterinary surgeon. She worked
hard to support her invalid
husband, to whom she was
devoted, and wept at the
thought that he was soon to
die. *La Terre.*

G

GABET (MÈRE), an old woman
who assisted the Huberts
with their washing. She became ill, and being in great
poverty, was assisted by Angelique, and later by Félicien.
Le Rêve.

GAGA, an elderly *demi-mondaine*
who had flourished in the
reign of Louis Philippe, and
was still notorious in the
Second Empire. She had a
daughter named Lili, who
became the mistress of the
Marquis Chouard. *Nana.*

GAGEBOIS, glass-works at Montsou. The strike of miners
led to the fires being extinguished. *Germinal.*

GAGNIÈRE, an artist, one of the
band of Claude Lantier. He
belonged to Melun, where his
well-to-do parents, who were
both dead, had left him two
houses ; and he had learned

painting, unassisted, in the
forest of Fontainebleau. His
landscapes were conscientious
and excellent in intent, but
his real passion was music.
Becoming more and more engrossed in this, he took lessons
in playing the piano from a
middle-aged lady whom he
married soon afterwards. He
established himself at Melun
in one of his two houses,
going to Paris two or three
times a month to attend a
concert, and he continued to
exhibit each year at the *Salon*
one of his little studies of
the banks of the Seine.
L'Œuvre.

GALISSARD, a haberdasher of
Plassans, whose daughter
married Professor Lalubie.
She was a pretty girl to whom
Claude Lantier and Sandoz
used to sing serenades.
L'Œuvre.

GARÇONNET, a Legitimist who
was Mayor of Plassans at
the time of the *Coup d'État.*
He was taken prisoner by the
insurgents. *La Fortune des
Rougon.*

GARTLAUBEN (VON), captain in
the Prussian Army. During
the occupation of Sedan he
was billeted on Delaherche.
He was a person of some
importance, as his uncle had

been made Governor-General at Rheims, and exercised sovereign power over the district. Fascinated by Gilberte Delaherche, his chief wish was to be taken for a man of refinement, and not for a barbarous soldier. He was able to render some services to the Delaherches, and to make the Prussian occupation easier for them. *La Débâcle.*

GASC, proprietor of a racing-stable. One of his horses, named Boum, ran in the Grand Prix de Paris. *Nana.*

GASPARINE, a tall, handsome girl of Plassans, with whom Achille Campardon fell in love. She had no money, however, and he married her cousin Rose Domergue, who had a dowry of thirty thousand francs. Tears and recriminations followed, and Gasparine went to Paris, where for some time she had a situation in the shop of Madame Hédouin. Madame Campardon having fallen into ill-health, her husband returned to his first love, and a *liaison* existed between him and Gasparine for a considerable time. Ultimately she went to live with the Campardons, and managed their household affairs. *Pot-Bouille.*

GASTON was the son of a General, and was the same age as the Prince Imperial, though much stronger than he. The Emperor frequently made inquiries regarding the child. *Son Excellence Eugène Rougon.*

GAUDE, bugler in the 106th regiment of the line. "He was a big, skinny, sorrowful, taciturn man, without a hair on his chin, and blew his instrument with the lungs of a whirlwind." On the 1st September, during the defence of the Hermitage, he became seized with the madness of heroism, and continued to blow after his comrades had been slain and until he himself was shot down. *La Débâcle.*

GAUDIBERT (ISIDORE), Mayor of Barbeville since 1850, wrote some poetry on political subjects, and was decorated by the Minister of State, Eugène Rougon. *Son Excellence Eugène Rougon.*

GAUDRON, husband of Madame Gaudron. He was described as having the sluggishness of a beast. *L'Assommoir.*

GAUDRON (MADAME), a wool-carder who lived with her husband and their large family in the same tenement-house as the Coupeaus and the

Lorilleux. She was one of the guests at the Coupeaus' wedding. *L'Assommoir.*

GAUDRON FILS, the eldest child of the Gaudrons, was a journey-man carpenter. *L'Assommoir.*

GAUJEAN (M.), a silk manu-facturer of Lyons who was dissatisfied with the monopoly created by the large establish-ments, such as that of Octave Mouret, and thought it could be broken by the creation of special shops in the neigh-bourhood, where the public could find a large and varied choice of articles. With this object he assisted Robineau to purchase Vinçard's business by giving him credit to a large amount ; the scheme was not successful, and he lost heavily. *Au Bonheur des Dames.*

GAUTIER, a wine-grower at Saint-Eutrope, with whom François Mouret had dealings at one time. *La Conquête de Plassans.*

GAVARD, originally kept a *rôtisserie* or poultry-roasting establishment in the Rue Saint-Jacques, at which time he became acquainted with Florent and Quenu. In 1856 he retired from this business, and to amuse himself took a stall in the poultry-market. " Thenceforth he lived amidst ceaseless tittle-tattle, ac-quainted with every little scandal in the neighbour-hood." Gavard was a leading spirit in the revolutionary circle which met in Lebigre's wine-shop, and was the means of bringing Florent to attend the meetings there. He was arrested at the same time as Florent and was transported. *Le Ventre de Paris.*

GAVAUDAN (JOSÉPHINE), a market - woman of Plassans who married Antoine Mac-quart in 1826. She was much addicted to drink, but worked in order to keep her husband in idleness. She died in 1850. *La Fortune des Rougon.*

GÉDÉON, an ass which belonged to Mouche. It was very mis-chievous, and on one occasion got access to a vat of new wine, with the result that it became extremely drunk. *La Terre.*

GEORGES, a young man whose acquaintance Renée Saccard made by chance while walking one day on the Quai Saint-Paul. Her fancy for him passed without her ever having asked his family name. *La Curée.*

GÉRALDINE, a character in *La Petite Duchesse*, played by Clarisse Besnus at the Théâtre des Variétés. It was originally intended that the part should be played by Nana. *Nana.*

GILQUIN (THÉODORE), a lodger at Madame Correur's hotel at the same time as Eugène Rougon and Du Poizat. A man of shady character, he was frequently employed by Rougon, and by a fortunate accident was able to give him warning of the Orsini plot against the life of the Emperor. He was rewarded with the appointment of Commissary of Police at Niort. On the order of Rougon, he arrested Martineau, Madame Correur's brother. He was removed from his position on account of having compromised himself by taking a bribe to procure a conscript exemption from service. *Son Excellence Eugène Rougon.*

GIRAUD (TATA) kept at Plassans a boarding-school for children, where the sculptor Mahoudeau had known Pierre Sandoz and other comrades who met later in Paris. *L'Œuvre.*

GODARD (ABBÉ), curé of Bazoches-le-Doyen. The authorities of Rognes, which was in his parish, refused to provide for a priest of their own, and Abbé Godard, in order to perform Mass, had to walk each Sunday the three

kilometres which separated the two communes. He was a short, stout man of hasty temper, who was disgusted with the indifference and irreligion of his parishioners, and his services were the shortest and baldest possible. In spite of his temper, he had, however, a passion for the miserable, and to these he gave everything—his money, his linen, almost the clothes off his back. *La Terre.*

GODEBŒUF, a seller of herbs who occupied the shop in Rue Pirouette which formerly belonged to Gradelle, the porkbutcher. *Le Ventre de Paris.*

GODEMARD, a pupil of Dequersonnière, the architect. *See* Gorju. *L'Œuvre.*

GOMARD, the keeper of a working-man's café in Rue de la Femme-sans-Tête, under the sign *Au Chien de Montargis.* Claude Lantier occasionally took his meals there. *L'Œuvre.*

GONIN, a family of fisher-folks who lived at Bonneville. It consisted of Gonin, his wife, and one little girl. A cousin of the wife, named Cuche, came to live with them after his house had been washed away by the sea. Gonin soon after fell into bad health, and his wife and Cuche treated him so badly that the police talked of an inquiry. Pauline Quenu tried to reform the little girl, who had been allowed to grow up wild. *La Joie de Vivre.*

GORJU, a pupil of Dequer-sonnière, and himself a future architect. On one of the walls of the studio one could read this brief statement : " The 7th June, Gorju has said that he cared nothing for Rome. Signed, Gode-mard." *L'Œuvre.*

GOUJET, a blacksmith from the Département du Nord, who came to Paris and got em-ployment in a manufactory of bolts. " Behind the silent quietude of his life lay buried a great sorrow : his father in a moment of drunken madness had killed a fellow-workman with a crowbar, and after arrest had hanged himself in his cell with a pocket-handkerchief." Goujet and his mother, who lived with him, always seemed to feel this horror weighing upon them, and did their best to redeem it by strict upright-ness. " He was a giant of twenty-three, with rosy cheeks and blue eyes, and the strength of a Hercules. In the work-shop he was known as Gueule d'Or, on account of his yellow

beard. With his square head, his heavy frame, torpid after the hard work at the anvil, he was like a great animal, dull of intellect and good of heart." For a time the Coupeaus were his neighbours, and he came to love Gervaise with a perfectly innocent affection, which survived all disillusionments, and sub-sisted up to the time of her death. It was he who lent her money to start a laundry, and afterwards repeatedly as-sisted her when in difficulties. *L'Assommoir.*

GOUJET (MADAME), mother of the preceding, was a lace-mender, and lived with her son in part of the house first occupied by the Coupeaus. She showed much kindness to them, though she was dis-tressed by her son's infatua-tion for Gervaise, and did not altogether approve of his lend-ing her money to start a laundry. Notwithstanding this, she continued to assist Gervaise until neglect of work entrusted made it impossible to do so longer. She died in October, 1868, of acute rheu-matism. *L'Assommoir.*

GOURAUD (BARON) was made a Baron by Napoleon I, and was a Senator under Napoleon III. " With his vast bulk, his bovine face, his elephantine movements, he boasted a delightful rascality ; he sold himself majestically, and committed the greatest infamies in the name of duty and conscience." *La Curée.*

GOURD (M.), at one time valet to the Duc de Vaugelade, and afterwards doorkeeper in the tenement-house in Rue de Choiseul which belonged to M. Vabre, and was occupied by the Campardons, the Josserands, and others. He spent much of his time spying on the tenants, and posed as guardian of the morals of the establishment. *Pot-Bouille.*

GOURD (MADAME), wife of the preceding. She was the widow of a bailiff at Mort-la-Ville, and she and her present husband owned a house there. She was exceedingly stout, and suffered from an affection of the legs which prevented her from walking. *Pot-Bouille.*

GRADELLE, brother of Madame Quenu, senr., and uncle of Florent and Quenu. He was a prosperous pork-butcher in Paris, and after Florent's arrest he took young Quenu into his business. He died suddenly, without leaving a will, and Quenu succeeded

to the business, and to a considerable sum of money which was found hidden at the bottom of a salting-tub. *Le Ventre de Paris.*

GRAND-DRAGON (LE), one of the band of brigands led by Beau-François. *La Terre.*

GRANDE (LA), elder daughter of Joseph Casimir Fouan, and sister of Père Fouan, Michel Mouche, and Laure Badeuil. Married to a neighbour, Antoine Péchard, she brought to him seven acres of land against eighteen which he had of his own. Early left a widow, she turned out her only daughter, who, against her mother's will, wished to marry a poor lad named Vincent Bouteroue. The girl and her husband died of want, leaving two children, Palmyre and Hilarion, whom their grandmother refused to assist. At eighty years of age, respected and feared by the Fouan family, not for her age but for her fortune, she exacted the obedience of all, and still directed the management of her land. She bitterly reproached her brother Louis for dividing his property between his children, and warned him that he need not come to her when they had turned him into the street, a threat which she carried into effect. She took delight in the squabbles of the Fouan family, exciting their cupidity by promising them a share of her property at her death. Meantime she made a will which was so complicated that she hoped it would lead to endless lawsuits amongst her heirs. *La Terre.*

GRANDGUILLOT, a notary at Plassans. He embezzled large sums belonging to his clients, among whom was Dr. Pascal Rougon, and thereafter fled to Switzerland. *Le Docteur Pascal.*

GRANDJEAN (M.), son of a sugar-refiner of Marseilles. He fell in love with Hélène Mouret, a young girl of great beauty, but without fortune ; his friends bitterly opposed the match, and a secret marriage followed, the young couple finding it difficult to make ends meet, till the death of an uncle brought them ten thousand francs a year. By this time Grandjean had taken an intense dislike for Marseilles, and decided to remove to Paris. The day after his arrival there he was seized with illness, and eight days later he died, leaving his wife with one daughter, a young girl of ten. *Une Page d'Amour.*

GRANDJEAN (MADAME HÉLÈNE), wife of the preceding. *See* Hélène Mouret.

GRANDJEAN (JEANNE), born 1842, was the daughter of M. Grandjean and Hélène Mouret, his wife. She inherited much of the neurosis of her mother's family along with a consumptive tendency derived from her father, and from an early age had been subject to fits and other nervous attacks. One of these illnesses, more sudden and severe than usual, caused her mother to summon Doctor Deberle, and thus led to an intimacy which had disastrous results. Jeanne's jealous affection for her mother amounted almost to a mania, and when she came to suspect that Dr. Deberle had become in a sense her rival, she worked herself into such a nervous state that she exposed herself to a chill, and having become seriously ill, died in a few days, at the age of thirteen. *Une Page d'Amour.*

GRANDMORIN (LE PRÉSIDENT), one of the directors of the Western Railway Company. " Born in 1804, substitute at Digne on the morrow of the events in 1830, then at Fontainebleau, then at Paris, he had afterwards filled the posts of procurator at Troyes, advocate-general at Rennes, and finally first president at Rouen. A multi-millionaire, he had been member of the County Council since 1855, and on the day he retired he had been made Commander of the Legion of Honour." He owned a mansion at Paris in Rue du Rocher, and often resided with his sister, Madame Bonnehon, at Doinville. His private life was not unattended by scandal, and his relations with Louisette, the younger daughter of Madame Misard, led to her death. A somewhat similar connection with Séverine Aubry, a ward of his own, had less immediately serious consequences, as he arranged for her marriage to Roubaud, an employé of the railway company, whom he took under his protection. Three years later Roubaud learned the truth by chance, and murdered Grandmorin in the Havre express between Malaunay and Barentin. The President left a fortune of over three and a half million francs, among other legacies being one to Séverine Roubaud of the mansion-house of Croix-de-Maufras. *La Bête Humaine.*

GRANDMORIN (BERTHE), daughter of the preceding, was the wife of a magistrate, M. de Lachesnaye. She was a narrow-minded and avaricious woman, who affected ignorance of her father's real character, and the influence of her husband tended to increase her meanness. After the murder of President Grandmorin, when vague suspicions fell on Roubaud, Berthe took up a position antagonistic to her old playfellow Séverine Roubaud, in the hope that a legacy left by Grandmorin to her would be cut down. *La Bête Humaine.*

GRANDSIRE (M.), the justice of peace who assisted the Huberts in making the necessary arrangements for their adoption of Angelique. *Le Rêve.*

GRANOUX (ISIDORE), one of the group of conservatives who met in Pierre Rougon's yellow room to declaim against the Republic. *La Fortune des Rougon.*

GRAS (MADAME), an old lady living in the Rue des Orties, who boarded and lodged young children for a small sum. When Denise Baudu got a situation in "The Ladies' Paradise," she put her young brother Pépé under the charge of Madame Gras for a time. *Au Bonheur des Dames.*

GRÉGOIRE (CÉCILE), daughter of Léon Grégoire. Her parents were devoted to her, and brought her up in happy ignorance, allowing her to do much as she liked. They taught her to be charitable, and made her dispense their little gifts to the poor ; these were always in kind, as they held that money was likely to be misused. When the great strike broke out at Montsou, Cécile could comprehend nothing of the revolt of the poor, or the fury with which they regarded those better off than themselves, and when she fell into the hands of a fierce crowd was almost paralysed under the attack of La Brûlé and of Père Bonnemort, from which she escaped with difficulty. A little later she chanced to call on a charitable errand at Maheu's house, and unfortunately was left alone for a few moments with Bonnemort, who was now supposed to be helpless. The sight of her seemed, however, to waken memories in the old man, for in an accession of madness he found strength to throw himself upon the poor girl and strangle her. *Germinal.*

GRÉGOIRE (EUGÈNE), grandfather of Léon Grégoire. He inherited the share in the Montsou mine bought by his father, but the dividends at that time were small, and as he had foolishly invested the remainder of the paternal fortune in a company that came to grief, he lived meanly enough. The share passed to his son Félicien. *Germinal.*

GRÉGOIRE (FÉLICIEN), son of the preceding and father of Léon Grégoire. The family fortune began with him, for the value of the share in the Montsou mine had greatly increased, and he was able to buy the dismembered estate of Piolaine, which he acquired as national property for a ludicrous sum. However, bad years followed ; it was necessary to await the conclusion of the revolutionary catastrophes, and afterwards Napoleon's bloody fall. The little fortune of Félicien Grégoire passed to his son Léon. *Germinal.*

GRÉGOIRE (HONORÉ), great-grandfather of Léon Grégoire. He was in 1760 steward on the estate of Piolaine, a property which belonged to Baron Desrumaux. When the Montsou treaty was made, Honoré, who had laid up savings to the amount of some fifty thousand francs, yielded tremblingly to his master's unshakable faith. He gave up ten thousand francs, and took a share in the Montsou Company, though with the fear of robbing his children of that sum. When he died his share passed to his son Eugène. *Germinal.*

GRÉGOIRE (LÉON), great-grandson of Honoré Grégoire. It was he who profited at a stupefying rate of progress by the timid investment of his ancestor. Those poor ten thousand francs grew and multiplied with the company's prosperity. Since 1820 they had brought in cent for cent ten thousand francs. In 1844 they had produced twenty thousand ; in 1850, forty. During two years the dividend had reached the prodigious figure of fifty thousand francs ; the value of the share, quoted at the Lille Bourse at a million, had centrupled in a century. Six months later an industrial crisis broke out ; the share fell to six hundred thousand francs. But Léon refused to be alarmed, for he maintained an obstinate faith in the mine. When the great strike broke out he would not be persuaded of its serious-

ness, and refused to admit any danger, until he saw his daughter struck by a stone and savagely assaulted by the crowd. Afterwards he desired to show the largeness of his views, and spoke of forgetting and forgiving everything. With his wife and daughter Cécile he went to carry assistance to the Maheus, a family who had suffered sadly in the strike. Cécile was unfortunately left alone with old Bonnemort, Maheu's father, who in a sudden frenzy attacked the girl and strangled her. This terrible blow entirely shadowed the lives of Grégoire and his wife. *Germinal.*

GRÉGOIRE (MADAME LÉON), wife of the preceding, was the daughter of a druggist at Marchiennes. She was a plain, penniless girl, whom he adored, and who repaid him with happiness. She shut herself up in her household, having no other will but her husband's. No difference of tastes separated them, their desires were mingled in one idea of comfort ; and they had thus lived for forty years, in affection and little mutual services. *Germinal.*

GRESHAM, a jockey who, it was said, had always bad luck. He

rode Lusignan in the Grand Prix de Paris. *Nana.*

GROGNET, a perfumer in Rue de Grammont, whose business was ruined by the growth of Octave Mouret's great establishment. *Au Bonheur des Dames.*

GROSBOIS, a Government surveyor who had also a small farm at Magnolles, a little village near Rognes. Liable to be summoned from Orgères to Beaugency for purposes of survey, he left the management of his own land to his wife, and in the course of these constant excursions he acquired such a habit of drinking that he was never seen sober. That mattered little, however ; the more drunk he was the better he seemed to see ; he never made a wrong measurement or an error in calculation. People listened to him with respect, for he had the reputation of being a sly, acute man. *La Terre.*

GUENDE (MADAME DE), a friend of the Saccards. She was a woman well known in the society of the Second Empire. *La Curée.*

GUEULE-D'OR, the sobriquet of Goujet. *L'Assommoir.*

GUEULIN, nephew of Narcisse Bachelard, was a clerk in an insurance office. Directly after office hours he used to meet his uncle, and never left him, going the round of all the *cafés* in his wake. " Behind the huge, ungainly figure of the one you were sure to see the pale, wizened features of the other." He said that he avoided all love affairs, as they invariably led to trouble and complications, but he was ultimately caught by his uncle in compromising circumstances with Mademoiselle Fifi, who was a *protégée* of the old man. Bachelard insisted on their marriage, and gave the girl a handsome dowry. *Pot-Bouille.*

GUIBAL (MADAME), wife of a barrister well known at the Palais de Justice, who led, it was said, a somewhat free life. The husband and wife were never seen together, and Madame Guibal consoled herself with M. de Boves, from whom she derived such large sums of money that he found difficulty in carrying on his own establishment. She was a tall, thin woman, with red hair, and a somewhat cold, selfish expression. *Au Bonheur des Dames.*

GUICHON (MADEMOISELLE), the office-keeper at the railway station of Havre. She was a slim, fair woman about thirty years of age, who owed her post to M. Dabadie, the chief station-master, with whom it was generally believed she was on intimate terms. Nevertheless Madame Lebleu, who lived on the same corridor and kept perpetual watch, had never been able to discover anything. *La Bête Humaine.*

GUIGNARD, a peasant who belonged to the same village as Zéphyrin Lacour. He desired to sell his house, and Zéphyrin and Rosalie, his sweetheart, looked forward to buying it. *Une Page d'Amour.*

GUILLAUME, a peasant of Rognes. He owned a piece of land beside the hovel of Hyacinthe Fouan. *La Terre.*

GUILLAUME, a young swineherd at La Borderie. He afterwards became a soldier. *La Terre.*

GUIRAUD (M. DE), a magistrate of Paris, who was a friend of Doctor Deberle and visited at his house. *Une Page d'Amour.*

GUIRAUD (MADAME DE), wife of the preceding. She was on intimate terms with Madame Deberle, and took part in the amateur theatricals arranged by that lady. *Une Page d'Amour.*

GUIRAUDE (MADAME), mother of Sophie and Valentin, patients of Dr. Pascal. Her husband died of phthisis, and she herself suffered from a slow decomposition of the blood. She died soon after her son Valentin. *Le Docteur Pascal.*

GUNDERMANN, the great Jew banker, master of the Bourse and of the financial world. He was a man of over sixty years of age, who had long suffered from ill-health. Constantly engaged in business of the greatest magnitude, he never went to the Bourse himself; indeed, he even pretended that he sent no official representative there. He was not on friendly terms with Saccard, and when the Universal Bank was started he placed himself in antagonism towards it. The wild speculation in the shares of the bank gave him his chance; his principle was that when a share rose above its true value a reaction was bound to follow. Accordingly, when the bank shares rose to two thousand francs he began to sell, and though Saccard by steady buying forced them to over three thousand francs, he continued to sell. His losses meantime were, of course, enormous, but having got information through Baroness

Sandorff that Saccard's resources were at an end, he
made a final effort, with the
result that a panic ensued, the
price of the shares broke, and
Saccard, along with the bank,
was ruined. *L'Argent.*

GUNTHER (OTTO), captain in
the Prussian Guard. He was
a cousin of Weiss on the
mother's side. His feelings
were strongly anti-French,
and he refused to give any
assistance to Henriette Weiss
after the death of her husband,
when she was searching for
his body. *La Débâcle.*

GUSTAVE, Maxime Saccard's
hairdresser. *La Curée.*

GUTMANN, a soldier in the
Prussian Army, who took
part in the attack on Bazeilles.
It was he who tore Henriette
Weiss from the arms of her
husband, who, being a civilian,
was about to be executed for
firing upon the Prussian troops.
Henriette found him later
in the ambulance at Remilly.
He was unable to speak, a
ball having carried away half
his tongue, and they could
only guess from the sounds he
made that his name was
Gutmann. Henriette, moved
by pity, remained with him
to the end, and she alone
followed him to the place of
burial. *La Débâcle.*

GUYOT (ABBÉ), a priest of Saint-
Eutrope. He took duty
temporarily at Artaud while
Abbé Mouret was ill. *La
Faute de l'Abbé Mouret.*

GUYOT-LAPLANCHE, a man of
considerable importance in
the Second Empire, whom
Clorinde Balbi gained to the
cause of Eugène Rougon.
Son Excellence Eugène Rougon.

H

HAFFNER, a well-known manufacturer, at Colmar. He was
a multi-millionaire, and became a politician during the
time of the Second Empire.
He was the husband of
Suzanne Haffner. *La Curée.*

HAFFNER (MADAME SUZANNE),
wife of a celebrated manufacturer of Colmar, a millionaire twenty times over, whom
the Empire was transforming
into a politician. She was the
inseparable companion of the
Marquise d'Espanet, and had
been a schoolfellow of Madame
Renée Saccard. *La Curée.*

HALLEGRAIN(CAPTAIN JACQUES),
the father of Christine. He
was a Gascon from Montau-
ban. A stroke of paralysis
in the legs caused his retirement from the army, and he
settled at Clermont with his
wife and daughter. One day,

when they were at church, he died of a second attack of paralysis. *L'Œuvre.*

HALLEGRAIN (MADAME), wife of the preceding. She survived him for five years, remaining at Clermont, managing as well as she could on her scanty pension, which she eked out by painting fans, in order to bring up her daughter as a lady. During these five years Madame Hallegrain became each day paler and thinner, until she was only a shadow ; one morning she could not rise, and she died, looking sadly at Christine, with her eyes full of great tears. *L'Œuvre.*

HALLEGRAIN (CHRISTINE), daughter of the preceding, was born at Strasburg. Her father died · when she was twelve years old, and her mother, who had a severe struggle to make a living for herself and her child, only survived him five years. Christine was left penniless and unprotected, without a friend, save La Mère des Saints-Anges, the Superior of the Sisters of the Visitation, who kept her in the convent until she got a situation as reader and companion to Madame Vanzade, an old lady who lived in Paris. Chance led

to a meeting between Christine and Claude Lantier on the evening of her arrival in the city, and the acquaintanceship ripened into love. Ultimately she ran off with him, and they took up house at Bennecourt, where they lived happily for several years, a son being born to them in 1860. She was devoted to Claude, who was engrossed in his art, and when she saw that he was becoming discontented in the country she urged his return to Paris. There he became obsessed by the idea of a masterpiece, by means of which he was to revolutionize the world of art, and Christine allowed him to sacrifice their child and herself to his hopes of fame. They began to encroach on the principal of their small fortune, and while this lasted were not unhappy, though Claude's increasing mental disturbance already gave cause for anxiety. Their marriage had taken place some time previously, and this had tended to make her position more comfortable. The exhaustion of their means was followed by great hardships, but Christine continued to sacrifice everything to her husband. The death of their child drew him away from his task for a time, but he again took it up, his mind becoming more and more unhinged. Christine made a last effort to detach him, but the call of his masterpiece was too strong, and one morning she found him hanging in front of the picture, dead. She fell on the floor in a faint, and lay there to all appearance as dead as her husband, both of them crushed by the sovereignty of art. *L'Œuvre.*

HAMELIN (CAROLINE), sister of Georges Hamelin, accompanied him to Paris after the death of their father. She took a situation as governess, and soon after married a millionaire brewer in whose house she was employed. After a few years of married life, she was obliged to apply for a separation in order to avoid being killed by her husband, a drunkard who pursued her with a knife in fits of insane jealousy. Living with her brother, in the flat of the Orviedo mansion above that occupied by Saccard, she made the acquaintance of the latter, becoming after a time his housekeeper and subsequently his mistress. During the absence of her brother in the East, after the foundation of the Universal

Bank, she did everything she could to protect his interests, and tried to persuade Saccard to discontinue the gambling in the shares of the bank which ultimately led to its ruin. Like her brother, she sold all her shares in the bank, and after the final crash divested herself of all her means in the assistance of ruined shareholders. She followed her brother in his flight to Rome. *L'Argent.*

HAMELIN (GEORGES), son of a Montpellier physician, a remarkable *savant*, an enthusiastic Catholic, who had died poor. After his father's death he came to Paris, along with his sister Caroline, and entered the Polytechnic school. He became an engineer, and having received an appointment in connection with the Suez Canal, went to Egypt. Subsequently he went to Syria, where he remained some years, laying out a carriage road from Beyrout to Damascus. He was an enthusiast, and his portfolio was full of schemes of far-reaching magnitude. Having met Saccard in Paris, he joined with him in the formation of the Universal Bank, which was intended to furnish the means of carrying out some at least of his schemes. Against his wish, Hamelin was made chairman of the bank, and he thus became liable for the actions of the other directors, though he was himself absent in the East forming the companies in which the bank was interested. He was a man of high honour, and when the gamble in the shares of the bank reached an excessive point, he did all he could to restrain it, even selling his own shares. The money received for these was subsequently used in relieving other shareholders who lost their all. When the crash came, Hamelin was arrested along with Saccard, and, after trial, was sentenced to five years' imprisonment and a fine of three thousand francs. By a technicality of law they were allowed a month to appeal, during which they were at liberty. With the connivance of Eugène Rougon they fled the country, Hamelin going to Rome, where he secured a situation as an engineer. *L'Argent.*

HAMELIN (FRANÇOISE), sister of M. Hamelin, a farmer, who lived at Soulanges. She brought up Angelique Marie, who was handed over to her

by the Foundling Hospital when only a few days old. Angelique remained with her until she went to Paris with Madame Franchomme, some years later. *Le Rêve.*

HARDY, tax-collector at Cloyes. *La Terre.*

HARTMANN (BARON), Director of the Crédit Immobilier, a concern which had large interests in property immediately adjoining " The Ladies' Paradise." The Baron had been a lover of Madame Desforges, and through her influence he agreed to give financial support to Octave Mouret, thereby enabling him to carry out the large schemes of extension to which he had long looked forward. *Au Bonheur des Dames.*

HAUCHECORNE, principal assistant in the draper's shop known as the *Vieil Elbeuf.* He married Désirée, the daughter of his employer, and succeeded to the business, which he ultimately handed over to Baudu, his own son-in-law. *Au Bonheur des Dames.*

HAUCHECORNE (MADAME), wife of the preceding. *See* Désirée Finet.

HAUCHECORNE (ELIZABETH), daughter of the preceding. *See* Madame Baudu.

H

HautecœÉur (Monseigneur Jean d') was a member of one of the oldest and proudest families in France. He was for some time in the army, and until he was forty years of age he led an adventurous life, travelling everywhere and having many strange experiences. At last he chanced to meet Mademoiselle Pauline, daughter of the Comte de Valençay, very wealthy, marvellously beautiful, and scarcely nineteen years of age. They were married, but at the end of a year Pauline had a son and died. A fortnight later M. d'Hautecœur entered into Holy Orders, and soon became a priest ; twenty years afterwards he was made a bishop. During all that time he refused to see Félicien, his son, who had been brought up by an old abbot, a relation of his wife. He intended to have his son brought up as a priest, but the lad having no vocation, he gave up the idea and brought him to live at Beaumont. There Félicien met and fell in love with Angelique, but the Bishop sternly forbade any thought of marriage between them, and even went the length of arranging a marriage between his son and Claire de Voincourt. A touch-

ing personal appeal by Angelique had no effect in gaining the Bishop's consent, but he was secretly much moved, and when she fell into ill-health he himself came to administer the last rites of the Church. Her semi-miraculous recovery led to the Bishop consenting to his son's marriage, which was celebrated a few months later in the cathedral of Beaumont. *Le Rêve.*

Hautecœur (Marquise Jean XII de). *See* Paule de Valençay.

Hautecœur (Angelique de). *See* Angelique Marie.

Hautecœur (Félicien d'), only child of Jean d'Hautecœur, who was afterwards Bishop of Beaumont. Félicien's mother having died at his birth, his father took Holy Orders, and refused to see him for over twenty years. Having ultimately come to live with his father at Beaumont, Félicien met and fell in love with Angelique, the adopted daughter of Hubert, the chasuble-maker. The Bishop having absolutely refused to consent to the marriage, the Huberts endeavoured to separate the lovers by persuading Angelique that Félicien no longer cared for her. They were aided in this by a rumour that Félicien was to marry Claire de Voincourt. A meeting between Angelique and Félicien cleared away the mists, but by this time the girl had fallen into ill-health and appeared to be dying. The Bishop, who had formerly been secretly moved by an appeal made to him by Angelique, came to administer to her the last rites of the Church. A semi-miraculous recovery followed, and, the Bishop having consented, Félicien was married to Angelique in the cathedral of Beaumont. The recovery had, however, been a mere spark of an expiring fire, for as Félicien led his new-made wife to the cathedral porch, she slipped from his arm, and in a few moments was dead. *Le Rêve.*

HAZARD, a horse in the Mechain stable. It ran in the Grand Prix de Paris. *Nana.*

HÉDOUIN (CHARLES), originally a salesman in the draper's shop known as *Au Bonheur des Dames*, he became a partner by marrying Caroline Deleuze, a daughter of one of the proprietors. He fell into ill-health, but when he died the business was left in a flourishing condition. *Pot-Bouille.*

HÉDOUIN (MADAME CAROLINE), wife of M. Hédouin, the proprietor of a draper's shop in Paris known as "The Ladies' Paradise." She was a handsome woman with strong commercial capabilities, and during the frequent absences of her husband she undertook the management of the business. When Octave Mouret came to Paris, he first got employment at "The Ladies' Paradise," and with a view to establishing his position he conceived the idea of becoming Madame Hédouin's lover. She discouraged his advances, however, and he gave up his situation. M. Hédouin died soon afterwards, and his widow, finding the responsibilities of business too heavy, invited Octave Mouret to return ; a few months afterwards they were married. *Pot-Bouille.*

After her marriage with Octave Mouret the business extended rapidly, and an enlargement of the shop soon became necessary. While the work was in progress she met with an accident which resulted in her death three days later. *Au Bonheur des Dames.*

HÉLÈNE (DUCHESSE), the principal character in *La Petite Duchesse,* a piece by Fauchery played at the Théâtre des Variétés. The part was originally given to Rose Mignon, but was played by Nana, who was a complete failure in it. *Nana.*

HÉLOÏSE, an actress at the Folies. She was plain-looking, but very amusing. *Au Bonheur des Dames.*

HENNEBEAU, general manager of the Montsou Mining Company, was born in the Ardennes. In his early life he had undergone the hardships of a poor boy thrown as an orphan on the Paris streets. After having followed the courses of the École des Mines, at the age of twenty-four he became engineer to the Sainte-Barbe mine, and three years later he became divisional engineer in the Pas-de-Calais, at the Marles mines. When there he married the daughter of the rich owner of a spinning factory at Arras. For fifteen years they lived in the same small provincial town, and no event broke the monotony of existence, not even the birth of a child. An increasing irritation detached Madame Hennebeau, who was disdainful of this husband who gained a small salary with such difficulty. The misunderstandings between them became more pronounced, but with the view of pleasing his wife Hennebeau accepted a situation in an office in Paris. But Paris only completed their separation, for she immediately threw herself into all the luxurious follies of the period. During the ten years spent there she carried on an open intrigue with a man whose desertion nearly killed her. It was then that her husband accepted the management of the Montsou mines, still hoping that his wife might be changed down there in that desolate black country. When the great strike of miners broke out he at first minimized its seriousness, thinking that it would not last a week. By his lack of decided action he forfeited to some extent the confidence of his directors, but he regained this by the subsequent measures taken by him for bringing the strike to an end, and ultimately received the decoration of an officer of the Legion of Honour. His domestic life was, however, once more embittered by the discovery of a *liaison* between his wife and his nephew, Paul Négrel. *Germinal.*

HENNEBEAU (MADAME), wife of the preceding, was the daughter of a rich spinner at Arras. She did not get on well with her husband, whom she despised for his small success, and after she accompanied him to Paris she entered into a notorious *liaison* with a man whose subsequent desertion nearly killed her. For a time after their removal to Montsou she seemed more contented, but this did not last long, and she ultimately consoled herself with her husband's nephew, Paul Négrel. She was angry at the strikers, as they interfered with the arrival of provisions for a dinner-party which she was giving ; but she was incapable of understanding the sufferings of the miners and their families in the hardships they were forced to undergo. *Germinal.*

HÉQUET (CAROLINE), a well-known *demi - mondaine* in Paris. Her father, who was a clerk in Bordeaux, was long since dead, and her mother, accepting the situation, looked after Caroline's financial affairs with the strictest regularity. She bought the estate known as *La Mignotte* after Nana tired of it. *Nana.*

HÉQUET (MADAME), mother of the preceding. She was a model of orderliness, who kept her daughter's accounts with severe precision. She managed the whole household from some small lodgings two stories above her daughter's, where, moreover, she had established a work-room for dressmaking and plain sewing. *Nana.*

HERBELIN, a great chemist whose discoveries revolutionized that science. Lazare Chanteau, who was for some time in his laboratory as an assistant, got from him the idea of extracting chemicals from seaweed by a new process. *La Joie de Vivre.*

HERMELINE, a student of rhetoric at the college of Plassans. He was in love with Sister Angèle, and once went the length of cutting his hands with his penknife to get an opportunity of seeing and speaking to her while she dressed his self-inflicted hurts. In the end the student and the Sister ran off together. *L'Œuvre.*

HIPPOLYTE, valet to Duveyrier. *Pot-Bouille.*

HIPPOLYTE, valet to Hennebeau, the manager of the Montsou Mining Company. *Germinal.*

HOMME NOIR (L'), an apparition said to haunt the Voreux pit. It was said to take the form of an old miner who twisted the necks of bad girls. *Germinal.*

HONORINE, a maid-servant with the Grégoires. She was a girl of some twenty years, who had been taken in as a child and brought up in the house. *Germinal.*

HONORINE, a servant in the employment of the Badeuils. When dismissed for misconduct she became insolent. *La Terre.*

HORN (LÉA DE), a Parisian *demi-mondaine* whose drawing-room was frequented by some of the old ministers of Louis Philippe. *Nana.*

HORTEUR (ABBÉ), parish priest of Bonneville, was a thick-set man of peasant-like build whose red hair was still unsilvered by his fifty years. Much of his time was spent in cultivating a small plot of ground in the churchyard, which he had enclosed as a vegetable garden. With regard to religion, he had come to be contented with the observance of outward ceremonies, and his tolerance had degenerated into a state of indifference as to the spiritual condition of his flock. He was on good terms with Chanteau, with whom it was his custom to play draughts every Saturday. *La Joie de Vivre.*

HOTON, a sugar - refinery at Montsou. Its prosperity was greatly affected by the strike of miners. *Germinal.*

HOURDEQUIN (ALEXANDRE), born 1804, was the only son of Isidore Hourdequin. He studied at the college of Châteaudun, but made little progress, as his only interest was in farming, for which he had an absolute passion. On the death of his father he became master of La Borderie, which he cultivated on the latest principles of agriculture, spending large sums upon it. He married a sister of Bailliehache, the notary, who brought him a considerable sum, which also went into the land. His wife died in a few years, leaving him with two children, a son named Léon, who to his great disappointment became a soldier, and a daughter who died young. In spite of these misfortunes he retained all his passion for the land, and in it he gradually sunk all his fortune, getting little from it in return. A *liaison* with Jacqueline Cognet, followed, and she gradually acquired complete influence over him.

He died as the result of an accident brought about by Tron, one of his own servants, who was also a lover of Jacqueline. *La Terre.*

HOURDEQUIN (MADAME), wife of the preceding. *See* Mademoiselle Baillehache. *La Terre.*

HOURDEQUIN (ISIDORE), born 1767, was the descendant of an old peasant family of Cloyes, which had educated and elevated itself into a middle-class position in the sixteenth century. They had all been employed in the administration of the salt monopoly, and Isidore, who had early been left an orphan, was worth sixty thousand francs, when, at twenty-six, the Revolution cost him his post. As a speculation he bought the farm of La Borderie for a fifth of its value, but the depreciation of real estate continued, and he was unable to resell it at the profit of which he had dreamed. He therefore determined to farm it himself, and about this time he married the daughter of a neighbour, who brought him an additional hundred and twenty acres of land. He had one son, Alexandre, and died in 1831. *La Terre.*

HOURDEQUIN (LÉON), son of Alexandre Hourdequin. He had an intense hatred of the soil and became a soldier, being promoted Captain after Solferino. He did not visit his home more than once a year, and was much annoyed to discover the *liaison* between his father and Jacqueline Cognet. He endeavoured to get the latter into disgrace, but the only effect was to make a complete breach between his father and himself. *La Terre.*

HOURDEQUIN (MADEMOISELLE), the second child of Alexandre Hourdequin. She was a delicate and charming girl, tenderly loved by her father. She died young, a short time after her mother. *La Terre.*

HOUTELARD, a fisherman of Bonneville, whose house was washed away after the destruction by the sea of the barricade erected by Lazare Chanteau. *La Joie de Vivre.*

HUBERT, a chasuble-maker who lived in a house immediately adjoining the cathedral of Beaumont. "For four hundred years the line of Huberts, embroiderers from father to son, had lived in this house." At twenty years of age he fell in love with a young girl of sixteen, Hubertine, and as her mother refused to give her consent to their union they ran away and were married. On the morning after Christmas, 1860, he found the child Angelique lying in a fainting condition in the snow outside the cathedral door. Having taken her into his house, he and his wife soon became attached to her, and as they had no children, ultimately adopted her as their daughter. *Le Rêve.*

HUBERTINE, wife of the preceding. At the age of sixteen she fell in love with Hubert, the chasuble-maker, and as her mother, widow of a magistrate, would not give her consent, they ran away and were married. A year later she went to the deathbed of her mother, who, however, disinherited her and gave her her curse. " So affected was she by the terrible scene that her infant, born soon after, . died." The Huberts had no other children, and after twenty-four years they still mourned the little one they had lost. She warmly approved of the adoption by her husband and herself of the foundling child Angelique, whom she treated with the greatest kindness. From the bitterness of her own experience she had a horror of

disobedience to parents, and when she found that the consent of Monseigneur d'Hautecœur could not be obtained to a marriage between his son Félicien and Angelique, she did all she could to sever the lovers. In this she was successful for a time, until the illness of Angelique, and her miraculous recovery, induced the Bishop to give his consent. *Le Rêve.*

HUE (M.), a retired Government official, who was a sincere lover of art. He was unfortunately not rich enough to be always buying pictures, and could only bewail the blindness of the public which allowed a genius to die of starvation ; for he himself, convinced, had selected Claude Lantier's crudest works, which he hung by the side of his Delacroix, predicting an equal fortune for them. *L'Œuvre.*

HUGON (MADAME), mother of Philippe and Georges Hugon. She was the widow of a notary, and lived quietly at Fondettes, an old family property near Orléans, but had retained a house in Paris in Rue de Richelieu. She had been an old friend of the Marquise de Chouard, and was on intimate terms with her daughter, the Comtesse

Sabine. A woman of high principles, she believed that one should overlook much in others in order that something might be pardoned in oneself. In this she contrasted strongly with her old friend the Marquis de Chouard, who professed the most rigorous virtue while he secretly lived a shameful life. She was, however, unable to bear with equanimity the eccentricities of Nana, her neighbour in the country, who led Philippe Hugon into dishonour, and his brother Georges to suicide. *Nana.*

HUGON (GEORGES), the younger son of Madame Hugon. At seventeen years of age he became infatuated with Nana, and a *liaison* with her followed. His mother, having discovered the state of affairs, interfered, and kept him at Fondettes for some months after Nana had returned to Paris, but he ultimately followed her there. Though he was not affected by the knowledge that Nana had other lovers, he was driven to frenzy when he learned that his brother Philippe had become one of the number. He implored Nana to marry him, and when she refused to take his offer seriously he plunged a pair of her scissors into his breast. The injury was not immediately fatal, but he died a few months afterwards ; some said as the result of the wound reopening, while others spoke of a second and successful attempt at suicide. *Nana.*

HUGON (PHILIPPE), the elder son of Madame Hugon. A tall, handsome youth, he quickly attained the rank of lieutenant in the army, and was stationed first in the garrison at Bourges, and afterwards at Vincennes. His mother imprudently sent him to endeavour to release Georges from the toils of Nana, with the result that he was himself ensnared. He had little money of his own, and, as the demands of Nana were unceasing, he began to take small sums from the regimental funds, of which he was treasurer. The thefts went on for a considerable time, and when discovery was made they amounted to twelve thousand francs. Philippe was arrested, and when he was released from prison some months afterwards, dishonoured for ever, he was only in time to join his mother at the death-bed of her other son, who was also a victim to Nana's unhappy influence. *Nana.*

HUGUENIN held a sinecure worth six thousand francs at the Ministry of the Interior. When he died Eugène Rougon, the Minister, gave the post to Léon Bejuin. *Son Excellence Eugène Rougon.*

HUPEL DE LA NOUE (M.), *préfet* of the district for which M. Mareuil was member. He arranged the *tableaux vivants* at the great party given by Aristide Saccard. *La Curée.*

HURET, a member of the Chamber of Deputies who obtained his election through the influence of Eugène Rougon. His very existence depended on the favour of the Minister of State, towards whom he conducted himself as a sort of general servant. " By following this calling for a couple of years he had, thanks to bribes and pickings, prudently realized, been able to increase his estates." Having ascertained that Rougon would not oppose the foundation of the Universal Bank, Huret became a director ; later on, when the shares had risen to their highest point, he sold out in the knowledge that Rougon had decided to abandon his brother and that a catastrophe would be inevitable. *L'Argent.*

HUTIN, a salesman in the silk department of " The Ladies' Paradise." " He had managed after eighteen months' service to become one of the principal salesmen, thanks to a natural flexibility of character, a continual flow of caressing flattery under which was concealed a furious rage for business." Having conspired against Robineau, the " second hand " in his department, he succeeded him, only to be conspired against in turn by his own subordinates. When Denise Baudu first came to " The Ladies' Paradise " Hutin showed her some kindness, for which she was grateful, but ultimately he made statements about her which were entirely without foundation. *Au Bonheur des Dames.*

HUTIN (MADAME), a woman who lived in the vicinity of the *Halles Centrales*, and was spied on by Mademoiselle Saget, whose penetrating eye allowed none of her neighbours to escape notice. *Le Ventre de Paris.*

I

ISABELLE, a character in *La Petite Duchesse*, a piece by Fauchery, played at the Théâtre des Variétés. The part was taken by Simonne Cabiroche. *Nana.*

J

JABOUILLE, a herbalist, whose shop was situated in Rue du Cherche-Midi. He was a widower, and married for the second time a woman named Mathilde. His shop was at one time prosperous, but business fell away until what was left was only that of an equivocal character. He died of syncope induced by phthisis. *L'Œuvre.*

JABOUILLE (MADAME MATHILDE), wife of the preceding. She was a woman of about thirty, plain-looking, and exceedingly thin. From the time of her marriage to Jabouille, his business began to decrease, and this, it would appear, was due to her reputation, which alarmed the more respectable customers. Her *liaisons* were numerous, and included Mahoudeau, Chaîne, and Jory, but after the death of her husband she married the last named, settling down into respectability and ruling him with a rod of iron. *L'Œuvre.*

JACOBY, a Jew from Bordeaux, between whom and Mazaud there was keen rivalry. "Though of great experience and shrewdness, he was sorely handicapped by his passion for speculation, and in spite of considerable profits always seemed on the eve of a catastrophe. His money melted away on settling days." He acted as broker for Daigremont, and also for Gundermann. The great gamble in the shares of the Universal Bank resolved itself into a duel between Jacoby and Mazaud, the one selling on behalf of Gundermann, and the other buying on behalf of Saccard ; and the final catastrophe was hastened by Jacoby warning Daigremont of Gundermann's determination to crush out the bank. *L'Argent.*

JALAGUIER (MADAME), a *protégée* of Madame Correur, who induced Eugène Rougon, the Minister, to increase the old lady's pension considerably. *Son Excellence Eugène Rougon.*

JALAGUIER FILS, son of the preceding. Madame Correur took an interest in him, and asked Eugène Rougon to secure a scholarship for him. *Son Excellence Eugène Rougon.*

JANTROU, an ex-professor of the University of Bordeaux, who in consequence of some misconduct was obliged to leave for Paris, without caste or position. At the age of twenty-eight, he landed at the Bourse, where for ten years he dragged out existence as a *remisier* or broker's tout. At the time of the foundation of the Universal Bank he suggested to Saccard the purchase of a newspaper to be employed in the interest of the company. The purchase was carried out, and Jantrou was appointed editor. Subsequently other papers were acquired, which he manipulated so as to keep the bank continually before the public. He gave information to Baroness Sandorff which she repeated to Gundermann, who was induced thereby to continue his attack on the bank. *L'Argent.*

JEANBERNAT, the caretaker of the deserted estate of Paradou in Provence. He lived by himself with his niece Albine in an old house on the border of the demesne. In an attic he had found a large number of books which had been saved from a fire in the old mansion, and these he had studied for twenty years, imbibing from them the rationalistic theories of the eighteenth century. He had no respect for religion, and particularly disliked Brother Archangias, who insulted both him and his niece. After the death of Albine he attacked Archan-

gias, and cut off his right ear with a pocket-knife. *La Faute de l'Abbé Mouret.*

JENARD, a partner of the firm of Cornille and Jenard, which developed in the eighteenth century the mineral concession of Joiselle. *Germinal.*

JÉSUS CHRIST, the sobriquet of Hyacinthe Fouan. *La Terre.*

JEUMONT (M. AND MADAME) were well known in society during the Second Empire. The Emperor admired Madame Jeumont, and her husband was decorated by him. *L'Argent.*

JOBELIN (AUGUSTE), son of Colonel Jobelin. Contrary to regulations, Eugène Rougon took him into the office of the Minister of the Interior without the necessary bachelor's degree. *Son Excellence Eugène Rougon.*

JOBELIN (COLONEL), a friend of Eugène Rougon, through whose aid he hoped to secure a nomination as commander of the Legion of Honour, and an appointment for his son. He was a cousin of M. Bouchard. After Rougon's return to office he received the appointment as commander. *Son Excellence Eugène Rougon.*

JOIRE (ABBÉ), Curé of Montsou. He pretended not to interest

himself in anything, so as not to vex either the workers or the masters. During the strike he took his walks at night, to prevent himself from being compromised by the miners. He obtained promotion, and was replaced by Abbé Ranvier. *Germinal.*

JONCQUIER, a lover of Rose Mignon, who deserted her for a time in favour of Laure. *Nana.*

JONCQUOY (MADAME DU), an old friend of the Muffats. Years ago she had met Bismarck, who struck her as stupid ; she was unable to understand his later success. *Nana.*

JORDAN (PAUL), a journalist, whose father, a Marseilles banker, had committed suicide in consequence of some disastrous speculations. He married a daughter of M. Maugendre, to whom he had been betrothed in more prosperous days. His wife brought him no dowry, as her parents were against the marriage on the ground of Jordan's occupation and want of means. Having made the acquaintance of Saccard, he received an appointment on the staff of the newspaper purchased to support the policy of the Universal Bank. He did not

speculate, however, and remained in comparative poverty, until the success of a novel which he had written put him in more comfortable circumstances, and even enabled him to give assistance to his wife's parents after they were ruined by the failure of the bank. *L'Argent.*

JORDAN (MADAME MARCELLE), wife of the preceding. She was the only child of M. Maugendre, who was ruined by the failure of the Universal Bank. *L'Argent.*

JORY (EDOUARD) was the son of a magistrate of Plassans, whom he drove crazy by his profligate conduct. In the end he ran off with a music-hall singer under the pretext of going to Paris to follow the literary profession. Notwithstanding the fact that his profligacy went to even greater lengths in the city, he was successful in journalism, and soon earned between seven and eight thousand francs a year as a leader-writer and art critic. His first success was gained in a series of articles in a little newspaper called *Le Tambour*, in which he fell foul of the accepted canons of art, and hailed Claude Lantier and his companions as the founders of a new school. Later he claimed to have made Fagerolles by his articles, in the same manner as he formerly took credit for making Lantier. He gradually dropped his old friends, however, finding that the public only laughed at their productions, and in excuse pleaded that he had not a journal in which he could support their cause; but when, still later, he became director of a great Art review, he preserved the same silence. After innumerable love affairs, he ended by marrying Mathilde Jabouille. *L'Œuvre.*

JORY (MADAME), wife of the preceding. *See* Mathilde Jabouille.

JOSEPH, a butler in the employment of Nana at La Mignotte. *Nana.*

JOSEPH, an old soldier who secured a situation in "The Ladies' Paradise" through the influence of Lhomme, whose foster-brother he was. He married Mlle. de Fontenailles, a shop-girl in the establishment. *Au Bonheur des Dames.*

JOSEPH (MADAME), the *concierge* of the house on Quay Bourbon where Claude Lantier lived. *L'Œuvre.*

JOSSE (MADEMOISELLE) kept a little school for young children in Rue Polonceau. Anna Coupeau was her pupil, and made herself such a nuisance that twice Mademoiselle Josse sent her away, taking her back each time in order not to lose the small fees. *L'Assommoir.*

Nana in later years exchanged reminiscences with Satin, who, like herself, had been a pupil at Mademoiselle Josse's school. *Nana.*

JOSSERAND PÈRE, the father of Josserand, the cashier at the Saint-Joseph glassworks. He was originally a solicitor at Clermont. *Pot-Bouille.*

JOSSERAND, cashier at the St. Joseph glass-works. His salary was not a large one, and in consequence of the determination of his wife to keep up a greater style than they could afford, he was engaged in a continual struggle to make ends meet; to gain a few extra francs he frequently spent much of the night addressing circulars for a firm of publishers. Worn out by hard work and by the continual bickerings of his wife and daughters, he was not in a condition to stand the disgrace of his daughter

Berthe's *liaison* with Octave Mouret, and he was struck down by paralysis, which soon after resulted in his death. *Pot-Bouille.*

JOSSERAND (MADAME ÉLÉANORE), wife of the preceding. Her two objects in life were to appear better off than she really was, and to secure husbands for her daughters. In the latter quest she had many disappointments, and her temper, never good, correspondingly suffered, her unfortunate husband bearing the brunt. A marriage having ultimately been arranged between Berthe Josserand and Auguste Vabre, Madame Josserand made a strong effort to induce her brother, Narcisse Bachelard, to pay the dowry which he had long ago promised to his niece. As he refused to do so, Madame Josserand overcame the difficulty by a subterfuge of doubtful honesty. *Pot-Bouille.*

JOSSERAND (BERTHE), second daughter of M. Josserand. After several ineffectual efforts to secure a husband she became engaged to Auguste Vabre, the elder son of her father's landlord. Difficulties as to a dowry followed, but these were surmounted by somewhat shady means, and the marriage took place. Vabre's health was not good, and Berthe soon became discontented, a state of mind largely induced by the bad advice of her mother. About this time Octave Mouret came to be assistant in Vabre's shop, and Berthe, carried away by his attentions, entered upon an unfortunate *liaison* with him. Discovery by Vabre led to Berthe's return to her parents' home, and it was only after a considerable time that a reconciliation was brought about by the efforts of Abbé Mauduit. *Pot-Bouille.*

JOSSERAND (HORTENSE), elder daughter of M. Josserand. Her mother endeavoured to secure a husband for her, but she made her own choice, selecting one Verdier, a lawyer. The marriage was put off from time to time as Verdier had got entangled with a woman from whom he found separation difficult. *Pot-Bouille.*

JOSSERAND (LÉON), elder son of M. Josserand. He was a young man of ambition, who hoped to rise through the influence of Madame Dambreville, whose lover he became. Ultimately she arranged a marriage between him and her niece Raymonde, who brought him a large dowry. Soon afterwards by the same means he was appointed *Maître des Requêtes. Pot-Bouille.*

JOSSERAND (MADAME LÉON), wife of the preceding. *See* Raymonde. *Pot-Bouille.*

JOSSERAND (SATURNIN), younger son of M. Josserand. He was a powerful young man of twenty-five, whose mind had been seriously affected by an attack of brain fever ; though not actually insane, he was subject to fits of blind fury whenever anybody annoyed him. When his sister Berthe was a little girl, he nursed her through a long illness, and since he saved her life he adored her with a deep, passionate devotion. The preparations for her marriage to Auguste Vabre affected him so seriously that his removal to an asylum became necessary, and he remained there for some time. On his release he went to live with his sister and her husband, but domestic trouble having arisen, his mind again became so unhinged that he made an attempt on the life of his brother-in-law and had again to be taken to an asylum. *Pot-Bouille.*

JOUVE (ABBÉ), an officiating priest at Notre Dame de Grâce, the parish church of Passy. He had known M. Grandjean at Marseilles, and showed much kindness to Hélène after the death of her husband, assisting her in settling up her affairs. Along with M. Rambaud, his half-brother, he was a regular visitor at Hélène's house, and later endeavoured to arrange a marriage between her and his brother. He was devoted to Jeanne Grandjean, and helped to nurse her during her fatal illness. An amiable, kind-hearted man, he was greatly beloved by his parishioners. *Une Page d'Amour.*

JOUVE, a retired captain in the army, and afterwards one of the four inspectors at " The Ladies' Paradise." In addition to acting as a spy on the staff he watched the customers, and it was he who detected Madame de Boves in the act of stealing some fine lace. He made certain advances to Denise Baudu which she resented, and in consequence he afterwards showed considerable ill-will towards her. *Au Bonheur des Dames.*

JUILLERAT (DOCTOR), an old physician who attended most

of the inhabitants of the Rue de Choiseul. He was a man of only average abilities who had built up a large practice by hard work. His views were somewhat advanced, and he had many arguments with Abbé Mauduit, with whom he frequently came in contact at the bedsides of his patients. *Pot-Bouille.*

JULES, the lover of La Sarriette. He lived on her earnings as a fruit-dealer. *Le Ventre de Paris.*

JULES, one of the soldiers sent to Montsou during the strike. He was born at Plogof, where his mother and sister still resided. One night while he was on guard at the Voreux mine he was murdered by Jeanlin Maheu, who with the assistance of Étienne Lantier carried the body to a gallery of the mine, where they buried it under a fall of rock. *Germinal.*

JULES (MADAME), Nana's dresser at the Théâtre des Variétés. *Nana.*

JULIE, cook in the employment of the Duveyriers. *Pot-Bouille.*

JULIEN, butler in the employment of Nana in the Avenue de Villiers. He left the house with a large sum, as Comte Muffat, being jealous, wished to be freed from his presence. *Nana.*

JUSSELIN (PIERRE-FRANÇOIS), a *protégée* of M. de Marsy. Eugène Rougon refused to nominate him as an officer of the Legion of Honour, and gave the decoration which had been intended for him to Béjuin. *Son Excellence Eugène Rougon.*

JUZEUR (MADAME), a neighbour of the Josserands in the Rue de Choiseul. Her husband had left her after ten days of married life, and thenceforth she lived alone in quiet lodgings. Very little was known of her circumstances or mode of life. *Pot-Bouille.*

K

KAHN (M.), son of a Jewish banker at Bordeaux ; a deputy who was engaged in a scheme for the construction of a railway from Niort to Angers. He was chiefly anxious for this, as the proposed line would pass through Bressure, where he had some blast-furnaces, the value of which it would considerably increase. Rougon supported him energetically, and had almost secured the grant when his retirement from office de-

I

layed the scheme for some years. Soon after Rougon's appointment as Minister of the Interior the grant was obtained, and he accompanied Kahn to Niort to attend the inauguration of the scheme. *Son Excellence Eugène Rougon.*

KAHN (MADAME), wife of the preceding. She lived a very retired life at Paris. *Son Excellence Eugène Rougon.*

KELLER (LES), well - known leaders of society in Paris. It was at their house that Baroness Sandorff first met Gundermann. *L'Argent.*

KOLB (M.), a banker whose business consisted to a large extent in gold arbitrage, buying foreign coins, and melting them into gold bars. He was a man of Jewish origin, and having heard that Daigremont was to be connected with the Universal Bank, he readily agreed to become a director. Being a cautious man, however, he sold all his shares before the final collapse. *L'Argent.*

L

LABORDETTE, a young man who was well known in racing circles, and was specially popular with women, as he was always ready to render them little services. Through his relations with the world of trainers and jockeys he had always the latest information as to races. He made himself very useful to Nana when she was setting up a stable of her own, and assisted her in the selection of servants. *Nana.*

LACAILLE, a customer of Madame François, the market gardener. He attended the Revolutionary meetings in Lebigre's café. *Le Ventre de Paris.*

LACAMP. *See* Puech and La-camp.

LACASSAGNE, a dealer in feathers and artificial flowers, whose business was ruined by the competition of Octave Mouret's great establishment. *Au Bonheur des Dames.*

LACHESNAYE (DE), judge at the Rouen Court of Appeal, was the husband of Berthe Grandmorin, whom he somewhat resembled in character. He was a little man, dry and yellow, who had been a judge at the Court of Appeal from the age of thirty-six; he had been decorated, thanks to the influence of his father-in-law, and to the services which his father had rendered on the High Commissions at the time of the *Coup d'État.* He was disliked by Denizet, the examining magistrate, in whose eyes he represented the class of judicial functionary who attained position by wealth and influence. Lachesnaye was incensed at the will of his father-in-law, Grandmorin, who left fully half of his fortune to women of all classes, most of them unknown to his family. *La Bête Humaine.*

LACHESNAYE (MADAME DE), wife of the preceding. *See* Berthe Grandmorin. *La Bête Humaine.*

LACOUR (ZÉPHYRIN), a young lad from the same village as Rosalie, whose sweetheart he was. He was drawn in the conscription and sent to Paris, where, by permission of Madame Grandjean, he came to see Rosalie, her maid, every Sunday. He was a simple, good - hearted lad, whose ambition was to get out of the army, marry Rosalie, and return to his native village. *Une Page d'Amour.*

LADICOURT (BARONNE DE), a lady who lived at Vouziers. Captain Beaudoin lunched at her house on 26th August, 1870, at the hour when the Seventh Army Corps was taking up its position for battle. *La Débâcle.*

LADRICOURT (COMTE DE), father of the Baroness Sandorff. He was a confirmed gambler, and a man of brutal manners. He died of apoplexy, completely ruined, after a series of disgraceful failures. *L'Argent.*

LA FALOISE (HECTOR DE), a youth who came from the country to Paris in order to complete his education. Thanks to the death of an uncle, he was very rich, and his chief ambition was to be in everything ultra Parisian. He posed as a man who had experienced everything, and who no longer thought anything worthy of being taken seriously. Introduced behind the scenes of the Théâtre des Variétés by his cousin Fauchery, he met Nana, who did him the honour of ruining him without much loss of time. When his money was done, he returned to the country in the hope of marrying a distant relation who was both ugly and pious. *Nana.*

LAFOUASSE, a tavern-keeper in the neighbourhood of Plassans, between the old demesne of Paradou and the village of Artaud. He was treated by Dr. Pascal Rougon for ataxy, but died after a hypodermic injection of a serum with which the doctor was experimenting. *Le Docteur Pascal.*

LAGARDE (EDMOND), a sergeant in the 6th Regiment of the line. At the most his age was twenty-three, but he did not appear more than eighteen. He took part in the battle of Sedan, and was wounded in the left arm, which was broken by a bullet. His father, who was a shopkeeper in Paris, was a customer of Delaherche, and he was removed to the house of the manufacturer, where he was treated as one of the family. A handsome lad, he aroused the pity of Gilberte Delaherche, whose lover he became. *La Débâcle.*

LAGRIFOUL (MARQUIS DE), the Legitimist Deputy for Plassans. His election came as a severe blow to the Government, and to M. Péqueur des Saulaies, the sub-prefect of Plassans, who was held responsible for it. In reality, the election had been largely influenced by the clergy, combined with the old nobility. It was to counteract this influence that the Government sent Abbé Faujas to Plassans. The Marquis being a man of poor abilities, whose public appearances were disappointing, his overthrow was rendered easier and more complete. *La Conquête de Plassans.*

LA JOLIE DAME, a customer at Octave Mouret's shop, *Au Bonheur des Dames.* She was a favourite with all the salesmen, and as no one knew her name she was always referred to as "The Pretty Lady." *Au Bonheur des Dames.*

LALUBIE, teacher of the sixth form at the college of Plassans. He found one day his room transformed into a *chapelle ardente*, thanks to his pupils led by Pouillard. After he recovered from his fright he set a heavy punishment for the whole class. He married the daughter of Galissard, the haberdasher at Plassans. *L'Œuvre.*

LAMBERTHIER, an assistant at the *Halles Centrales.* Josephine Déjoie was at one time cook in his house. *L'Argent.*

LAMBERTHON (M. DE), a Deputy who discussed with M. La Rouquette the wisdom of the Emperor conceding the privilege of presenting an address to the Crown. *Son Excellence Eugène Rougon.*

LAMBOURDIEU, a shopkeeper at Cloyes, who sold Parisian novelties in all the villages within a radius of five or six miles. *La Terre.*

LANDOIS (AUGUSTE), assistant in Quenu's business. He came to Paris from Troyes to perfect himself in his trade, and having little money, intended to set up for himself as a pork-butcher. He was engaged to his cousin Augustine Landois, who was also employed by Quenu. He took a dislike to Florent, and wrote an anonymous letter denouncing him to the Prefect of Police. *Le Ventre de Paris.*

LANDOIS (AUGUSTINE) came to Quenu's establishment to learn shop management. She was engaged to be married to her cousin Auguste Landois. *Le Ventre de Paris.*

LANGLADE (DE), Prefect of Deux-Sèvres. He was accused of dissolute conduct, and was superseded in his office by Du Poizat. *Son Excellence Eugène Rougon.*

LANTIER (AUGUSTE), the lover of Gervaise Macquart ; he accompanied her to Paris, when she left home with their two children. *La Fortune des Rougon.*

Soon after their arrival in Paris, he deserted Gervaise for a girl named Adèle, with whom he lived for several years, during which he appears to have done little work. After Adèle left him he renewed friendship with Gervaise and Coupeau, her husband, and induced them to take him into their house as a lodger. Once established there, he paid nothing for his support, and soon Gervaise was supporting him as well as her husband, who by this time was doing nothing. Gervaise, having become disgusted with her husband's intemperance, resumed her old relations with Lantier, and these continued till she was financially ruined, and her shop was taken over by Virginie Poisson. Lantier, having transferred his affections to Virginie, was allowed to retain his old position as lodger, and soon resumed his former tactics of paying no rent and living off his landlord. In course of time he succeeded in eating the Poissons' stock of sweetmeats and bringing them to ruin, and then began to look out for some one else to support him. *L'Assommoir.*

LANTIER (CLAUDE), son of Gervaise Macquart and Auguste Lantier, was born at Plassans in 1842. He was brought up by his paternal grandmother, but when she died, in 1850, he was taken to Paris by his parents. *La Fortune des Rougon.*

After Lantier's desertion of Gervaise, and her subsequent marriage to Coupeau, Claude continued to reside with his mother, but a few years later an old gentleman of Plassans, a lover of pictures, who had been greatly struck by some daubs done by the child, offered to pay for his education. The offer was accepted, and Claude returned to Plassans. *L'Assommoir.*

Some years later his benefactor died, leaving him an income of a thousand francs a year, enough to prevent him dying of hunger in the artistic career which he had decided to follow. Having come to Paris with an intense hatred of romanticism, he was struck by the artistic possibilities of the *Halles Centrales*, the great provision markets of Paris, which he haunted in search of subjects for his brush. He was induced by Florent to attend one of the republican meetings in Lebigre's café, but was not in sympathy with the movement, and declined to take part in it. He occasionally visited his aunt, Madame Lisa Quenu, but revolted against her complete indifference to art, and her middle-class selfishness. *Le Ventre de Paris.*

He was appointed a member of the family council which nominally had charge of Pauline Quenu's fortune. *La Joie de Vivre.*

He established himself in a studio near the roof of an old house close to the river, and there lived the life of a Bohemian, with an absolute disdain for everything not related to art. He revolted against the canons of the schools, and tried to achieve truth in painting by adopting an exaggerated realism. His hopes became centred in a large painting, which he called *Plein Air*, intended for exhibition in the *Salon*. The picture was rejected, and when shown at a minor exhibition was greeted with derision by the public. About this period began his connection with Christine Hallegrain, with whom he lived for several years, and ultimately married. They took up house at Bennecourt in an old cottage, and there some years passed happily enough, a son named Jacques Louis being born in 1860. But Claude gradually became discontented, and the little family returned to Paris, where there began a long struggle against poverty, a struggle beginning in high anticipation and ending in despair. After a long search for a subject for the picture which was to be his masterpiece, Claude selected a stretch of the river near Notre Dame, and into this he intended to put all those new theories of art with which he hoped to revolutionize the world. Everything was sacrificed to this picture ; the small fortune left him by his early benefactor was gradually realized to provide food, and when it was exhausted there was little but starvation for the artist and his dependants. The work was begun in a frenzy of genius, but was constantly interrupted by doubts and indecision ; it became a monomania, and under its influence Claude's mind gradually became unhinged ; the family virus was at last showing itself. Christine was wholly taken up with her husband, and their child died of an illness due greatly to neglect. By this time Claude was incapable of any real feeling save for art, and the death of his child only served to give him a subject for a picture. Having torn himself away from his intended masterpiece for a time, he painted *L'Enfant Mort*, which was exhibited in the *Salon*, and met with an even

more contemptuous reception from the public than his *Plein Air*. Christine used all her influence to prevent her husband from returning to his task, but his brain had become obsessed by the great idea, which his hand proved powerless to execute as his mind became increasingly deranged. At length, in a moment of delirium, he hanged himself in front of the picture which had proved the means of his undoing. His genius was incomplete, and he was unable to carry out his own theories, but they were adopted by other and less able successors with better results. He was buried in the cemetery of Cayenne at Saint-Ouen. *L'Œuvre.*

LANTIER (MADAME CHRISTINE), wife of the preceding. *See* Christine Hallegrain. *L'Œuvre.*

LANTIER (ÉTIENNE), the youngest son of Auguste Lantier and Gervaise Macquart, was born in 1846, and accompanied his parents to Paris in 1850. *La Fortune des Rougon.*

After his mother had been married to Coupeau for some time, and had started her laundry, Étienne was found somewhat in the way, and on the suggestion of Goujet was sent to work in the rivet making factory where he himself was employed. Later the boy was sent to Lille, where he was apprenticed to an old master of Goujet, an engineer in that town. When Gervaise had fallen into poverty, Étienne, who was by that time a stoker on an engine, was able to send his mother a five-franc piece occasionally. *L'Assommoir*.

In a moment of passion Étienne struck his chief, and was at once dismissed from his employment. An industrial crisis existed at the time, and, finding it impossible to get work, he tramped from place to place till eventually he arrived at Montsou, worn out with fatigue and want. At the Voreux pit he chanced to get work in a gang led by Maheu, and went underground for the first time. The work was hard and distasteful to him, but he was unwilling to give it up, and was perhaps influenced by the bright eyes of Catherine Maheu, who toiled alongside him. He became more and more impressed with a sense of the hardships of the miners' lives, and his mind was also influenced by Souvarine, a confessed anarchist, beside whom he lodged. Gradually Étienne began to indoctrinate his companions with a spirit of revolt, and when the great strike broke out he became the leader. He did not, however, accept the extreme doctrines of Souvarine, and endeavoured to dissuade the strikers from doing damage to property. In this he was not altogether successful, and his influence became considerably lessened, until he was blamed by his comrades for the hardships they had to endure during the strike, and for its ultimate collapse. He returned to work, and in the terrible catastrophe brought about by Souvarine he was cut off at the bottom of the pit with Chaval and Catherine Maheu. He had always loved Catherine, and notwithstanding their peril, an old jealousy revived, and in a struggle with Chaval Étienne killed him. Days elapsed before rescue came, and by that time Catherine was dead. After six weeks in hospital, Étienne left for Paris. *Germinal*.

At Paris, later on, he took part in the Communist rising, and was condemned to death. He was respited, and transported to Noumea, where he married, and became father of a little girl. *Le Docteur Pascal*.

LANTIER (JACQUES), the second son of Gervaise Macquart and Auguste Lantier, was born at Plassans in 1844. He was six years old when his parents went to Paris with his brothers, Claude and Étienne, leaving him with his godmother, Aunt Phasie, who sent him to the School of Arts and Crafts. After two years passed on the Orléans Railway, he became an engineer of the first-class on the Western Railway. At twenty-six he was a tall, handsome man, with dark hair and a clear complexion. From childhood he had suffered from a complaint which the doctors did not understand, a pain in the head, behind the ears, accompanied by fever and an intense melancholy, which tempted him to hide like a suffering animal. When about sixteen years of age he became affected by a curious form of insanity, the desire to murder any woman of whom he became fond. " On each occasion it seemed like a sudden outburst of blind rage, an ever-recurring thirst to avenge some very ancient offence, the exact recollection of which escaped him. Did it date from so far back, from the harm women had done to his race, from the rancour

laid up from male to male since the first deceptions in the depths of the caverns ? " Even with his cousin Flore, who loved him from childhood, the same terrible instinct arose, and could only be stilled by flight.

By chance, Jacques was a momentary witness of the murder of President Grandmorin, and when suspicion fell upon the Roubauds he came to be of opinion that it was well-founded, a belief which was confirmed by a subsequent confession to him by Séverine. This avowal by Séverine placed her in his mind in a different category from all other women ; she had killed, and was a person sacred and apart, a woman he could love without his lust for blood being evoked. At the request of Séverine, Jacques promised to kill Roubaud, her husband, whom she had come to hate ; but, though all the preparations were made, it was Séverine herself whom he killed, in an accession of that homicidal rage which he imagined he had conquered. He escaped all suspicion, and calmly allowed Roubaud and Cabuche to be punished for the crime. In order to see whether the murder of Séverine had cured him of his blood lust, he made love to Philomène Sauvagnat, thereby arousing the jealousy of her lover, Pecqueux, who was stoker on the engine driven by Lantier. A quarrel between the two men on the footplate of the engine resulted in both of them falling off, and being cut in pieces beneath the wheels. *La Bête Humaine.*

LANTIER (JACQUES LOUIS), born 1860, was the son of Claude Lantier and Christine Hallegrain. He was allowed to grow up wild at Bennecourt until he was two and a half years old, when his parents removed to Paris, taking him with them. Life in the city did not agree with the child, who to make matters worse was much neglected, his mother being wholly taken up with her lover, and his father with art. He grew up puny, serious like a little man ; at five years his head had grown quite out of proportion to his height, but as his skull increased in size his intelligence diminished. His head alone continued to grow, verging on cretinism, until, in 1869, the unfortunate child died of some obscure form of mal-nutrition. *L'Œuvre.*

LAPOULLE, a soldier in the 106th Regiment of the line, in the squad of Corporal Jean Macquart. He came from the Marshes of Sologne, and was so ignorant that when he joined the regiment he asked to be shown the King. He had great strength, and consequently all the heavy work of his company was assigned to him. After the battle of Sedan, he was one of the prisoners on the Isle d'Iges, where driven frantic by famine, and instigated by Chouteau, he killed Pache, who had hidden some bread from his companions. The following night he attempted to escape by swimming the Meuse, but was killed by a bullet fired by a Prussian sentinel. *La Débâcle.*

LAQUERRIÈRE (FLORENT), an unfortunate man who died of yellow fever in Dutch Guiana in the arms of Florent. It was by the aid of his papers that Florent, who had escaped from Cayenne, was able to return to France, and to evade the notice of the police. *Le Ventre de Paris.*

LA ROUQUETTE (M.), a member of the Chamber of Deputies. His sister, Madame de Llorentz, was one of the ladies-in-waiting of the Empress Eugénie. *Son Excellence Eugène Rougon.*

LA ROUQUETTE (MADEMOI-
SELLE DE). *See* Madame de
Llorentz.

LARSONNEAU, formerly a clerk
at the Hôtel de Ville along
with Aristide Saccard ; he
was dismissed for prying into
the préfet's private drawers.
He acted for Saccard in many
of the shady transactions in
which he could not himself
appear, and being entirely
unscrupulous ultimately a-
massed such a sum of money
that he was able to start a
small banking establishment.
La Curée.
He became immensely rich.
It was through him that Busch
came to know the past life
of Aristide Saccard. *L'Argent.*

LAURE, an actress for whom
Joncquier had an infatuation.
Nana.

LAURE, a performer in a singing-
hall at Montmartre. Hutin,
one of Octave Mouret's salesmen, and his friend Liénard
applauded her performance
so noisily that the police
threatened to intervene. *Au
Bonheur des Dames.*

LAURENT, a peasant in easy circumstances who lived near
Artaud. Père Bambousse was
anxious to have him as son-in-
law. *La Faute de l'Abbé
Mouret.*

LAURENT, the Recorder at the
Court of Rouen who assisted
Denizet at the inquiry into
the murder of Grandmorin.
He was skilful in selecting
the essential parts of evidence,
so as not to put down anything useless. *La Bête Humaine.*

LAURENT, a gardener at Bazeilles. He was a man of
thirty years of age who had
recently lost his mother and
his wife, who had both died of
the same fever. During the
battle of 1st September, 1870,
he took part in the defence
of Weiss's house, and having
only his own body to care
for, he determined to sell it
dearly, and at each shot to
bring down one of the enemy.
He continued firing till his
ammunition was exhausted,
when he was taken prisoner
by the Prussians, who finding
that he was a civilian removed
him, along with Weiss, for
instant execution. In the
face of the firing party he
retained all his calmness,
standing with his hands in
his pockets till the fatal shots
were fired. *La Débâcle.*

LAUWERENS (DE), a well-known
financier who was both
wealthy and avaricious. He
went the length of refusing
to pay his wife's milliner's
bill. *La Curée.*

LAUWERENS (MADAME DE), wife of the preceding. Notwithstanding certain well-authenticated scandals, she managed to keep her high position in society. She was a friend of Renée Saccard. *La Curée.*

LAVIGNIÈRE, was one of the auditors at the Universal Bank, Rousseau being the other. Their duties were delicate, and in the circumstances useless. Lavignière was disposed to approve of everything, being consumed with a desire to become a member of the board later on. *L'Argent.*

LA VIGNIÈRE (CHEVALIER DE), grandfather of Madame Chanteau. *La Joie de Vivre.*

LA VIGNIERE (EUGÉNIE DE). *See* Madame Chanteau.

LA VILLARDIÈRE (DE), deputy for the department of the Côté d'Or. He was a friend of La Rouquette. *Son Excellence Eugène Rougon.*

LÉA, a customer at the Café Anglais. *Nana.*

LEBEAU, a man of considerable influence in the Second Empire, whom Clorinde Balbi was able to gain over to the cause of Eugène Rougon. *Son Excellence Eugène Rougon.*

LEBLEU, the cashier at Havre railway station. *La Bête Humaine.*

LEBLEU (MADAME), wife of the preceding, was a woman of forty-five, so stout that she was in constant danger of choking. Between her and Séverine Roubaud there was ill-feeling of long standing, arising from a question of their houses in the Station, the Lebleus occupying that which should by rights have belonged to the Roubauds, who on account of the generosity of their predecessor were relegated to rooms little more cheerful than a prison. She had a mania for spying upon her neighbours, and in the end caused so much irritation, that she was ordered to exchange houses with the Roubauds, thus letting them have the one to which they were entitled. The annoyance, and the change to a dismal house, proved fatal to Madame Lebleu, and she died four months afterwards. *La Bête Humaine.*

LEBIGRE, proprietor of the wine shop where Florent and his friends held their meetings. He was a police spy. Ultimately he married Louise Méhudin. *Le Ventre de Paris.*

LEBIGRE (MADAME). *See* Louise Méhudin.

LEBOUCQ, Counsellor at the Court of Rouen. He was

assessor at the trial of Roubaud and Cabuche. *La Bête Humaine.*

LEBOUCQ (MADAME), wife of the preceding. She was a handsome woman, for whose receptions the barristers of Rouen were beginning to desert those of Madame Bonnehon, her rival. It was said that to the influence of Madame Leboucq was largely due the result of the trial of Roubaud, a result not favourable to the family of President Grandmorin. *La Bête Humaine.*

LECŒUR (MADAME), a butter and cheese merchant at the *Halles Centrales.* She was sister-in-law to Gavard, and had an idea of marrying him after the death of his wife. He made no advances, however, and she subsequently regarded him with bitter ill-will. Along with Mlle. Saget, she took an active share in the gossip which partly led to the arrest of Florent and Gavard, and wrote an anonymous letter denouncing them to the police. Accompanied by La Sarriette, her niece, she went to Gavard's house after his arrest, and took possession of his money, which they divided between them. *Le Ventre de Paris.*

LECOMTE (MADAME), an acquaintance of the Deberles. *Une Page d'Amour.*

LEFÈVRE (MADAME), wife of a manufacturer at Raucourt, whose house was pillaged by the Prussians after the battle of Beaumont. *La Débâcle.*

LEGOUGEUX, a miner at Joiselle. He was an associate of Pluchart. *Germinal.*

LEGRAIN (GENERAL), a deputy at the Corps Législatif. He was devoted to the Emperor, and notwithstanding a severe attack of gout, attended at the Chamber in order to vote the funds for the baptism of the Prince Imperial. *Son Excellence Eugène Rougon.*

LEHONGRE (LES), grocers in Rue Neuve de la Goutte-d'Or. *L'Assommoir.*

LÉHUDIER, a child to whom Charvet gave lessons. *Le Ventre de Paris.*

LELORRAIN, a notary in Rue Sainte Anne. In his office was executed the deed which established the joint - stock company of the Universal Bank. *L'Argent.*

LEMBALLEUSE, a family who lived in a ruined mill near the cathedral of Beaumont. It consisted of a grandmother, her daughter, and three grand-daughters, all of whom lived by begging. Angelique did all she could for them, giving them food and even clothes. *Le Rêve.*

LENFANT, the keeper of a dram-shop at Montsou. *Germinal.*

LENGAIGNE, a dealer in tobacco and tavern-keeper at Rognes. He cultivated a small piece of land, while his wife weighed tobacco and looked after the cellar. He also shaved and cut the hair of the village, a trade learned by him when he was in the army. He professed strong Republican principles, though he was afraid to express his opinions too strongly, in case of losing his licence. An old rivalry subsisted between him and Macqueron, a neighbouring tavern-keeper, with whom he was always on the point of blows. *La Terre.*

LENGAIGNE (MADAME FLORE), wife of the preceding. She was always quarrelling with Cœlina Macqueron. *La Terre.*

LENGAIGNE (SUZANNE), daughter of the two preceding. She was apprenticed to a dressmaker at Châteaudun, but after six months ran off to Paris, where she led a gay life. Her return to her native village clad in silks caused quite a sensation, of which her parents were very proud. *La Terre.*

LENGAIGNE (VICTOR), brother of Suzanne. Before he was drawn in the conscription he was an awkward youth, but he returned a swaggering braggart, who could hardly be recognized with his moustache and beard. *La Terre.*

LENORE, a racehorse; mother of Frangipane. *Nana.*

LÉON, a lad of about fifteen years of age, apprentice to Quenu. He was a gentle-looking lad, given to stealing stray bits of ham and sausage, which he concealed under his pillow and ate during the night. *Le Ventre de Paris.*

LÉONCE (MADAME), the door-keeper of the house where Gavard lived in the Rue de la Cossonnerie. She acted also as Gavard's housekeeper. *Le Ventre de Paris.*

LÉONIE, an artificial-flower maker employed by Madame Titreville. She left her trade in order to be married. *L'Assommoir.*

LÉONIE, aunt of Louise Thibaudier. Louise went to her house after leaving Bonneville, driven away by Pauline Quenu. *La Joie de Vivre.*

LEPALMEC, a peasant at Plogof, in Brittany. *Germinal.*

LEQUEU, the schoolmaster at Rognes. His parents were

peasants, and he had an intense hatred of the class from which he had sprung, looking upon them as little better than barbarians. In politics he had advanced views, but in consequence of his position he concealed them to a great extent. Disappointed in the hope which he had long nourished of marrying Berthe Macqueron, he ended by preaching the doctrines of anarchy. *La Terre.*

LERAT (MADAME), *née* Coupeau, was a sister of Coupeau and Madame Lorilleux. She was a widow of thirty-six years of age, and was forewoman in the manufactory of artificial flowers carried on by Madame Titreville. The eldest of the Coupeau family, she was "a tall, skinny, mannish-looking woman, who talked through her nose "; she lived a hard-working, cloisteral existence, but she had a perfect mania for making improper allusions, so very obscure that only she herself could understand them. *L'Assommoir.*

For a long time she lost sight of her niece Nana, but later she found her in a position of apparent wealth. Madame Lerat had abandoned her trade of artificial flower-maker and lived upon her savings, scraped together sou by sou. Nana rented a small house for her aunt, and gave her an allowance of a hundred francs per month to look after her little son Louiset. *Nana.*

LERENARD, the keeper of a café in the neighbourhood of Montsou. *Germinal.*

LEROI, *alias* CANON, a journeyman carpenter, who deserted Paris on account of some trouble, and preferred to live in the country, tramping from village to village, doing a week here and a week there, and offering his services from one farm to another when his employer did not want him. When there was a scarcity of work he begged on the highroads, living partly on the vegetables he stole. He professed strong revolutionary principles, which he was fond of airing in village ale-shops. He was a friend of Hyacinthe Fouan. *La Terre.*

LETELLIER, father of Madame Deberle and her sister Pauline. He owned an extensive silk warehouse on the Boulevard des Capucines. "Since his wife's death he had been taking his younger daughter about everywhere, in search of a rich husband for her." *Une Page d'Amour.*

LETELLIER (JULIETTE). *See* Madame Deberle.

LETELLIER (PAULINE), the younger daughter of M. Letellier, a wealthy silk merchant, and sister of Madame Deberle. She was a giddy young girl who went about everywhere with her father in the hope of securing a rich husband, and was a constant visitor at the house of her sister. *Une Page d'Amour.*

LETURC (MADAME), widow of a captain, was a *protégée* of Madame Correur, who obtained a tobacco licence for her. *Son Excellence Eugène Rougon.*

LEVAQUE, a neighbour of the Maheus. He was of intemperate habits, and beat his wife on little provocation. During the strike he was among the most reckless, and at the assault on the Voreux pit he was taken prisoner by the troops. His arrest made him a sort of hero, and by the Paris newspapers he was credited with a reply of antique sublimity to the examining magistrate. *Germinal.*

LEVAQUE (ACHILLE), the eldest child of Zacherie Maheu and of Philomène Levaque. He was three years old when his parents were married. *Germinal.*

LEVAQUE (BÉBERT), son of the Levaques, was a little boy of twelve, who already worked in the pit. Along with Lydie Pierron, he was a companion of Jeanlin Maheu in many escapades. As Jeanlin became more daring and unscrupulous, Bébert and Lydie were drawn together in an affection born of their common fear of him. The three children were present at the attack on the Voreux pit, and Bébert and Lydie, killed by the volley fired by the troops, fell dead in one another's arms. *Germinal.*

LEVAQUE (DÉSIRÉE), the youngest child of Philomène, aged nine months. *Germinal.*

LEVAQUE (PHILOMÈNE), daughter of the Levaques, had two children to Zacharie Maheu before her marriage to him. She had a delicacy of the chest and was unable to work underground. After the death of her husband she left Montsou with her two children, in the company of a miner from the Pas-de-Calais. *Germinal.*

LEVAQUE (LA), wife of Levaque the miner, and mother of Philomène and Bébert. She was a bad housekeeper, and was roughly treated by her husband, who, however, did not take exception to her relations with Bouteloup, their lodger. *Germinal.*

LEVASSEUR (MADAME), an acquaintance of Madame Deberle. *Une Page d'Amour.*

LEVASSEUR, chief clerk at "The Ladies' Paradise." *Au Bonheur des Dames.*

LEVASSEUR, a tax-collector at Chêne Populeux. His father was one of the heroes of the army of the first Napoleon. He married a peasant woman named Fouchard, who died in bringing Maurice and his twin sister Henriette into the world. He sacrificed everything to make his son a gentleman, and the bad conduct of the lad hastened his end. *La Débâcle.*

LEVASSEUR (HENRIETTE), daughter of the preceding, and twin sister of Maurice. After the death of her father she gave up the whole of her share of his property in order to retrieve to some extent the foolish conduct of her brother. Fortunately she had the chance soon after to marry Weiss, with whom she lived happily. On the morning of the battle of Sedan, Henriette, fearing that her husband was in danger at Bazeilles, where he had gone to look after a house he had re-

cently bought, decided to follow him there. By this time fighting was going on fiercely, and when, after the greatest difficulties and dangers, she arrived at Bazeilles, she was only in time to see her husband shot before her eyes. She took refuge at Remilly, at the house of her uncle Fouchard, and devoted herself to the care of the wounded in the battle. Among these was Jean Macquart, who along with Maurice had escaped from captivity. After the war with Prussia was over, Maurice unfortunately threw in his lot with the Communists, and when Henriette followed him to Paris it was to find that he had been fatally wounded in the fighting there. By an extraordinary chance, the wound was inflicted by his former comrade, Jean Macquart, who had remained in the regular army when Maurice joined the Communist ranks. The death of Maurice in this way put an end to the possibility of a dawning love idyll between Henriette and Jean Macquart. *La Débâcle.*

LEVASSEUR (MAURICE), twin brother of the preceding. Everything was sacrificed by his father and sister in order

K

that he might become an advocate, but when he went to Paris to complete his education he took part in every kind of foolishness and dissipation. In July, 1870, he had just been admitted to the Bar, when the outbreak of war found him full of enthusiasm, and he at once enlisted in the 106th Regiment of the line, commanded by Colonel de Vineuil. He was put into the squad of Jean Macquart, against whom he had at first an aversion. Later, the kindness of Jean when he was worn out with fatigue practically saved his life, and they became close comrades, Maurice in turn saving Jean by carrying him, severely wounded, from the battlefield of Sedan. Maurice was of a highly strung, nervous temperament, and the repeated disasters of the campaign drove him to madness. He threw himself into the Communist struggle, and sought for death when defeat became certain. It was Jean Macquart, his old comrade, who, by an extraordinary chance, was fated to deliver the fatal blow. *La Débâcle.*

LÉVÊQUE (MADAME), sister-in-law of Durieu, the brewer. *L'Argent.*

LÉVÊQUE, a solicitor at Plassans. He interested himself in the affairs of Dr. Pascal Rougon after Grandguillot absconded, and was able to recover a considerable sum which Pascal had believed to be entirely lost. *Le Docteur Pascal.*

LÉVÊQUE (MADEMOISELLE), daughter of the preceding, was an old friend of Clotilde Rougon, who was three years older than her. She married Dr. Ramond. *Le Docteur Pascal.*

LHOMME (M.), chief cashier at "The Ladies' Paradise." "Son of a tax-collector at Chablis, he came to Paris as a clerk in the office of a merchant of the Port-aux-Vins. Then, while lodging in Rue Cuvier, he married the daughter of his *concièrge*, and from that day he bowed submissively before his wife, whose commercial ability filled him with respect. She earned more than twenty thousand francs a year in the dress department of "The Ladies' Paradise," whilst he only drew a fixed salary of five thousand francs." The loss of his right arm in an omnibus accident did not interfere with his work, and did not prevent him from playing upon a specially constructed French horn, an instrument of which he was passionately fond. *Au Bonheur des Dames.*

LHOMME (MADAME AURÉLIE), wife of the preceding. The daughter of a small tailor, she had keen business instincts, and, as head of the dress department at " The Ladies' Paradise," was able to make a large income. She was far from friendly to Denise Baudu, but seeing ultimately that Mouret was in love with the girl, she changed her methods in the hope of rendering her own position more secure. *Au Bonheur des Dames.*

LHOMME (ALBERT), son of the preceding. He was an idle and vicious youth, who could keep no situation, and only got a post in the pay-desk of " The Ladies' Paradise " through the influence of his mother. He was careless in his work, and was repeatedly reprimanded, causing his parents much anxiety ; ultimately it was discovered that he had conspired with some of the salesmen in a long series of frauds, and his dismissal followed. *Au Bonheur des Dames.*

LIARDIN, a relation of the Quenu's. He was a member of Pauline's family council, and consented to her emancipation. *La Joie de Vivre.*

LIÉNARD, son of a rich Angers draper, came to Paris and got a situation in " The Ladies' Paradise." His spare time was spent in idleness and debauchery, and when his father recalled him to Angers he refused to leave Paris. *Au Bonheur des Dames.*

LIEUTAUD (M.), the diocesan architect at Plassans. He was consulted by Madame Mouret and Abbé Faujas regarding the Home for Girls which they founded, and he subsequently prepared the plans for the building. *La Conquête de Plassans.*

LIEVIN, a townsman of Plassans, who was amongst those enrolled and armed by Pierre Rougon to rescue the Town Hall, which had been occupied by the Republicans. He was so excited that he fired in the air without intending to do so. *La Fortune des Rougons.*

LILI, pet name of Amélie, the daughter of Gaga. *Nana.*

LINGUERLOT (LES), neighbours of the Lorilleux in Rue de la Goutte-d'Or. *L'Assommoir.*

LIOTARD (VEUVE HENRI), a firm of shipowners who joined the transport syndicate formed by Aristide Saccard. *L'Argent.*

LISA, a peasant girl of Les Artaud. Like the others of her class, she was void of any religious feeling, and when she came to decorate the church for the festival of the Virgin, she engaged in all sorts of irreverent pranks. *La Faute de l'Abbé Mouret.*

LISA, a workwoman employed by Madame Titreville, the artificial flower-maker. *L'Assommoir.*

LISA, Madame Campardon's housemaid. She was active and intelligent, and her conduct was regarded as irreproachable. This was, however, a somewhat too favourable estimate, and her companionship was by no means beneficial to the Campardons' young daughter, Angèle. *Pot-Bouille.*

LISON (LA), the name of the express engine driven by Jacques Lantier up to the time of the terrible railway accident caused by Flore. *La Bête Humaine.*

LLORENTZ (MADAME DE), one of the ladies-in-waiting of the Empress Eugénie and sister of M. La Rouquette, was the widow of General de Llorentz. She carried on an intrigue with De Massy, and was said to hold three compromising letters from him regarding

certain august personages. *Son Excellence Eugène Rougon.*

LOGRE, a fish auctioneer at the *Halles Centrales.* He attended the revolutionary meetings in Lebigre's wine-shop, and made violent speeches there, but was in reality an agent of the Police. *Le Ventre de Paris.*

LOISEAU, a municipal councillor of Rognes. He was devoted to the Mayor, Alexandre Hourdequin, on whose farm his son worked. He was an uncle of Macqueron. *La Terre.*

LONJUMEAU, a member of the band of brigands led by Beau-François. *La Terre.*

LORET (MADAME), a woman who lived in the neighbourhood of the *Halles Centrales.* Mademoiselle Saget made ill-natured remarks regarding her. *Le Ventre de Paris.*

LORILLEUX, a maker of gold chains, who was married to Coupeau's sister. He was a little man who looked much older than his age, and suffered from a constant cough. Miserly and spiteful, he was jealous of the Coupeaus in their success, and rejoiced at their downfall. *L'Assommoir.*

LORILLEUX (MADAME), wife of the preceding, was a sister of

Coupeau, who married Gervaise Macquart. Along with her husband, she worked at the trade of gold chain-making ; like him, she was so avaricious that her custom was to examine the soles of her visitors' boots lest they should depart with any adhering gold dust. From the first she resented her brother's marriage, and took every opportunity of being disagreeable to Gervaise. Though she was willing to accept the Coupeaus' hospitality in their prosperous days, she refused to do anything to assist them after their downfall. *L'Assommoir.*

LORILLON (LES), peasants at Rognes, who were said to have been cured of illness by the bone-setter Sourdeau. *La Terre.*

LOUBET, a soldier in the 106th Regiment of the line ; in the squad of Corporal Jean Macquart. He was unwilling to fight, and during the battle of 1st September, 1870, he assisted his comrade Chouteau to carry Sapin to the ambulance, spending the rest of the day in a tavern. After the capitulation of the French army, Loubet was made a prisoner. Along with Chouteau he made a determined effort to escape, and would have done so had not his companion treacherously tripped him up in order to increase his own chance. *La Débâcle.*

LOUHETTE, an elderly draper in Rue Neuve Saint-Augustin. He was the father of Madame Théophile Vabre. *Pot-Bouille.*

LOUHETTE (MADAME), wife of the preceding, and mother of Madame Théophile Vabre. *Pot-Bouille.*

LOUHETTE (VALÉRIE). *See* Théophile Vabre.

LOUIS, Irma Bécot's butler at her house in the Avenue de Villiers. *L'Œuvre.*

LOUIS, cousin of Gabuche, and, like him, a quarryman. He drove Cabuche's wagon on the evening of the murder of President Grandmorin. *La Bête Humaine.*

LOUIS, an artillery gunner, in the same battery as Honoré Fouchard and Adolphe. He was mated with Adolphe, who was inclined to treat him as an inferior. In the attack by the Prussians on the Calvary d'Illy Louis fell, killed by the same shot as his comrade, and the two died entwined in one another's arms. *La Débâcle.*

LOUIS (LA MÈRE), a wine-seller, who was famous for her "hen feet." *L'Assommoir.*

LOUISE, an actress at the Palais-Royal. *Nana.*

LOUISE, a young girl who was brought up in an Orphanage. At fifteen she went as maid-servant to Madame Jazeur, but not proving satisfactory, was sent back to the Orphanage. *Pot-Bouille.*

LOUISET, the pet name of Louis Coupeau, son of Nana, born 1867. Left at first with a nurse in the country, he was afterwards taken charge of by his aunt, Madame Lerat, who removed him to Batignolles. He was a delicate child, pale and scrofulous, bearing a legacy of ill-health derived from an unknown father. He died in July, 1870, of small-pox, which he communicated to his mother, who had just returned from Russia. *Nana.*

LOUISETTE, the younger daughter of Madame Misard (Aunt Phasie). She was a fair and sweet child who had a strong affection for Cabuche, a man who was regarded by nearly everyone as an outcast. As a maid-servant in the house of Madame Bonnehon, she attracted the notice of President Grandmorin, and fleeing from him, half-mad with fear, she came to the hut of Cabuche, who tenderly nursed her till she died of brain fever a few days later. *La Bête Humaine.*

LOULOU, a dog which belonged to Pauline Quenu. *La Joie de Vivre.*

LULU, a dog which belonged to Nana. *Nana.*

LUSIGNAN, a racehorse in the stable of Vandeuvres. Mounted by Gresham, it was the favourite in the race for the Grand Prix de Paris. *Nana.*

M

MACQUART, a poacher and smuggler who lived at Plassans in a hovel adjoining the Fouque property. His reputation was of the worst, and "although no crimes had actually been brought home to him, the first suspicions always fell upon him whenever a theft or murder had been perpetrated in the country." He frequently disappeared for long periods, but during his short sojourns in the town he drank to great excess. He became the lover of Adélaïde Fouque in 1789, less than a year after the death of her husband, and had two children by her, Antoine and Ursule Macquart. A man of violent and unrestrained passions, and of incorrigibly lazy habits, he retained complete influence over Adélaïde, and they lived in the same relationship for over twenty years. About 1810, Macquart was killed on the frontier by a custom-house officer while he was endeavouring to smuggle a cargo of Geneva watches into France. Adélaïde was sole legatee, the estate consisting of the hovel at Plassans and the carbine of the deceased, which a smuggler loyally brought back to her. *La Fortune des Rougon.*

MACQUART (ANTOINE), born 1789, son of Macquart the smuggler and Adélaïde Fouque ; was drawn in the conscription in 1809. On his return to Plassans, he found that his half-brother Pierre had sold the family property and had appropriated the proceeds. Being a confirmed drunkard, he was averse from work of any kind, but in order to support himself he learned the trade of basket-making. In 1826 he married Joséphine Gavaudan, a market-woman, whom he afterwards allowed to support him. They had three children, Lisa, Gervaise, and Jean. His wife died in 1850, and soon after his daughter Gervaise and his son Jean, who had assisted to keep him in idleness, ran off. He had a bitter ill-will towards his brother Pierre Rougon, and, chiefly with a view to his annoyance, expressed strong Republican principles. For the same reason he took every opportunity of teaching these principles to his young nephew Silvère Mouret. After the *Coup d'État* he took an active share in the agitation which resulted in a Republican rising. When the Insurgents left Plassans, he remained with a few men to overawe the inhabitants. He and his whole band were, however, taken prisoners by the citizens under the leadership of Pierre Rougon. He was assisted to escape by Madame Félicité Rougon, who promised him a sum of money on condition that he would bring about an attack on the Town Hall by the Republicans. He did so the same night, and an ambush having been prepared by the Rougons, a number of lives were sacrificed. He thereafter left the country. *La Fortune des Rougon.*

Some time afterwards he returned to France, and bought a small house at Les Tulettes, about three leagues from Plassans. He fitted up his establishment by degrees, and even became possessed of a horse and trap. Where the money came from no one knew, but it was believed that his brother Pierre Rougon was keeping him. Notwithstanding this, he had great ill-will towards the Rougons, and lost no opportunity of annoying them. Partly with this object, and partly at the instigation of Abbé Fenil, who wished to be revenged on Abbé Faujas, he contrived the escape of François Mouret from the asylum at Les Tulettes ; as result, Mouret returned to Plassans, and setting fire to his house, caused the death of Abbé Faujas, himself perishing in the flames. *La Conquête de Plassans.*

Macquart lived to an old age at Les Tulettes, though he increasingly gave way to drunkenness. His relations with the Rougons were friendly, but he was hated by Félicité on account of his knowledge of the origin of the family fortune. At eighty-four years of age he was still healthy, but his flesh was so saturated with alcohol that it seemed to be preserved by it. One day, as he was sit-

ting helpless with drink and smoking his pipe, he set fire to his clothes, and his body, soaked as it was with ardent spirits, was burned to the last bone. Félicité Rougon chanced to enter the house just as the conflagration began, but she did nothing to stop it, and went silently away. The combustion was so complete that there was nothing left to bury, and the family had to content itself with having masses said for the repose of the dead. When Macquart's will was opened, it was found that he had left all his money for the erection of a magnificent tomb for himself, with weeping angels at the head and foot. *Le Docteur Pascal.*

MACQUART (MADAME ANTOINE), wife of the preceding. *See* Joséphine Gavaudan.

MACQUART (GERVAISE), born 1828, was a daughter of Antoine Macquart, and was slightly lame from birth. She was apprenticed to a laundress, but at an early age had two children to a journeyman tanner named Lantier.*

* These two are the only children of Gervaise and Lantier mentioned by M. Zola in *La Fortune des Rougon*, *L'Assommoir*, *L'Œuvre*, and *Germinal*. In *La Bête Humaine*, however, the hero, Jacques Lantier, is stated to have been a child of these parents.

Soon after the death of her mother, in 1850, she ran off to Paris with Lantier and her children, Claude, a boy of eight, and Étienne, aged four. *La Fortune des Rougon.*

The party had only been in the city a few weeks when Lantier ran off with a girl named Adèle, leaving Gervaise and the children unprovided for. She got work in the laundry of Madame Fauconnier, and not long after received an offer of marriage from Coupeau, a respectable zinc-worker, which after some hesitation she accepted. The marriage took place, and for a considerable time things prospered, one child, a daughter named Nana being born. An accident to Coupeau, who fell from a roof and was seriously injured, led to a gradual change ; formerly temperate and industrious, he became unwilling to work, and began to spend his time in public-houses. Gervaise had meantime taken a shop with money borrowed from the Goujets, and had started a laundry in it. She was at first successful, but in time grew lazy and fond of good living, while Coupeau continued idle and became increasingly intemperate. Business began to go, and Ger-

vaise became more careless, even taking more drink occasionally than she had been wont to do. About this time Lantier, her former lover, appeared again, and made friends with Coupeau, who agreed to take him into the house as a lodger. After that, the descent of Gervaise was rapid. Lantier never paid anything for his support, Coupeau drank more heavily than ever, and Gervaise, who was gradually drifting into intemperance, resumed her old connection with her lover. All the time work was being neglected, and debts were accumulating with alarming rapidity. Eventually Madame Virginie Poisson took over the shop, and with it Lantier, who transferred his affections along with the lease, and the Coupeaus removed into a small house high up in the same building. Coupeau suffered from repeated attacks of *delirium tremens,* and eventually died in an asylum. Gervaise continued to sink still lower, until no work was too menial or too repulsive for her to undertake for the price of drink, and one day in the winter of 1869 she was found dead in a garret of that great tenement house where she had passed so much of her life. *L'Assom-moir*.

Her sister, Lisa Quenu, the pork-butcher, did not come to her assistance. Lisa did not like people who were unfortunate, and she was ashamed that Gervaise should have married a workman. *Le Ventre de Paris.*

Her son Étienne sent her small sums of money from time to time while he was in a situation at Lille. *Germinal.*

MACQUART (JEAN), born 1811, son of Antoine Macquart, was apprenticed to a carpenter. A quiet, industrious lad, Jean's father took advantage of his simple nature and made him give up his whole earnings to assist in keeping him in idleness. Like his sister Gervaise, he ran off soon after the death of his mother. *La Fortune des Rougon.*

He entered the army, and, after seven years of soldiering was discharged in 1859. When he had left the ranks he turned up at Bazoches-le-Doyen with a comrade, a joiner like himself ; and he resumed his occupation with the latter's father, a master carpenter in the village. But his heart was no longer in his work, and having been sent to La Borderie to make some re-

pairs, he stayed on to assist at the harvest, and eventually became a regular farm servant. He was not popular, however, with the peasants, who resented his having had a trade before he came back to the soil. He became acquainted at Rognes with Mouche and his daughters, Lise and Françoise, and eventually married the latter, in spite of the determined opposition of her brother-in-law, Buteau. Notwithstanding his marriage, he remained a stranger, and, after the death of his wife, went away, leaving everything in the hands of her relatives. The war with Germany had just broken out, and Jean, disgusted with his life, again enlisted in the service of his country. *La Terre.*

He was made corporal in the 106th Regiment of the line, commanded by Colonel Vineuil. An excellent soldier, and invaluable by reason of his former experience, his want of education prevented him being promoted to higher rank. Maurice Levasseur was in his company, and between the two men there was at first deep antagonism, caused by difference of class and education, but little by little Jean was able to gain over the other, till the two men became close friends. In the fierce fighting at Sedan, each in turn saved the other's life. After the battle, they were made prisoners, but escaped, Jean receiving a severe wound during their flight. They took refuge at Remilly in the house of Fouchard, and Jean was nursed by Henriette Weiss, Levasseur's sister. Under her care, the wounded man came to dream of the possibility of a life of happiness with this woman, so tender, so sweet, and so active, whose fate had been so sad. But the chances of war were too hard ; Maxime returned to Paris, and after the conclusion of the war took part in the Communist rising, which Jean assisted to quell. By an extraordinary chance, the two men, loving one another as brothers, came to be fighting on opposite sides, and it was the hand of Jean that was fated to inflict the fatal wound upon his friend. He had killed the brother of the woman he loved, and henceforth there could be nothing between them, so he passed from her life, returning to assist in that cultivation of the soil which was needed to rejuvenate his country. *La Débâcle.*

He settled at Valqueyras, near Plassans, where he married Mélanie Vial, the only daughter of a peasant farmer in easy circumstances, whose land he cultivated. Calm and sensible, always at his plough, his wife simple and strong, he raised a large and healthy family to assist in replenishing the soil exhausted by the horrors of war. *Le Docteur Pascal.*

MACQUART (MADAME JEAN), first wife of the preceding. *See* Françoise Mouche. *La Terre.*

MACQUART (MADAME JEAN), second wife of Jean Macquart. *See* Mélanie Vial. *Le Docteur Pascal.*

MACQUART (LISA), born 1827, daughter of Antoine Macquart. When a child of seven she was taken as maidservant by the wife of the postmaster at Plassans, whom she accompanied to Paris on her removal there in 1839. *La Fortune des Rougon.*

The old lady became very much attached to the girl, and when she died left her all her savings, amounting to ten thousand francs. Gradelle, a pork-butcher, who had become acquainted with Lisa by seeing her in his shop with her mistress, offered her a situation. She accepted, and soon the whole place seemed to belong to her; she enslaved Gradelle, his nephew Quenu, and even the smallest kitchen-boy. She became a beautiful woman, with a love of ease and the determination to secure it by steady application to duty. After the sudden death of Gradelle, she married Quenu, who had succeeded to the business, and they had one daughter, Pauline. Soon their affairs became so prosperous that Lisa induced her husband to remove to a larger shop. On Florent's return from exile, she received him kindly, and at once proposed to hand over to him his share of the money and property left by Gradelle, his uncle, which, however, he refused to accept. After a time she became tired of always seeing her brother-in-law about the house doing nothing, and was the means of making him accept the situation as Inspector at the Fish Market. When she heard of the Revolutionary meetings in Lebigre's wine-shop and of the leading part taken by Florent, she became greatly alarmed, more especially as Quenu had begun to accompany his brother occasionally. She succeeded in frightening her husband into giving up the meetings, and made it clear to Florent that he was no longer welcome in her house. Alarmed by the gossip of Mlle. Saget and others as to the progress of the conspiracy, she determined, after consultation with Abbé Roustan, to secure the safety of her husband and herself by informing the police of the plot. On going to the prefect, however, she learned that he had all along known of Florent's presence in Paris, and of the meetings, and was only waiting a favourable opportunity of arresting the plotters. She concealed the impending arrest from her husband and from Florent. Notwithstanding her action in this matter, Lisa was not an ill-natured or callous woman. She was only determined that nothing should come between her and a life of ease. In her there was much of her father's nature, though she did not know it. She was merely a steady, sensible Macquart with a logical desire for comfort, and to procuring this she gave all her time and thought. *Le Ventre de Paris.*

She died in 1863 from decomposition of the blood. *La Joie de Vivre.*

MACQUART (URSULE), born 1791, daughter of Macquart and Adélaïde Fouque ; married in 1810 a hatter named Mouret and went to live at Marseilles. She died of consumption in 1840, leaving three children. *La Fortune des Rougon.*

MACQUERON, a grocer and tavern-keeper at Rognes. He was a municipal councillor, and deputy Mayor. He made some money by speculating in wines, and had since become incorrigibly lazy, spending his time in fishing and shooting. Had his wife listened to him, they would have shut up the shop, but she was so fiercely set on money-making that she would not do so. There was a rivalry of long standing between the Macquerons and the Lengaignes, which frequently broke out in open quarrels. Having succeeded in undermining Hourdequin's position as Mayor, Macqueron succeeded him, but his triumph was of short duration, for some official scandal having arisen, he was obliged to resign. *La Terre.*

MACQUERON (MADAME CŒLINA), wife of the preceding, had a true passion for money-making. She was continually quarrelling with her neigh-bour, Madame Lengaigne. *La Terre.*

MACQUERON (BERTHE), daughter of the preceding, was educated at a boarding-school at Cloyes, and had learned to play the piano. She tolerated the attentions of Lequeu, the schoolmaster, whom she heartily disliked, as she felt flattered by the notice of the only man of education whom she knew. She had a fancy for the son of a neighbouring wheelwright, whom her parents would not allow her to see, and she ultimately compromised herself so seriously with him that they had to consent to her marriage. *La Terre.*

MADELEINE, a little girl of ten years of age who was an inmate of the institute founded by Princess d'Orviedo. Her mother was unable to look after her properly, and placed her there in the hope that she would be well cared for. *L'Argent.*

MADELINE (ABBÉ), was sent to Rognes, when that commune decided to have a *curé* to itself. He came from a mountainous district, and disheartened by the flatness of the vast plain of La Beauce, and especially by the religious indifference of his parishioners, he soon fell into ill-health, on one occasion fainting while he was saying Mass. At the end of two years and a half he left Rognes in a dying state, and returned to his native mountains. *La Terre.*

MADINIER (M.) carried on business as a cardboard manufacturer in part of the tenement occupied by the Coupeaus and the Lorilleux. The business was not prosperous, as he spent all his earnings on drink. He was one of Coupeau's witnesses on the occasion of his marriage to Gervaise Macquart, and was present at the wedding dinner. *L'Assommoir.*

MAFFRÉ (M.), a magistrate of Plassans and honorary Canon of Saint-Saturnin's church. Politically he was a Legitimist, and he was a friend of M. Rastoil, at whose house the party was in the habit of meeting. *La Conquête de Plassans.*

MAFFRÉ (ALPHONSE), second son of the magistrate at Plassans, aged eighteen years. Restrained too much by their father, the two brothers Maffré were especially intimate with Guillaume Porquier, who frequently led them into mischief. *La Conquête de Plassans.*

MAFFRÉ (AMBROISE), elder son of the magistrate at Plassans, aged twenty. *La Conquête de Plassans.*

MAGINOT, inspector of woods at Mézières. He married Gilberte de Vineuil, but died a few years afterwards. *La Débâcle.*

MAGINOT (MADAME). *See* Gilberte de Vineuil.

MAHEU (ALZIRE), the fourth child of Toussaint Maheu, aged nine years. She was deformed and delicate, but of precocious intelligence, and was able to assist her mother in many ways, sacrificing herself always for others. She died of cold and hunger during the strike at Montsou. *Germinal.*

MAHEU (CATHERINE), second child of Toussaint Maheu, worked as a putter in the Voreux pit along with the other members of her family. She liked Étienne Lantier, but became the mistress of Chaval, who treated her so abominably that she eventually returned home. As a result of the terrible catastrophe brought about by Souvarine, she was imprisoned at the bottom of the pit along with Chaval and Étienne. A struggle between the two men ensued, and Chaval was killed. Days elapsed before rescue arrived, but before then Catherine had died in the arms of Étienne, whom she had really loved all along. *Germinal.*

MAHEU (ESTELLE), seventh child of Toussaint Maheu, aged three months. Her constant crying disturbed the household. *Germinal.*

MAHEU (GUILLAUME), great-grandfather of Toussaint Maheu. When a boy of fifteen, he found rich coal at Réquillart, the Montsou Company's first pit, and the seam he discovered was named after him. He died of old age at sixty. *Germinal.*

MAHEU (HENRI), sixth child of Toussaint Maheu, aged four years. *Germinal.*

MAHEU (JEANLIN), third child of Toussaint Maheu, aged eleven years. He was employed at the Voreux pit, and earned twenty sous a day. His nature was vicious, and he forced his companions Bébert Levaque and Lydie Pierron to commit petty thefts, with the proceeds of which he concealed himself in a disused mine. His criminal tendencies increased,

until he was unable to resist the inclination to kill one of the soldiers who guarded the Voreux pit during the strike. He accordingly waited till night, and leaping on the shoulders of Jules, a little soldier from Brittany, thrust a knife into his throat and killed him. *Germinal.*

MAHEU (LÉNORE), fifth child of Toussaint Maheu, aged six years. She was always fighting with her brother Henri, who was very like her in appearance, both having large heads with light yellow hair. *Germinal.*

MAHEU (NICOLAS), grandfather of Toussaint Maheu. He was killed by a landslip in the pit, when he was barely forty years old. *Germinal.*

MAHEU (TOUSSAINT), son of old Bonnemort, and husband of La Maheude. He was considered one of the best workmen in the Voreux pit, did not drink, and was liked and respected by all his companions. He had been for a considerable time under the influence of the doctrines taught by Étienne Lantier when he was selected by his comrades to place their views before the officials of the company. In the great strike which followed he took part, and in the attack on the troops sent to guard the pit he was driven on by his wife to join the aggressors. He fell, shot through the heart, after the fatal volley fired by the soldiers. *Germinal.*

MAHEU (VINCENT). *See* Bonnemort.

MAHEU (ZACHARIE), eldest child of Toussaint Maheu. He worked in the Voreux pit along with his father, but was lazy and seized any opportunity of pleasure. He was married to Philomène Levaque, by whom he already had two children. The strike interested him very little, and he spent most of his time playing *crosse* with Mouquet. But when his sister Catherine was entombed in the pit he was one of the first to come forward to the rescue, and he worked day and night with frantic energy. The ninth day, in his haste, he was imprudent enough to open his lamp, and a sudden explosion of gas reduced him to a calcined, unrecognizable mass. *Germinal.*

MAHEUDE (LA), wife of Toussaint Maheu. She was at first against the miners' strike, but moved by the hardship of her lot and the poverty in which she was forced to bring up her family, she ultimately urged her husband to take an active part. Even after she had seen him killed by the bullets of the soldiers, she was furious with those who talked of submitting. But further tragedies broke her spirit; her son Zacharie was killed in an attempt to rescue his sister, entombed at the bottom of the Voreux pit. Out of charity the company allowed the afflicted woman to go underground again, though she was past the usual age, and found employment for her in the manipulation of a small ventilator. *Germinal.*

MAHOUDEAU, a sculptor. The son of a stonemason at Plassans, he attained great success at the local art competitions, and came to Paris as the *lauréat* of his town, with an allowance of eight hundred francs per annum for four years. In the capital, however, he found his level, failing in his competitions at the School of Arts, and merely spending his allowance to no purpose; so that in order to live he was obliged at the end of his term to enter the employment of a manufacturer of church statues. Later, however, he met with Claude Lantier and other companions from Plassans, and under their influence his ambitions revived. He installed himself in a studio in Rue du Cherche-Midi, and there set about the production of a colossal work entitled *La Vendangeuse* (the Vintage Girl), for which Madame Mathilde Jabouille served as model. For a time Chaîne, who also came from Plassans, lived with Mahoudeau, but they quarrelled over Mathilde, and ultimately separated. After this Mahoudeau lived alone, in considerable poverty, until he got employment from a manufacturer of artistic bronzes. He then began to produce work which suited the popular taste, and his productions began to be seen on middle-class chimney-pieces. *L'Œuvre.*

MAIGRAT, the principal shopkeeper in Montsou. He was originally an overseer at the Voreux pit, but, assisted by the company, started a business which grew to such proportions that he ultimately crushed out most of the other retail traders. He was a greedy, rapacious man, and during the strike made the women furious by refusing credit. For other reasons also they hated him, and his shop was one of the first places attacked by the maddened strikers. In terror Maigrat took refuge on the roof, but his foot slipped, and he was dashed to the ground, being killed on the spot. Even this did not satisfy his assailants, for the frenzied women, led by La Brûlé, rushed forward and mutilated the still quivering body. *Germinal.*

MAIGRAT (MADAME), wife of the preceding. She was a pitiful creature who passed all her days over a ledger without even daring to lift her head. On the day of the attack by the strikers she was a witness of the death of her husband and of the terrible events which followed. Up at the window she stood motionless ; but beneath the last gleams of the setting sun the confused faults of the window-panes deformed her white face, which looked as though it were laughing. *Germinal.*

MALGRAS (LE PÈRE), a picture-dealer with whom Claude Lantier had frequent dealings. He was a thick-set old man, with close-cropped white hair, and wore a dirty old coat that made him look like an untidy cabman. Beneath this disguise was concealed a keen

L

knowledge of art, combined with a ferocious skill in bargaining. As a superb liar, moreover, he was without an equal. He was satisfied with a small profit, but never purchased in the morning without knowing where to dispose of his purchase at night. He viewed with disdain the modern methods of picture-dealing introduced by Naudet, and like a cautious man he retired with a modest fortune to a little house at Bois-Colombes. *L'Œuvre.*

MALIGNON (M.), a young stock-broker who was supposed to have a large fortune and accordingly was received everywhere in society. He posed as a critic of art, literature, and the drama, and pretended to be bored with everything. Madame Deberle, being carried away by his attentions, was foolish enough to promise to meet him at a flat which he had taken, but Madame Hélène Grandjean having warned her that Dr. Deberle had got wind of the affair, the intended *liaison* came to nothing. *Une Page d'Amour.*

MALIVERNE (ROSE). *See* Madame Rose Fouan.

MALIVOIRE, a coach-hirer at Arromanches. He was the owner of the omnibus which ran between Arromanches and Bayeux. *La Joie de Vivre.*

MALOIR (MADAME), a respectable-looking elderly woman, was Nana's friend, chaperone, and companion, writing for her such letters as she required. She was always ready to receive the secrets of others, but never told anything about herself. It was said that she lived upon a mysterious pension, but she never appeared to carry any money with her. She had a mania for doing up all her hats afresh. *Nana.*

MAMAN NINI, the pet name given by Angelique to François Hamelin. *Le Rêve.*

MANGUELIN (MADAME), a young, retiring woman, who was to some extent dependent on the bounty of Madame Deberle. *Une Page d'Amour.*

MANOURY, a salesman at the Central Markets in Paris. He was the employer of Logre and Clémence. *Le Ventre de Paris.*

MARCEL, a vegetable-dealer at the Paris *Halles Centrales.* *Le Ventre de Paris.*

MARDIENNE FRÈRES, manufacturers of church ornaments in Rue Saint-Sulpice. Mademoiselle Menu worked in their establishment. *Pot-Bouille.*

MARÉCHAL, a bookmaker who had formerly been coachman to Comte de Vandeuvres. ' As the result of a racing swindle by Vandeuvres, Maréchal lost a large sum over a filly named Nana, and, his suspicions having been aroused, he caused such a scandal that the Comte was disqualified by the racing committee. *Nana.*

MARESCOT (M.), a cutler in the Rue de la Paix, who had once turned a grindstone in the streets and was now said to be worth several millions. He was a man of fifty-five, large, bony, with the huge hands of an old workman ; one of his delights was to carry off the knives and scissors of his tenants, which he sharpened himself for his own amusement. He owned the large tenement-house on the Rue Goutte d'Or, in which resided the Coupeaus, Lorilleux, and others, and though a fair landlord, would brook no delay in payment of rent, turning out defaulters without mercy. *L'Assommoir.*

MAREUIL (M. DE), a retired sugar-refiner of Havre whose real name was Bonnet. After amassing a large fortune, he married a young girl of good birth, whose name he assumed. He was ambitious and hoped to become a member of the Corps Législatif through the influence of his friend Saccard, whose brother Eugène Rougon was a Minister of State. To secure this he agreed to a marriage between his daughter and Maxime Saccard. He was a man of solemn and imposing appearance, but was absolutely without brains. *La Curée.*

MAREUIL (MADAME HÉLÈNE DE), wife of the preceding. She came of a noble and wealthy family, but lived such a fast life that she died young, worn out by pleasure. *La Curée.*

MAREUIL (LOUISE DE), daughter of a retired sugar-refiner of Havre. Slightly deformed and plain-looking, but with fascinating manners, she married Maxime Saccard, to whom she brought a large dowry. Six months afterwards she died of consumption in Italy. *La Curée.*

MAREUIL (COMTESSE DE), employed Clara Prunaire in her house to attend to the mending of linen. *Au Bonheur des Dames.*

MARGAILLAN, a great building contractor, many times a millionaire, who made his fortune out of the great public works of Paris, running up whole boulevards on his

own account. He was a man
of remarkable activity, with
a great gift of administration,
and an instinctive knowledge
of the streets to construct and
the buildings to buy. Moved
by the success of Dubuche
at the School of Art, and by
the recommendations of his
masters there, Margaillan took
the young architect into partnership, and agreed to his
marriage with his daughter
Régine. Unfortunately, Dubuche showed deplorable in-
capacity in carrying into practice the theories which he had
learned at the School of Art,
and Margaillan, after losing
considerable sums, returned
to his original methods of
construction, thrusting his
son-in-law to one side. He
possessed a magnificent estate
named *La Richaudière*, near
Bennecourt. *L'Œuvre.*

MARGAILLAN (MADAME), wife of
the preceding. She was a
girl of the middle-classes,
whose family history was a
bad one, and after suffering
for years from anæmia, she
ultimately died of phthisis.
L'Œuvre.

MARGAILLAN (RÉGINE), daughter of the preceding, and
wife of Louis Dubuche. She
was very delicate, and suffered
from a phthisical tendency

derived from her mother,
which in turn she handed
down to her two children,
Gaston and Alice. It was
frequently necessary for her
to leave home for the benefit
of her health, and during her
absences the children were left
at *La Richaudière* in charge of
their father. *L'Œuvre.*

MARIA, an actress at the Théâtre
des Variétés. *Nana.*

MARJOLIN, a boy who was found
in a heap of cabbages at the
Paris market. It was never
known who his parents were,
and he became the adopted
child of the place, always
finding a lodging with one or
other of the market-women.
Later on he lived with Madame Chantemesse, who had
adopted Cadine, another
foundling, and the two children grew up together, becoming inseparable. Marjolin
was always of slow intellect,
and as the result of an injury
to his head he became practically an idiot. Gavard gave
him employment in the
poultry market. *Le Ventre de
Paris.*

MARSOULLIER, proprietor of the
Hotel Boncœur, where Ger-
vaise Macquart and Lantier
put up when they came to
Paris. *L'Assommoir.*

MARTIN, coachman to Dr. Cazenove. He was an old man who formerly served in the navy, and had his leg amputated by Cazenove. *La Joie de Vivre.*

MARTINE, the old servant of Dr. Pascal, with whom she had been for thirty years. She brought up Clotilde Rougon, whose affection for the doctor excited her jealousy later on. Martine, who was devoted to her master, desired to force him to be reconciled with the Church, but Clotilde, at first her accomplice, escaped from religious influences and gave herself entirely to Pascal, leaving Martine with no other resource but prayer. She was extremely avaricious, but when the doctor was ruined, her devotion was such that she used some of her own money to purchase the necessaries of life for him. Distracted at the sudden death of her master, and in the hope of saving him from damnation, she assisted Madame Félicité Rougon to destroy his great work on heredity, which in her narrow-minded bigotry she believed was intended to subvert true religion. The work of destruction completed, she went away to live by herself at Sainte-Marthe, as she refused to serve any other master than the one she had been with so many years. *Le Docteur Pascal.*

MARTINEAU (M.), a notary of Coulonges, and brother of Madame Correur. He ignored his sister for many years, but his principles would not allow him to disinherit her, and he made a will under which his property would be divided between her and his wife. Soon thereafter, Madame Correur, knowing him to be in bad health, denounced him as a dangerous Republican to Rougon, then Minister of the Interior, and his arrest followed. The shock, together with the unnecessary harshnesses displayed by Gilquin, the commissary of police, caused Martineau's death, and the subsequent popular outcry had much to do with Rougon's second resignation of office. *Son Excellence Eugène Rougon.*

MARTINEAU (MADAME), wife of the preceding. *Son Excellence Eugène Rougon.*

MARSY (COMTE DE), Minister of the Interior before Eugène Rougon, who succeeded him on his appointment as President of the Corps Législatif. Marsy, who was said to be the son of a queen, was brilliant, immoral, and unscrupulous. He was the chief political opponent of Eugène Rougon and had great influence at the Court of Napoleon III. *Son Excellence Eugène Rougon.*

MARTY (M.), a master at the Lycée Bonaparte, who was being ruined by the extravagance of his wife, and was obliged to double his salary by giving private lessons, in order to meet the constantly growing household expenses. *Au Bonheur des Dames.*

MARTY (MADAME), wife of the preceding, was a woman of about thirty-five years of age, whose face, never beautiful, was now much marked by small-pox. She had a perfect mania for spending money on clothes, and never visited "The Ladies' Paradise" without buying innumerable articles for which she had no need. As a result of her extravagance, her husband was nearly ruined, and was forced to increase his earnings by giving private lessons. *Au Bonheur des Dames.*

MARTY (VALENTINE), daughter of the preceding, a young girl of fourteen years of age, who was used by her mother as an excuse for some of her extravagance, as she dressed

her like herself, with all the fashionable novelties of which she submitted to the irresistible seduction. *Au Bonheur des Dames.*

MASCART (PÈRE), a blind paralytic to whom Angelique showed much kindness. *Le Rêve.*

MASSACRE, one of the dogs of old Soulas, the shepherd. It shared the hatred of its master of La Cognette. *La Terre.*

MASSIAS, a frequenter of the Paris Bourse, where he gained a living by bringing business to stockbrokers, from whom he received a commission on each transaction. He was employed by Saccard after the foundation of the Universal Bank, and by speculating in the shares he made a considerable fortune. With the downfall of the institution, he lost everything, and found himself in debt for a large sum. By borrowing from friends, and pledging his entire life, he paid his debts and started afresh. *L'Argent.*

MASSICOT, a tradesman of Plassans who was enrolled and armed by Pierre Rougon to deliver the Town Hall from the Republicans who had occupied it. He was so excited that when he got into the building he fired in the air without knowing he had done so. *La Fortune des Rougon.*

MASSON (COLONEL), commander of the troops which crushed the Republican rising in 1851. *La Fortune des Rougon.*

MATHIAS, an old hunchback who worked on the farm of La Borderie. *La Terre.*

MATHIEU, a large dog which belonged to the Chanteaus at Bonneville and was a great favourite of the family. The death of this animal greatly accelerated the unreasoning fear of inevitable mortality with which the mind of Lazare Chanteau was becoming obsessed. *La Joie de Vivre.*

MATHILDE, an actress at the Théâtre des Variétés. *Nana.*

MATIGNON, a draper in Paris, whose shop was near that of Baudu. *Au Bonheur des Dames.*

MAUDIT (ABBÉ), Vicar of Saint-Roch, Paris, he counted among his parishioners the Josserands and the Duveyriers. Though well aware of the immorality that went on in his parish, he recognized the impossibility of stopping it, and did what he could to hide it under the cloak of religion. When the scandal arose about Madame Auguste Vabre, he was approached by her relations, and at their request acted as intermediary between the husband and wife. *Pot-Bouille.*

MAUGENDRE (M.), father of Madame Jordan ; was a retired awning manufacturer who had made a considerable fortune from his business. He disapproved of his daughter's marriage, and refused to give her any dowry, on the pretext that she would have his fortune intact when he was dead and gone. He was a careful man, averse from speculation, but having on one occasion made a small venture, he gradually became imbued with the craze. The phenomenal success of the Universal Bank induced him to purchase its shares more and more wildly, until, when the crash came, he was so deeply committed as to be ruined. Jordan, who by this time had met with some success in literature, came to his assistance. *L'Argent.*

MAUGENDRE (MADAME), wife of the preceding, was at first bitterly opposed to the small speculations entered into by her husband. She soon got infected with the craze, and became even more reckless than he, urging him to involve himself more and more deeply in the fortunes of the Universal Bank. *L'Argent.*

MAUGENDRE (MARCELLE). *See* Madame Marcelle Jordan.

MAURIAC (BARON DE), starter at the racecourse of Longchamp. *Nana.*

MAURIN, a hatter of Plassans, who was selected by the Republicans of that town as their candidate. At the election he only received about fifteen hundred votes against the rival candidate, M. Delangre. *La Conquête de Plassans.*

MAURIN, a notary at Tulettes, who was also Mayor of the Commune. It was he who drew up the certificate of death of Antoine Macquart from spontaneous combustion. *Le Docteur Pascal.*

MAZAUD, a broker on the Paris Bourse, who succeeded on the death of his uncle to one of the largest businesses in the city. He was young and pleasant-looking, with such remarkable activity and intuition that he soon came into the first rank. He was also assisted by the fact that he did business with all the great bankers, and was re-

puted to have a second cousin employed at the Havas News Agency. After the foundation of the Universal Bank, he became the official broker of that institution, and the great gamble in its shares resolved itself into a duel between him and Jacoby, the one buying for Saccard and the other selling for Gundermann. Mazaud did not speculate on his own account, but the failure of the bank led to so many of his clients being unable to meet their differences that he was ruined. After putting his affairs in order so far as possible, he committed suicide. *L'Argent.*

MAZAUD (MADAME), wife of the preceding. She married for love, and brought to her husband a considerable fortune. She had two children, a girl and a boy. The suicide of her husband completely overwhelmed her with grief. *L'Argent.*

MAZEL, a famous master at the School of Arts, and the last rampart of elegant conventionality. The first year that the Hanging Committee of the *Salon* was elected by the artists themselves, Mazel was chosen president. In the selection of pictures he was susceptible to influence, and was guided more by the name of the artist than by the quality of the work. *L'Œuvre.*

MÉCHAIN, proprietor of a racing-stable. Hazard, one of his horses, ran in the Grand Prix de Paris. *Nana.*

MECHAIN (MADAME), a woman in the employment of Busch, the money-lender and debt collector. She assisted him in tracing debtors, and in the purchase of securities of bankrupt companies. She was a cousin of Rosalie Chavaille, mother of Victor Saccard, on whose death she was left with the boy to bring up. On discovering the paternity of Victor some years later, she and Busch attempted to blackmail Saccard, but without success, though they had previously got a considerable sum from Caroline Hamelin, who wished to save Saccard from annoyance. *L'Argent.*

MÉGOT (JUSTINE), a young maid-servant of Renée Saccard. She had a son to Maxime Rougon in 1857, and was sent to live in the country with the child on a small annuity. *La Curée.*

Three years later she married Anselme Thomas, a harness-maker at Plassans. They had two children, and would have lived happily but

for the husband's dislike to her eldest child, Charles Rougon. Her conduct after marriage was exemplary in every way. *Le Docteur Pascal.*

MÉHUDIN (MADAME), originally came from Rouen to Paris, where she ever afterwards remained in the fish trade. As her two daughters, Louise and Claire, got on badly together, she ultimately divided her business between them, Louise going to the general fish-market, while Claire installed herself among the fresh-water fish. "From that time the old mother, although she pretended to have retired from business altogether, would flit from one stall to the other, still interfering in the selling of the fish, and causing her daughters continual annoyance by the foul insolence with which she at times spoke to customers." *Le Ventre de Paris.*

MÉHUDIN (CLAIRE), the second daughter of Madame Méhudin, was an idle, fair-complexioned girl, with a gentle manner. She had, however, a strong will, and was invariably at loggerheads with others. When Florent became Inspector at the Fish Market, Claire took his part against her mother and sister, but afterwards went to the opposite extreme when his relations with Louise had become friendly. It appeared that she had a real affection for him, however, as after his arrest she assaulted her sister in the belief that she had given information to the police. *Le Ventre de Paris.*

MÉHUDIN (LOUISE), commonly called La Normande. She was a beautiful woman who had at one time been engaged to be married to a clerk in the corn-market. He was, however, accidentally killed, leaving Louise with a son, who was known in the market by the nickname of *Muche.* When Florent was first appointed Inspector in the Fish Market, Louise, who had quarrelled with his sister-in-law, Lisa, did everything she could to annoy him. Afterwards, partly gratified by his kindness to her son, and partly to annoy Madame Lisa Quenu, she became reconciled to him. *Le Ventre de Paris.*

MEINHOLD (MADAME DE), a lady well-known in the Society of the Second Empire. She was a friend of Madame de Lauwerens and of the Saccards. *La Curée.*

MÉLANIE, cook in the employment of the Grégoires, with whom she had been for thirty years. *Germinal.*

MÉLANIE, the servant of Denizet, the examining magistrate at Rouen. The latter was anxious for promotion, in order that his old servant might be better fed and consequently better tempered. *La Bête Humaine.*

MÉLIE, niece of the Fancheurs. She was a girl from the village of Bennecourt, who waited on Claude Lantier and Christine in their cottage there, and greatly amused them by her stupidity. After the death of the Fancheurs, the inn came into the possession of Mélie, but soon lost favour on account of its dirt and disorder. *L'Œuvre.*

MENU (MADEMOISELLE), aunt of Fanny Menu, who lived with her. She had been an embroideress for thirty years, but her sight failed and she was obliged to give up work. Fortunately she received a small legacy from a relative, and on this, added to the earnings of her niece, she was able to live. *Pot-Bouille.*

MENU (FANNY), a young girl who was protected by Narcisse Bachelard. As he on one occasion found her with Gueulin, his nephew, under compromising circumstances, he insisted on their marriage, and gave her a handsome dowry. *Pot-Bouille.*

MERLE, usher at the Council of State. He was appointed by Eugène Rougon, through the influence of Madame Correur. *Son Excellence Eugène Rougon.*

MES BOTTES, the sobriquet of one of Coupeau's companions. He was a heavy drinker and an enormous eater, and on account of the latter gift he was occasionally asked by his friends to join such parties of pleasure as paid by contract for their entertainment, in order that they might watch the landlord's face lengthen at the rapid disappearance of food. Chiefly for this reason, he was asked to the Coupeaus' wedding party. *L'Assommoir.*

MEYER, owner of a Viennese bakery in faubourg Poissonnière. The Coupeaus bought their bread from him in order to please Lantier. *L'Assommoir.*

MICHELIN (M.), a surveyor of the Municipal Council. " His wife, a pretty woman, occasionally called to apologize to her husband's chiefs for his absence, when he stayed away through ill-health. He was often ill, but he obtained promotion at each illness." In order to secure Saccard's influence, Michelin assisted him in getting exorbitant prices for land sold to the city. *La Curée.*

MICHELIN (MADAME), wife of the preceding. By means of her good looks and a determination to get on at any cost, she secured the influence of her husband's superiors, and got rapid promotion for him in the office of the Municipal Council. *La Curée.*

MIETTE, the pet name of Marie Chantegreil (*q.v.*).

MIETTE, one of the peasant girls of Les Artaud who assisted to decorate the church for the festival of the Virgin. *La Faute de l'Abbé Mouret.*

MIGNON, a man who, beginning life as a bricklayer, had amassed a fortune by speculations in building land during the early days of the Second Empire. Along with Charrier, his partner, he had many business dealings with Aristide Saccard. *La Curée.*

MIGNON, husband of an actress at the Théâtre des Variétés. When Rose married him he was leader of the orchestra at a café concert where she sang. They were the best of friends, and lived together on the earnings of the wife, who exploited her beauty not less than her talents. Mignon was always on the best of terms with his wife's lovers, even assisting them occasionally to deceive her, with the view of bringing them back in penitence later on. *Nana.*

MIGNON (CHARLES), younger son of the preceding. *Nana.*

MIGNON (HENRI), elder son of Mignon. Along with his brother Charles he was educated at a boarding-school. *Nana.*

MIGNON (ROSE), wife of Mignon, was a star actress at the Théâtre des Variétés, being a fine *comédienne* and an admirable singer. She was dark and thin with that charming ugliness which is peculiar to the gamins of Paris. It was she who, annoyed by the rivalry of Nana, one day made Comte de Muffat aware of the *liaison* between his wife and Fauchery. She was, however, a good - hearted woman, and when she learned that Nana had contracted small-pox she arranged for her removal to the Grand Hotel, and nursed her there till she died. *Nana.*

MIGNOT, one of the salesmen in the glove department at "The Ladies' Paradise." He entered into a conspiracy with Albert Lhomme to defraud his employer, and this was successful to a considerable extent before its discovery; his dismissal followed, but there was no prosecution, as the firm preferred not to bring its internal affairs before the public eye. He afterwards got a situation as a traveller, and had even the boldness to call at "The Ladies' Paradise." *Au Bonheur des Dames.*

MIMI-LA-MORT, a pupil at the College of Plassans, who was also nicknamed *Le Squélette-Externe* (the Skeleton Day-Boarder) on account of his extreme thinness. Against the regulations of the College, he used to bring in snuff to the other scholars. *L'Œuvre.*

MINOUCHE, a white cat which belonged to the Chanteaus. *La Joie de Vivre.*

MISARD, signalman on the railway at Croix-de-Maufras, between Malaunay and Barentin. He was a little puny man, with thin, discoloured hair and beard, and a lean, hollow-cheeked face. His work was mechanical, and he seemed to carry it through without thought or intelligence. His wife, a cousin of Jacques Lantier, looked after the level-crossing which adjoined their house until failing health prevented her from leaving the house. For this little man, silently and without anger, was slowly poisoning his wife with a powder which he placed in the salt which she ate. This crime, patient and cunning, had for its cause a legacy of a thousand francs left to Aunt Phasie by her father, a legacy which she had hidden, and refused to hand over to Misard. But the old woman triumphed in the end, for though Misard searched day and night for the treasure, he was never able to find it ; she died taking her secret with her. An old woman of the neighbourhood, La Ducloux, whom he had employed to attend to the level-crossing after the death of his wife, induced him to marry her by pretending that she had discovered the secret hoard. *La Bête Humaine.*

MISARD (MADAME), wife of the preceding. *See* Phasie (Aunt).

MORANGE (CHARLOT), son of Silvine Morange and of Goliath Steinberg. Physically he resembled his father's race, whom, however, he was brought up to hate. Hidden behind his mother, he was at three years old a witness of the murder of his father by the francs-tireurs. *La Débâcle.*

MORANGE (SILVINE), servant with Fouchard at Remilly. Her mother, who was a worker in a factory at Raucourt, died when she was quite young, and her godfather, Dr. Dalichamp, got her a situation with Fouchard. Honoré Fouchard fell in love with her, and they became engaged, but the opposition of the old man was so great that Honoré went away from home and enlisted in the army. During his absence Silvine fell a victim to the wiles of Goliath Steinberg, and a child, Charlot, was born, Steinberg having previously disappeared. She had all along loved Honoré, and when he passed through Remilly on his way to fight the Prussians he forgave her, and promised to marry her on his return. When she heard that he had been killed in the battle of Sedan, she became nearly mad, and with Prosper Sambuc made a wild search of the battlefield for her lover's body. They found it eventually, and brought it back in a cart for burial. Goliath Steinberg, who was a German spy, again made advances to her, and, to save herself and her friends, she betrayed him to the francs-tireurs, who killed him in her presence. *La Débâcle.*

MORIZOT, a friend of Malignon, who took him to the children's party at Deberle's house. *Une Page d'Amour.*

MOSER, a speculator on the Paris Bourse. He was a short, yellow-skinned man, who suffered from liver complaint and was continually lamenting, in constant dread of some imminent catastrophe. In consequence of his views, he was known on the Bourse as " bear " Moser. Speculating heavily against the rise in the shares of the Universal Bank, he was at one time on the verge of ruin, but the collapse of that institution left him with an enormous fortune. *L'Argent.*

MOUCHE(LE PÈRE),the sobriquet of Michel Fouan, the third son of Joseph Casimir Fouan, and brother of La Grande, Père Fouan, and Laure Badeuil. When his father's estate was divided, he received the family dwelling-house and some land, but was dissatisfied with his share and continued to accuse his brother and sister, though forty years had elapsed, of having robbed him when the lots were drawn. He had been long a widower, and, a soured unlucky man, he lived alone with his two daughters, Lise and Françoise. At sixty years of age he died of an attack of apoplexy. *La Terre.*

MOUCHE (FRANÇOISE), younger daughter of Michel Fouan, *alias* Mouche. Her mother died early, and she was brought up by her sister Lise, to whom she was devotedly attached. She had a passion for justice, and when she had said " that is mine and that is yours," she would have been prepared to go to the stake in support of her rights. This execration of injustice gradually led to a change of feeling between the two sisters, for after the marriage of Lise to Buteau a division of the land should have been made. Buteau and his wife on various pretexts put off this division, and it was only on the marriage of Françoise to Jean Macquart that it was carried out. An entire estrangement between the two families followed, and constant quarrels took place. After a shameful assault by Buteau upon Françoise, his wife threw her upon a scythe which lay upon the ground near by, and the unfortunate girl received injuries from which she died a few hours later. A sense of loyalty to her family induced her to conceal the cause of these injuries, which were attributed to accident. *La Terre.*

MOUCHE (LISE), elder daughter of Père Mouche, and sister of the preceding. She had a son to her cousin Buteau, who, however, did not marry her for three years afterwards, when the death of her father made her heiress to some land. She was at first an amiable woman, but grew hardened under the influence of her husband, and ultimately her whole desire was to avoid the necessity of a division of her father's estate between her sister and herself. Moved by these feelings, her love for Françoise became transformed into a hatred so intense that she did not hesitate to assist her husband in attempting to bring about the girl's ruin. In the end, having assisted Buteau in a shameful assault on Françoise, she afterwards threw her upon a scythe which was lying on the ground near by, inflicting injuries which proved fatal. Père Fouan, having been a witness of the assault, was subsequently murdered by Lise and her husband, to ensure his silence and their own safety. *La Terre.*

MOULIN, an assistant station-master at Havre along with Roubaud. *La Bête Humaine.*

MOULIN (MADAME), wife of the preceding. She was a little woman, timid and weak, who was seldom seen. She had a large family of young children. *La Bête Humaine.*

MOUNIER, a tenor singer at the Opera, who gave the cue to Madame Daigremont at a performance in her house. *L'Argent.*

MOUQUE, father of Mouquet and of Mouquette. He had charge of the horses in the Voreux pit, and also acted as caretaker at a ruined mine known as the Réquillart, where the company had given him two rooms to live in. Almost every evening he received a visit from his old comrade Bonnemort. *Germinal.*

MOUQUET, son of the preceding, was an inseparable companion of Zacharie Maheu, along with whom he worked at the Voreux pit. During the strike he went out of curiosity to see the attack by the strikers on the soldiers who were guarding the mines, and was killed by a stray ball which struck him in the mouth. *Germinal.*

MOUQUETTE, daughter of Mouque. She was a putter in the Voreux pit, and lived with her father at the ruined mine of Réquillart, where he was caretaker. She was present at the attack by the strikers on the soldiers guarding the Voreux, and when the fatal volley was fired she was killed, in an instinctive attempt to save Catherine Maheu, before whom she placed herself. *Germinal.*

MOURET, a hatter of Plassans who married Ursule Macquart in 1810 and went to live at Marseilles. He was devoted to his wife, and a year after her death in 1839, he hanged himself in a cupboard where her dresses were still suspended. He left three children, Hélène, François, and Silvère. *La Fortune des Rougon.*

MOURET (MADAME), wife of the preceding. *See* Ursule Macquart. *La Fortune des Rougon.*

MOURET (DÉSIRÉE), born 1844, daughter of François Mouret, and sister of Octave and Serge. *La Fortune des Rougon.*

She was of feeble intellect, and when a girl of sixteen was still mentally like a child of eight. When her mother fell under the influence of Abbé Faujas, and began entirely to neglect her family, François Mouret removed Désirée to the home of her old nurse, in whose custody she remained. *La Conquête de Plassans.*

When her brother Serge was appointed priest of Les Artaud, she accompanied him there. By that time she had grown to be a tall, handsome girl, but her mind had never developed, and she was still like a young child. Her love of animals had become a passion, and at her brother's home she was able to indulge it to the fullest extent, and to her complete happiness. *La Faute de l'Abbé Mouret.*

She accompanied her brother to Saint Eutrope, where he became curé, and she continued innocent and healthy, like a happy young animal. *Le Docteur Pascal.*

MOURET (FRANÇOIS), born in 1817, son of Mouret and Ursule Macquart, his wife. He got a situation in the business of his uncle, Pierre Rougon, whose daughter Marthe he married in 1840. They had three children, Octave, Serge, and Désirée. On the retirement of his uncle, Mouret returned to Marseilles and established himself in business there. *La Fortune des Rougon.*

During fifteen years of close application on the part of Mouret and his wife, he made a fortune out of wines, oil and almonds, and then retired to Plassans, where he lived on his means, making an occasional deal in wine or oil when a chance occurred. He was not on good terms with his wife's relations, and placed himself politically in opposition to them by supporting the Legitimist candidate, the Marquis de Lagrifoul. In 1858, having two vacant rooms in his house, he was induced by the Abbé Bourrette to let them to Abbé Faujas, a priest who had been sent to Plassans by the Government to undermine the existing clerical influence there, which had been exercised in support of the Marquis de Lagrifoul. Mouret was a man of narrow and restricted intellect, and his peculiarities became more and more marked as the Abbé Faujas gradually came to dominate the household and induce Madame Mouret to neglect her husband and family for the service of the Church. By degrees Mouret came to be regarded as insane, and his wife having had several epileptic attacks, he was accused of having caused the

M

injuries she had really inflicted on herself. His wrongful removal to the asylum at Les Tulettes followed, and confinement soon confirmed the insanity which before had only threatened. In 1864, his uncle, Antoine Macquart, in order to annoy the Rougons contrived his escape from the asylum, and he returned by night to his home at Plassans. Finding it in the occupancy of Abbé Faujas and his relatives, he was overcome by the fury of madness, and set fire to the house in several places. So thoroughly did he do his work that all the inmates, including himself, perished in the flames. *La Conquête de Plassans.*

MOURET (MADAME MARTHE), wife of the preceding. *See* Marthe Rougon.

MOURET (HÉLÈNE), born 1824, daughter of Mouret and Ursule Macquart, his wife. *La Fortune des Rougon.*

When seventeen years old she married M. Grandjean, the son of a sugar-refiner of Marseilles, whose family were bitterly opposed to the match on account of her poverty. The wedding was a secret one, and the young couple had difficulty in making ends meet until an uncle died, leaving them ten thousand francs a year. " It was then that Grandjean, within whom an intense hatred of Marseilles was growing, had decided on coming to Paris, to live there for good." The day after their arrival Grandjean was seized with illness, and after eight days he died, leaving his wife with one daughter, a young girl of ten. Hélène, who was a woman of singular beauty, had no friends in Paris except Abbé Jouve and his half-brother M. Rambaud, but from them she received much kindness. Her daughter Jeanne was far from strong, having inherited much of the hereditary neurosis of her mother's family, along with a consumptive tendency from that of her father. A sudden illness of the girl led to an acquaintance with Doctor Deberle, and this ripened into love between him and Hélène, though considerations of duty kept them apart. Meantime, Hélène had discovered the beginnings of an intrigue between Madame Deberle and M. Malignon, and in order to break it off was herself placed in such a compromising position towards Doctor Deberle that he became her lover. The discovery of the fact by Jeanne, whose jealous love of her mother amounted to a mania, led to the child's illness and death, and to her mother's bitter repentance. Two years later Hélène married M. Rambaud, and went to live at Marseilles. *Une Page d'Amour.*

She lived for many years, very happy, and idolized by her husband, in a house which he owned near Marseilles, close to the seashore. She had no children by her second marriage. *Le Docteur Pascal.*

MOURET (OCTAVE), born 1840, son of François Mouret. *La Fortune des Rougon.*

A young man of high spirits and somewhat idle habits, he made little progress at college, and failed to pass the examinations for a degree. His father was much annoyed at this, and sent him off to Marseilles to enter a commercial business. The reports regarding him were, however, unsatisfactory, as it appeared that he showed no inclination to settle to hard work and was living a dissolute life.* *La Conquête de Plassans.*

* It is interesting to note that by a curious oversight M. Zola in *Pot-Bouille* refers to Octave Mouret as having passed the examination for his bachelor's degree before leaving Plassans, and states that at Marseilles the lad showed a passion for business life, being able during his three years' stay there to make a sum of five thousand francs (£200), which he took with him to Paris.

After the death of his parents, Serge Mouret, who was about to take Holy Orders, renounced his share of his father's fortune in favour of his brother Octave. *La Faute de l'Abbé Mouret.*

He was appointed a member of the family council which nominally had charge of Pauline Quenu's fortune. *La Joie de Vivre.*

After three years at Marseilles he came to Paris, where he secured an appointment as assistant at " The Ladies' Paradise " through the influence of the Campardons, who were old friends of his mother. He formed the project of advancing his prospects by making love to Madame Hédouin, wife of his employer, but she gave him no encouragement. He resigned his situation, and went as salesman to Auguste Vabre, a neighbouring silk merchant. Vabre's wife (*née* Berthe Josserand) was not on good terms with her husband, and a *liaison* was formed between her and Octave Mouret, which subsisted for some time before it was discovered by Vabre, who received information from Rachael, his maid-servant. Mouret returned to his former employment at " The Ladies' Paradise," and M. Hédouin

having died in the interval, he married the widow a few months afterwards. He had developed keen business ability, with large ideas, and under his management the shop became one of the most important in the district. *Pot-Bouille.*

In Mouret's hands the business of " The Ladies' Paradise " continued to grow, and repeated extensions of the building became necessary. While one of these was in progress, Madame Mouret, who was inspecting the work, fell into a hole, and as a result of her injuries died three days afterwards. Mouret remained a widower, and devoted himself to the extension of his business, though it was believed that a *liaison* with Madame Desforges was not the only entanglement of its kind. On the introduction of Madame Desforges he came to know Baron Hartmann, director of the Crédit Immobilier, who became interested in him, and eventually found the money necessary to carry out the vast schemes of extension which he had long had in mind. By this time Denise Baudu had come to " The Ladies' Paradise " as a saleswoman, and from the first Mouret had taken an interest in her. This was probably increased by the fact that she resisted all his advances, and refused all his offers. Ultimately he became so infatuated by her that he asked her to marry him, which she agreed to do. By this time the success of " The Ladies' Paradise " had become triumphant, and the smaller traders of the district were being crushed out of existence, and driven one by one into bankruptcy. *Au Bonheur des Dames.*

He assisted at the burial of his cousin, Claude Lantier the artist. By this time he had become very rich, was decorated with the Legion of Honour, and was desirous of giving the impression of an enlightened taste for art. *L'Œuvre.*

Octave Mouret, whose immense fortune continued to increase, had towards the end of 1872 a second child by his wife Denise Baudu, whom he adored, though he again began to lead a somewhat irregular life. Their little girl was puny, but the younger child, a boy, took after his mother, and grew magnificently. *Le Docteur Pascal.*

MOURET (MADAME CAROLINE), first wife of the preceding.

See Madame Caroline Hédouin.

MOURET (MADAME DENISE), second wife of Octave Mouret. *See* Denise Baudu.

MOURET (SERGE), born 1841, son of François Mouret. *La Fortune des Rougon.*

He was a young man of nervous temperament and of somewhat delicate health. Educated at Plassans, he took his degree at the college there, and it was intended that he should go to Paris to study for the bar. The state of his health caused his departure to be delayed, and meantime he, like his mother, fell under the influence of Abbé Faujas. Ultimately he decided to abandon the study of the law in order to become a priest, and against the wishes of his father he entered the Seminary at Plassans. *La Conquête de Plassans.*

After being ordained to the priesthood he was appointed curé of Les Artaud, a small village in Provence, to whose degenerate inhabitants he ministered with small success. From his parents he had inherited the family taint of the Rougon-Macquarts, which in him took the form of morbid religious enthusiasm bordering on hysteria. Brain fever resulted, and bodily recovery left the priest without a mental past. Dr. Pascal Rougon, his uncle, in the hope of saving his reason, removed him to Paradou, the neglected demesne of a ruined mansion, where he left him in the care of Albine, the keeper's niece. Here Serge slowly recovered his health, though the memory of his past was gone, and his mental development was that of a boy. In that enchanted garden, lush with foliage and with the scent of flowers, the drama of life unfolded, and Serge, loving Albine, and oblivious of his vows, unwittingly broke them. A chance meeting with Brother Archangais, and a glimpse of the world outside the Paradou, recalled to Serge the recollection of his priesthood, and, filled with horror, he tore himself from Albine and returned to his cure of souls. A fierce struggle between love and duty followed, but in the end the Church conquered, and Albine was left to die, while Serge threw himself even more feverishly than before into the observances of his faith. *La Faute de l'Abbé Mouret.*

Sent later to Saint-Eutrope, at the bottom of a marshy gorge, he was cloistered there with his sister Désirée. He showed a fine humility, refusing all preferment from his bishop, waiting for death like a holy man, averse to remedies, although he was already in the early stage of phthisis. *Le Docteur Pascal.*

MOURET (SILVÈRE), born 1834, son of Mouret, the hatter, and Ursule Macquart, his wife. After the death of his father, Silvère went to live with his grandmother Adélaïde Fouque. Though poorly educated, he was fond of reading, and his lonely life with this old half-imbecile woman increased his own tendency to visionary dreamings. " He was predisposed to Utopian ideas by certain hereditary influences ; his grandmother's nervous disorders became in him a chronic enthusiasm, striving after everything that was grandiose and impossible." His Uncle Antoine Macquart, who hoped through him to annoy the Rougons, encouraged him in his Republican views, and after the *Coup d'État* he joined the insurrection which then arose. Miette Chantegreil, a young girl to whom he was tenderly devoted, accompanied him, but was shot in an attack by regular troops. He was taken prisoner, and having been brought back to Plassans, was executed there. *La Fortune des Rougon.*

MOUSSEAU (ABBÉ), a priest at Plassans. *La Conquête de Plassans.*

MOURGUE, a peasant of Poujols, who, armed with a fork, had taken part in the insurrectionary rising against the *Coup d'État.* He was made prisoner, and was led to Plassans, tied by the arm to Silvère Mouret, who had also been arrested. He was shot at the same time as Silvère by Rengade, the gendarme. *La Fortune des Rougon.*

MOUTON, a cat which belonged to the Quenus, and was a favourite of little Pauline. *Le Ventre de Paris.*

MUCHE, the name by which Louise Méhudin's son was known in the market. He was befriended by Florent, who taught him to read and write. *Le Ventre de Paris.*

MUFFAT (MAMAN), wife of General Muffat de Beuville, who was created Comte by Napoleon I. She was an insufferable old woman, who was always hand-in-glove with the priests, and had an authoritative manner, which bent every one to her will. Her daughter-in-law, Comtesse Sabine, was entirely under her dominion, and was forced by her to lead an almost cloistered existence. *Nana.*

MUFFAT DE BEUVILLE (COMTE), son of the preceding and of General Muffat de Beuville. Brought up in the strictest manner by his mother, his life was one of cold and severe propriety, and being regarded with favour at the Court, he was appointed Chamberlain to the Empress. He married Sabine de Chouard, by whom he had one daughter, Éstelle. For seventeen years of married life his career was a pattern of all the virtues, until a chance meeting with Nana led to an infatuation amounting to mania. Everything was sacrificed to her, and no degradation to his self-respect seemed too high a price to pay for her favour. Disgusted for a time by her *liaison* with Fontan, he left her, and turned for amusement to Rose Mignon, but the infatuation for Nana reasserted itself, and he recovered her good graces by inducing Bordenave to give her a part which she greatly desired in *La Petite Duchesse,* a play by Fauchery. He spent vast sums upon Nana, giving her a magnificent house in the Avenue de Villiers. Her influence over him became complete, and he even accepted Daguenet, her former lover, as his son-in-law. He overlooked too his wife's numerous *liaisons*, as he required her signature to enable him to raise still more money for Nana. Muffat's means were coming to an end, however, and the scandal reached such a height that he was forced to resign his position at the Tuileries. It was only when he learned that Nana was carrying on a *liaison* with his own father-in-law, the aged Marquis de Chouard, that he finally broke with her, and coming once more under the influence of Venot, he sought forgetfulness of the past in an exaggerated devotion to the services of the Church. *Nana.*

MUFFAT DE BEUVILLE (COMTESSE), wife of the preceding. *See* Sabine de Chouard. *Nana.*

MUFFAT DE BEUVILLE (ÉSTELLE), daughter of the preceding. At sixteen she was thin and insignificant, seldom speaking, but after her marriage to Daguenet, she exhibited a will of iron, and completely dominated her husband. *Nana.*

MÜLLER (BLANCHE), a favourite actress at the Théâtre des Variétés. *La Curée.*

MUSSY (M. DE) was an admirer of Renée Saccard, and aspired to be her lover. He received an appointment on the staff of the London embassy. *La Curée.*

N

NANA. *See* Anna Coupeau.

NANA, name of a filly in the racing stable of Vandeuvres. She had been beaten in several races, and when run for the Grand Prix de Paris was looked on as an outsider. The success of the filly by fraudulent means led to the disqualification of the owner. *Nana.*

NAPOLEON III, Emperor of the French. Referred to in *Son Excellence Eugène Rougon* and in *La Débâcle.*

NATHANSOHN, a stockbroker. He came from Besançon, where his father was a watchmaker. He was very fortunate in his speculations, and soon became a man of consequence. His Jewish caution prevented him from becoming involved with Saccard in the affairs of the Universal Bank, and when that institution collapsed he was in a position to snatch a fortune from its ruin. *L'Argent.*

NAUD, a shoemaker in Rue d'Antin who felt severely the competition of Octave Mouret's great shop. *Au Bonheur des Dames.*

NAUDET, a cousin of the Quenus. He was a member of Pauline's family council, and consented to her emancipation. *La Joie de Vivre.*

NAUDET, a picture-dealer who for some years had been revolutionizing the trade. He put aside the old cautious methods, the watching for pictures by beginners, bought for ten francs and sold for fifteen. To judge by his appearance he might have been a nobleman, and his habits were in keeping ; he was, in fact, a pure speculator in pictures, caring nothing for art. But he unfailingly scented success ; he guessed what artists ought to be taken up, not the one likely to develop the genius of a great painter, but the one whose deceptive talent, set off by a pretended display of audacity, would command a premium in the market. He speculated, in fact, on the ignorance and vanity of amateurs. It was he who invented Fagerolles as a fashion, and made large sums out of his works. His success in forcing up the prices of pictures turned his head to some extent, and he even talked of crushing out all the other dealers. The exaggerated rise in the price of pictures came, as was inevitable, to an end, and in the fall which followed Naudet was practically ruined. *L'Œuvre.*

NÉGREL (MADAME), sister of M. Hennebeau, the manager of the Montsou mines. She was married to a captain, and after she became a widow lived at Avignon on a small income, contenting herself with little in order that she might properly educate her son Paul. *Germinal.*

NÉGREL (PAUL), son of the preceding. He was engineer at the Voreux pit, an appointment which he received from his uncle, M. Hennebeau, with whom he lived, being treated as one of the family. Madame Hennebeau, notwithstanding a *liaison* which subsisted between her and Négrel, planned for him a marriage with Cécile Grégoire, an arrangement which was only prevented by the murder of the girl by old Bonnemort. Négrel posed as taking no interest in the affairs of practical life, but in the terrible disaster at the Voreux pit he threw himself into the work of rescue with an ardour beyond praise. *Germinal.*

NOEMI, an actress at the Vaudeville. Madame Deberle admired the realistic manner in which she died in a piece she played. *Une Page d'Amour.*

NORINE, a vendor of salted provisions, who went round the neighbourhood of Cloyes. *La Terre.*

NORMANDE (LA), the sobriquet of Louise Méhudin. *Le Ventre de Paris.*

NOUGARÈDE, an old senator who was on the point of asking the hand of Clorinde Balbi after having seen her at a ball in the character of Diana the huntress. *Son Excellence Eugène Rougon.*

O

OCTAVE, the favourite lover of Blanche de Sivry. *Nana.*

ORVIEDO (PRINCE D') came to Paris from Spain with an immense fortune made on the Stock Exchange. There were strange stories told regarding the sources of his wealth ; stories not more creditable than those told of the armed bandits of former days, for his robberies, though less open, were more dangerous. For twenty years he took his share of booty in all the great financial swindles. He ultimately died of apoplexy. *L'Argent.*

ORVIEDO (PRINCESS D') was for a time one of the most curious notabilities of the Second Empire. At the command of her mother, the Duchesse de Combeville, she married the Prince in ignorance of the source of his regal fortune, estimated at three hundred millions of francs (twelve millions sterling). It was said that for twenty years the Prince had appropriated the lion's share of every great piece of financial rascality on the Bourses of France and Spain. After his sudden death from a stroke of apoplexy, the Princess shut up the great house in the Rue Saint-Lazare and retired with a maid to three rooms on the second floor, where she lived the life of a recluse. From thenceforth she lived solely for deeds of charity on a colossal scale. During five years she founded the St. Mary's Infant Asylum, the St. Joseph's Orphan Asylum, an Asylum for the aged at Chatillon, a hospital in the suburbs of Paris, and an institution known as *L'Œuvre du Travail,* in which were boarded three hundred waifs and strays from the streets of Paris. On these foundations, and on other charities, she spent in five years over a hundred millions of francs. For some time Saccard assisted her in a disinterested way in carrying out her schemes, and later he rented from her the premises in which he started the Universal Bank. As time went on, the Princess seemed to be swayed more and more by the desire of restitution to the poor of the uttermost remnants of her husband's fortune. In the end, when she had divided it all, she retired to a convent of Carmelites, walled off from the world. *L'Argent.*

OZIL, a pointsman at the junction for Dieppe, between the tunnel and the station of Malaunay. He was in love with Flore, who for a time seemed to encourage him. He was dismissed from his post on account of grave negligence caused by Flore, who distracted his attention in order that he might allow the Havre express to dash into a train loaded with ballast. The accident was only averted by a new automatic signalling apparatus. *La Bête Humaine.*

P

PACHE, a soldier in the 106th regiment of the line, in the squad of Corporal Jean Macquart. He brought from his native village strong religious principles, and was in the regular habit of saying his prayers outside his tent. The example of his companions, however, made him a bad soldier, and during the battle of 1st September, 1870, he left the ranks, and took refuge in a tavern. After the capitulation of Sedan, he was imprisoned along with his regiment on the promontory of Iges. Moved by famine, he concealed some bread from his companions ; but having been denounced by Chouteau, he refused to share the spoil, and was murdered by Lapoulle, who stabbed him with a knife. *La Débâcle.*

PAILLOT, a farmer in the neighbourhood of Montsou. *Germinal.*

PALETTE (LA MÈRE), a poultryseller at the Central Markets in Paris. *Le Ventre de Paris.*

PALOQUE, a judge. He and his wife were said to be the ugliest couple in Plassans, and in addition were far from popular. Madame Mouret having asked the assistance of

Madame Paloque in connection with the Home for Girls proposed by Abbé Faujas, she agreed to act on the Committee, and became Treasurer. At the opening ceremony, however, the Bishop omitted to make reference to her services, and she took great offence, becoming afterwards very irregular in her work, and declining to perform any duties that she did not fancy. This ultimately led to the appointment of a paid Secretary for the institution, Honoré Trouche, the brother-in-law of Abbé Faujas being selected. The Paloques were antagonistic to Faujas, but on getting a hint from Madame de Condamin that he had the backing of the Government and would see that they were rewarded, they came over to his side, and assisted him in "the conquest of Plassans" by the Bonapartist candidate. *La Conquête de Plassans.*

PARABOULOMENOS, a name given by the pupils of the college of Plassans to a youth who served in the kitchen. *L'Œuvre.*

PARALLELUCA, the sobriquet given by the pupils of the College of Plassans to a scullery-maid employed there. It was alleged that there was a love-idyll between her and Paraboulomenos, both of whom were extremely ugly. *L'Œuvre.*

PASCAL (LE DOCTEUR). *See* Pascal Rougon.

PATOIR, a veterinary surgeon at Cloyes. *La Terre.*

PAUVRE ENFANT, a young trooper in the 5th regiment of the line, who was fatally wounded at the battle of Sedan, and died in the ambulance at Remilly. He received the name because he continually repeated the words regarding himself, saying that his mother had always called him so. He died in the arms of Henriette Weiss, whom in his delirium he named "Mother." *La Débâcle.*

PAYAN, a stone-cutter from the South, whose friends had views of making him an artist. He was a lover of Clarisse Bocquet, and pilfered from her a large quantity of furniture given her by Duveyrier. *Pot-Bouille.*

PÉCHARD (ANTOINE), a neighbour of the Fouans. He owned eighteen acres of land when he married La Grande, who brought him seven acres more. He died young, leaving one daughter. *La Terre.*

PÉCHARD (MADAME), wife of the preceding. *See* La Grande. *La Terre.*

PÉCHARD (MADEMOISELLE), daughter of Antoine Péchard and Marianne Fouan, his wife. As she insisted on marrying a poor youth named Vincent Bouteroue, her mother cast her out. Misfortunes pursued the young couple, both of whom died within a few years, leaving two children in profound misery. *La Terre.*

PECQUEUX, a stoker in the employment of the Western Railway Company. He was married to Mère Victoire, the old nurse of Séverine Aubry. His original intention was to qualify as an engine-driver, but time passed without advancement, and later there was an insuperable barrier in his own conduct, for he was given to drinking bouts which converted him for the time into a savage animal, capable of any violence. His wife lived at Paris, while Philomène Sauvagnat helped him to pass the hours he was compelled to spend at Havre, an arrangement which had the concurrence of Victoire. Pecqueux had the devotion

of a dog for his comrade Jacques Lantier, who concealed his vices and shared with him a love for their engine, " La Lison." Philomène, however, excited his jealousy by her attentions to Lantier, and the former friendship of the two comrades became changed to fierce enmity. At length it happened that one night, as their engine was drawing eighteen trucks of soldiers towards the seat of war in Prussia, Pecqueux in a sudden access of madness attacked Lantier, and, after a fierce struggle on the narrow foot-plate, the two fell off, and were cut in pieces beneath the wheels. *La Bête Humaine.*

PEIROTTE, receiver of taxes at Plassans. He was taken as a hostage by the Republican insurgents and was inadvertently shot by the troops which crushed the rising. *La Fortune des Rougon.*

PÉQUEUR DES SAULAIES (M.), subprefect of Plassans. He fell into disfavour with the Government on account of the election of a Legitimist Deputy. For some time he was afraid to compromise himself with Abbé Faujas, but having received a hint from Madame de Condamin, who had influential friends in Paris, he allied himself with the Abbé. The result was the election of Delangre, who though nominally independent, was actually the Government candidate. *La Conquête de Plassans.*

PÉQUIGNOT, a friend of the Lorilleux. He was a furniture dealer. *L'Assommoir.*

PERDIGUET, a singer known to Malignon, who promised to take him to the children's party at Deberle's house. *Une Page d'Amour.*

PÈRE COLOMBE, owner of the *Assommoir*, a public-house which was largely the scene of the downfall of Coupeau and Gervaise Macquart, his wife. *L'Assommoir.*

PEROU (LA MÈRE), an old woman employed by Gourd, the *concierge*, to do cleaning work. Terrorized by his brutality she agreed to accept less wages. *Pot-Bouille.*

PHASIE (AUNT), was the wife of Misard, and the mother of Flore and Louisette. She was a cousin of the Lantiers and was godmother to Jacques, who was left in her charge when his parents went to Paris. Her first husband died, leaving her with two daughters, and she married for a second time Misard, a little man, cunning and avaricious, who was five years her senior. Jacques found them later, living in Normandy at Croix-de-Maufras on the line to Havre, where Misard was signalman, and his wife had charge of the level crossing. It was a miserable existence, without neighbours or any one to speak to, without even anything to look at, except the trains constantly rushing past. Aunt Phasie, as she had always been called by Jacques Lantier, was a tall, handsome woman, but since her second marriage she had aged so rapidly that at forty-five she looked over sixty. The truth was that between her and Misard there was going on a duel to the death ; Aunt Phasie had received a legacy of a thousand francs from her father, and this she obstinately refused to allow her husband to share, having indeed hidden the money to prevent him from taking it. Misard, overcome by avarice, slowly killed his wife with poison placed in the salt, but, though she had the strongest suspicions, she would neither take action against him nor tell him the hiding-place of her little hoard. And so she died, carrying the secret with her ;

but in the end she triumphed, for search as he might, Misard never discovered the hidden treasure. *La Bête Humaine.*

PICHINETTE, a horse entered for the Grand Prix de Paris. It was withdrawn before the race. *Nana.*

PICHON (JULES), a clerk who lived in the house in Rue de Choiseul occupied also by Octave Mouret. His means were small, and he was obliged to work hard, frequently till late at night, his wife being necessarily left much alone. *Pot-Bouille.*

PICHON (MARIE), wife of the preceding. She was a daughter of M. and Madame Vuillaume, by whom she was strictly brought up. A dreamy unpractical woman, she fell under the influence of Octave Mouret, her next-door neighbour, and a *liaison* existed between them for a considerable time, with results which caused much annoyance to her parents. *Pot-Bouille.*

PICHON (LILITTE), infant daughter of the preceding. *Pot-Bouille.*

PICHON (ROSALIE), Madame Hélène Grandjean's maidservant. She was an honest country girl who had been brought to Paris by Abbé Jouve on the recommendation of a village priest, in whose house she had been brought up. She served her mistress faithfully, and ruled Zéphyrin Lacour, her sweetheart, with a hand of iron. *Une Page d'Amour.*

PICOT, a soldier of infantry who belonged to the first division of the seventh Army Corps. After the defeats of Wissenbourg and Frœschwiller, Picot, half dead with fatigue and slightly wounded, was left behind in a ditch with his comrade Coutard of the first corps. They were only able to rejoin the army at Rheims on 22nd August, 1870, arriving with their clothes worn out and covered with mud, and having more the appearance of bandits than of soldiers. *La Débâcle.*

PICOU (M.), a townsman of Plassans who expressed disbelief in the success of the *Coup d'État. La Fortune des Rougon.*

PIED-DE-CÉLERI, a friend of Coupeau. He had a wooden leg, from which he received his nickname. *L'Assommoir.*

PIÉDEFER (LAURE), kept a cheap restaurant in Rue des Martyrs, which was much frequented by a certain class of *demi-*

mondaines. Laure appeared to be on intimate terms with her customers, as they usually kissed her when they entered. *Nana.*

PIÉDEFER (ZOÉ), an artist's model who lived in Rue Campagne-Première. She was a tall brunette. *L'Œuvre.*

PIERRE, Dr. Deberle's butler. *Une Page d'Amour.*

PIERRE, an employé at *Au Bonheur des Dames.* He was waiter in the dining-room of the shop assistants. *Au Bonheur des Dames.*

PIERRON, a miner employed at the Voreux pit. He was a widower with a little girl aged eight, Lydie, when he married for the second time, the daughter of La Brûlé. Though he took part in the strike he betrayed his companions, giving information to the company through Dansaert, his wife's lover. After the attack on the pit Pierron was arrested by mistake, and was taken off with handcuffs at his wrists as far as Marchiennes, to the great amusement of his mates. He was subsequently promoted to be captain of a gang, but his excessive zeal made him disliked by his men. *Germinal.*

PIERRON (LYDIE), daughter of the preceding, was a fragile child, who when ten years old was already working in the pit. Her constant companions were Jeanlin Maheu and Bébert Levaque, with whom she made many raids in search of food during the strike. She was killed by the volley fired by the troops at the strikers attacking the Voreux pit. *Germinal.*

PIERRONNE (LA), the second wife of Pierron, was a daughter of La Brûlé. She was allowed by the Company to sell sweetmeats and biscuits, which were a considerable source of revenue. Dansaert, the head captain of the Voreux pit, was her lover, and through him she obtained various favours, giving him in exchange information as to the intentions of the strikers. After the strike she was enabled to acquire the little *Estaminet du Progrès. Germinal.*

PIFARD, an usher at the college of Plassans, whose wonderful nose kept betraying his presence behind doors when its owner went eavesdropping. *L'Œuvre.*

PILLERAULT, a speculator on the Bourse, whose guiding principle was recklessness ; he declared that he plunged into catastrophes whenever he paused to reflect. He was ruined by the failure of the Universal Bank. *L'Argent.*

PIOT AND RIVOIRE, a firm of furniture-dealers, whose business was seriously affected when Octave Mouret added a furniture department to "The Ladies' Paradise." *Au Bonheur des Dames.*

PIQUETTE kept an *estaminet* at Montsou, where Chaval lodged. *Germinal.*

PLOUGUERN (M. DE) was a member of the Chamber of Deputies during the reign of Louis Philippe. After the Revolution of February, 1848, he manifested a sudden affection for the Republic, and later, when the Emperor granted him the refuge of the Senate, he was a Bonapartist. He was a man of high birth and breeding, and though a sceptic, defended religion and family life. During a journey in Italy he met Comtesse Balbi, whose lover he remained for thirty years. According to some, Clorinde Balbi was his daughter. *Son Excellence Eugène Rougon.*

PLUCHART, a former workman who was now secretary of a branch of the International Association of workers. He had been Étienne Lantier's foreman at Lille, and at his request came to Montsou to address the miners there. As a result of his visit ten thousand miners joined the International Association. *Germinal.*

POIRETTE (LE PÈRE), a countryman of Bennecourt, with small eyes and the face of a wolf. He was the owner of an old cottage, which Claude Lantier and Christine rented from him for two hundred and fifty francs a year. *L'Œuvre.*

POISSON (M.), who was originally a cabinet-maker, served his time as a soldier, and ultimately got a place as a policeman, which he considered more certain and respectable. He married Virginie, who afterwards went into business as a dealer in groceries and sweetmeats in the shop previously occupied by Gervaise Coupeau. Auguste Lantier, who had for some time lodged with the Coupeaus, remained with the Poissons, and lived at their expense. M. Poisson affected not to observe the resulting *liaison* between his wife and Lantier. *L'Assommoir.*

POISSON (MADAME), wife of the preceding. *See* Virginie. *L'Assommoir.*

POLAND, a pet rabbit which belonged to Rasseneur, and was a favourite of Souvarine. *Germinal.*

POMARÉ (LA REINE), a rag-picker, who had formerly been one of the handsomest women in Paris. Now, for the sake of a laugh, the women of the district made her drink absinthe, after which the street boys would chase her and throw stones. *Nana.*

PORQUIER (DR.), the fashionable medical man of Plassans. He had considerable influence, and this was secured by Abbé Faujas on behalf of the Government's candidate for the representation of Plassans by the promise of an appointment for his son Guillaume, a young man who had hitherto given him much trouble. *La Conquête de Plassans.*

PORQUIER (GUILLAUME), son of Dr. Porquier, had been sent to Paris to study, but did nothing there but get into debt. He caused his father much distress, and was supposed to afford the worst possible example to the youth of Plassans, whom he was believed to lead into all kinds of mischief. Ultimately, as a reward to his father, who had supported Delangre as representative of Plassans,

Porquier was appointed chief clerk at the post office. *La Conquête de Plassans.*

POUILLAUD, a fellow-pupil of Claude Lantier and Pierre Sandoz at the college of Plassans. While there he was an inveterate practical joker, one of his escapades being the transformation of Professor Lalubie's room into a *chapelle ardente. L'Œuvre.*

POWELL (MISS), second assistant in the corset department at *Au Bonheur des Dames.* She was able to play the piano, a talent of which the other assistants were jealous. *Au Bonheur des Dames.*

POZZO (LUIGI), Secretary to the Sardinian Minister at Paris. " Diplomatist, painter, musician, and lover." A friend of Clorinde Balbi. *Son Excellence Eugène Rougon.*

PRICE, an English jockey who mounted the filly Nana in the Grand Prix de Paris. *Nana.*

PRINCE IMPERIAL. Referred to in *Son Excellence Eugène Rougon.*

PROUANE, a retired non-commissioned officer in the navy, who acted as beadle to Abbé Harteur, as well as fulfilling the duties of Mayor's clerk. He eked out a livelihood by gathering shell-fish, but when

N

he had any money he was usually in a state of intoxication. *La Joie de Vivre.*

PRULLIÈRE, an actor at the Théâtre des Variétés, where he played in *La Blonde Venus* and *La Petite Duchesse. Nana.*

PRUNAIRE (LE PÈRE), a maker of sabots, who lived at Vivet. Furious at the conduct of his daughter Clara, he threatened to go to Paris and break her bones with kicks of his sabots. *Au Bonheur des Dames.*

PRUNAIRE (CLARA), daughter of a clog-maker in the forest of Vilet, came to Paris and got a situation in "The Ladies' Paradise." She lived a fast life, and, after alluring Colomban away from Geneviève Baudu, his intended wife, she ultimately disappeared. *Au Bonheur des Dames.*

PUECH, senior partner of the firm of Puech and Lacamp, oil-dealers in Plassans; was father of Félicité Puech. *La Fortune des Rougon.*

PUECH AND LACAMP, a firm of oil-dealers in Plassans, who were in financial difficulties when Pierre Rougon married Félicité, the daughter of the senior partner. The money put into the business by Rougon retrieved the position of the firm, and, the two partners

having retired soon afterwards, he acquired the sole interest in it. *La Fortune des Rougon.*

PUECH (FÉLICITÉ). *See* Madame Félicité Rougon.

PUTOIS (MADAME), one of the workwomen employed by Gervaise Coupeau in her laundry. She was a little, lean woman of forty-five, "who worked at her ironing table without even taking off her bonnet, a black bonnet trimmed with green ribbons turning yellow." In character she was severely respectable. *L'Assommoir.*

Q

QUANDIEU, the oldest captain of the Montsou mines. During the strike, the energetic position taken up by him saved the Mirou pit from destruction by the infuriated strikers. *Germinal.*

QUENU (MADAME) was a widow with one son when she married her second husband, M. Quenu, a clerk in the subprefecture at Le Vigan. Three years after, M. Quenu died, leaving a son. Madame Quenu lavished all her affection on Florent, her elder son, and stinted herself to the verge of starvation in order that he might continue his legal studies. Before these were completed she succumbed to the hardship of her life. *Le Ventre de Paris.*

QUENU, the half-brother of Florent. After the death of his mother, he was taken to Paris by Florent, who supported him by teaching. He was at first idle and unsettled, but after Florent's arrest he was taken in by his uncle Gradelle, to whose business of pork-butcher, as well as to a considerable sum of money, he ultimately succeeded. After his uncle's death he married Lisa Macquart, who had previously assisted in the shop, and they had a daughter, Pauline. Business prospered, and the Quenus were soon in a position to remove to larger premises. Florent on his return from exile was kindly received by Quenu, who later on took no part in the efforts made by his wife to induce his brother to leave voluntarily. He was ignorant of his wife's action with reference to the subsequent arrest of Florent. *Le Ventre de Paris.*

He died of apoplexy in 1863, six months after the death of his wife, leaving a will under which M. Chanteau, his cousin, became the guardian of his daughter Pauline. *La Joie de Vivre.*

QUENU (MADAME LISA), wife of the preceding. *See* Lisa Macquart.

QUENU (PAULINE), born 1852, daughter of Quenu, the pork-butcher, and Lisa Macquart, his wife. A quiet, amiable child, she unwittingly gave Mlle. Saget, who bullied her, information regarding her uncle Florent's history, which led to the clamour against him in the Market, and ultimately to his arrest. *Le Ventre de Paris.*

After the death of her father, who left her a fortune of a hundred and fifty thousand francs, Pauline went in 1863 to live at Bonneville with M. Chanteau, her guardian. She soon endeared herself to her relatives, and became much attached to her cousin Lazare. As she grew up and her nature developed, it became more and more her pleasure to sacrifice herself for her friends. She allowed her fortune to be squandered by the Chanteaus, and though engaged to be married to Lazare, she released him in order that he might marry another girl with whom he had become infatuated. After his mania became acute, it was she who endeavoured to comfort him, and to dispel his unreasoning fear of death. She never married. *La Joie de Vivre.*

After the death of Chanteau, she remained at Bonneville, resolved never to marry, in order that she might devote herself entirely to Lazare's little son, Paul. *Le Docteur Pascal.*

QUINETTE, a glover in Rue Neuve Saint - Augustine, whose business was seriously affected by the competition of "The Ladies' Paradise." *Au Bonheur des Dames.*

QUITTARD (AUGUSTE), son of Françoise Quittard. He was a child of six years of age, who was so ill of typhoid fever that he could not be removed from Bazeilles when the place was attacked by the Prussians. Early in the day, his mother was killed by a cannon ball, and the poor child lay for hours tossing with fever and calling for her. He was burned to death in his bed, as the Prussians, infuriated by the length of the struggle, wantonly set fire to the village. *La Débâcle.*

QUITTARD (FRANÇOISE), widow of a mason, and now care-taker of the dye-works at Bazeilles, which belonged to Delaherche. Before the battle all the workers made their escape into Belgium, but Françoise was unable to leave on account of the illness of her little son. Early in the attack by the Prussians, the unfortunate woman was killed by a cannon ball. *La Débâcle.*

R

RABIER, a tanner of Beaumont. He was a brother of Madame Franchomme, and after her death she left the child Angelique in the care of him and his wife. They treated the girl with such cruelty that she ultimately ran away, finding shelter with the Huberts. *Le Rêve.*

RACHAEL, the maid-servant in Auguste Vabre's household. As Octave Mouret and Madame Vabre did not bribe her sufficiently, she revealed their intrigue to Vabre. She acted as his housekeeper for some time, but had to leave after the reconciliation between him and his wife. *Pot-Bouille.*

RAMBAUD (M.), half-brother of Abbé Jouve, had a large business in the Rue de Rambuteau, where he sold oils and other southern produce. Along with Abbé Jouve he showed much kindness to Hélène Grandjean after the death of her husband, and was a constant visitor at her house. Later on, the Abbé tried to arrange a marriage between Rambaud and Hélène, but at her request the decision was delayed. Meantime the love episode with Doctor Deberle intervened, followed by the death of Jeanne. Two years afterwards the marriage took place, Rambaud having previously sold his Paris business and removed to Marseilles. *Une Page d'Amour.*

He retired from business and went to live at Marseilles. Having by his marriage become a cousin of Madame Lisa Quenu, he was appointed a member of the family council which nominally had charge of her daughter's fortune. *La Joie de Vivre.*

Rambaud led a happy life with his wife, whom he adored. *Le Docteur Pascal.*

RAMBAUD (MADAME), wife of the preceding. *See* Hélène Mouret.

RAMOND (DR.), a pupil and fellow-practitioner of Dr. Pascal. He wished to marry Clotilde Rougon, but she refused him, and he subsequently married Mademoiselle Lévêque. When Doctor Pascal was seized with an affection of the heart, Ramond diagnosed the nature of the illness, and subsequently attended him with unremitting care until his death. *Le Docteur Pascal.*

RAMOND (MADAME), wife of the preceding. *See* Mademoiselle Lévêque. *Le Docteur Pascal.*

RANVIER (ABBÉ), succeeded Abbé Jouve as curé at Montsou. He was of socialistic tendencies, and blamed the middle classes, who he said had formerly robbed the Church, for all the horrors produced by the strike at Montsou. Upon the troops who had been called on to fire upon the strikers, he called down the anger of God, predicting an hour of justice in which fire would descend from heaven to exterminate the *bourgeoisie.* He was finally removed by the bishop as too compromising. *Germinal.*

RASSENEUR kept a tavern with the sign *A l'Avantage* between the settlement of the Deux-Cent-Quarante and the Voreux pit. He was formerly a good workman, but as he was an excellent speaker, and placed himself at the head of every strike, he was dismissed by the Mining Company. His wife already held a licence, and when he was thrown out of work he became an innkeeper himself. It was in his house that Étienne Lantier found lodgings when he first came to Montsou, and Souvarine also lodged there. Rasseneur's readiness of speech gave him great influence with the miners, but a rivalry arose between him and Lantier, whose new theories caught the popular ear. This jealousy caused him to take a side against the strike, solely because it had been proposed by Lantier, and this attitude made him very unpopular. But after the failure of the strike, which he had all along predicted, the inconstancy of the crowd turned in his favour and he soon regained his old popularity. *Germinal.*

RASSENEUR (MADAME), wife of the preceding. At the time her husband was dismissed from the pit, she already held a licence, and they subsequently worked together to extend the business, in which they had considerable success. She was much more radical in politics than her husband, but during the strike trouble was careful to show extreme politeness to everyone. *Germinal.*

RASTOIL, a neighbour of François Mouret. He was a rich man about sixty years of age, who had been president of the civil tribunal of Plassans for over twenty years. He was a Legitimist, and his house was used as a convenient meeting-place for the party. For some time he refused to compromise his political position with Abbé Faujas, who had all along concealed his opinions. Ultimately, however, he supported the candidate for the representation of Plassans proposed by Faujas, for which he was rewarded by an appointment for his son. *La Conquête de Plassans.*

RASTOIL (MADAME), wife of the preceding, was a listless and somewhat prudish woman whose old entanglement with M. Delangre was still remembered with amusement in the cafés. She was consulted by Madame Mouret regarding the Home for Girls proposed by Abbé Faujas, and ultimately agreed to act on the committee. *La Conquête de Plassans.*

RASTOIL (ANGÉLINE), elder daughter of M. Rastoil, the president of the civil tribunal

of Plassans. Though twenty-
six years old, and now very
yellow and shrewish-looking,
she still adopted the *rôle* of a
young girl, and had hopes of
securing a husband. *La Conquête de Plassans.*

RASTOIL (AURÉLIE), second
daughter of M. Rastoil. Like
her sister Angéline, she was
plain-looking, and posed as a
girl fresh from school, in the
uncertain hope of gaining a
husband. *La Conquête de
Plassans.*

RASTOIL (SÉVERIN), son of M.
Rastoil, the president of the
civil tribunal of Plassans.
" He was a tall young man of
five and twenty, with a badly
shaped skull and a dull brain,
who had been just called to
the Bar, thanks to the position
which his father held. The
latter was anxiously dreaming
of making him a substitute,
despairing of his ever succeed-
ing in winning any practice
for himself." On the suggestion of Abbé Faujas he took a
share in starting the Club for
Young Men at Plassans. After
the election of M. Delangre as
representative of Plassans,
Rastoil received the appointment of assistant public procurator at Faverolles. *La
Conquête de Plassans.*

RAVAUD, a captain in the 106th
Regiment of the line, commanded by Colonel de Vineuil.
A young soldier in his company was the first of the
wounded to be taken to the
ambulance in Delaherche's
house on 1st September, 1870.
In March, 1871, captain
Ravaud was at Paris, in a
regiment of recent formation,
the 124th of the line. Jean
Macquart was corporal in his
company in this regiment. *La
Débâcle.*

READING (LORD), proprietor of a
racing stable. Bramah, one
of his horses, once gained the
Grand Prix de Paris. *Nana.*

REBUFAT, a farmer whose land
adjoined that inherited by
Adélaïde Fouque. He pur-
chased the Fouque property
when it was sold by Pierre
Rougon. After the death of
his wife Rebufat and his son
Justin treated her niece Miette
Chantegreil very harshly. *La
Fortune des Rougon.*

REBUFAT (MADAME EULALIE),
wife of the preceding ; " a
big, dark, stubborn shrew."
She was a sister of Chantegreil, and was therefore the
aunt of Miette, who lived
with her after her father's conviction. *La Fortune des Rougon.*

REBUFAT (JUSTIN), son of Re- bufat. "A youth about twenty years old, a sickly, squint-eyed creature, who cherished an implacable hatred against his cousin Miette." *La Fortune des Rou- gon.*

REMANJOU (MADEMOISELLE), an old lady who lived in the same tenement house in Rue de la Goutte d'Or as the Coupeaus and the Lorilleux, where she made a scanty livelihood by dressing dolls. She was one of the guests at the Coupeaus' wedding party. *L'Assommoir.*

RENAUDIN, a notary at Paris, who adjusted the Contract of Marriage between Auguste Vabre and Berthe Josserand. He acted in concert with Duveyrier in selling some heritable property to the loss of other members of the family. *Pot-Bouille.*

RENAUDIN, a medical man at Grenelle. Joséphine Déjoie was at one time cook in his house. *L'Argent.*

RENGADE, a gendarme whose eye was accidentally destroyed by Silvère Mouret during a struggle for possession of a carbine after the entry of the insurgents into Plassans. *La Fortune des Rougon.*

REUTHLINGUER (BARON DE), a banker, and possessor of one of the largest fortunes in Europe. He was a friend of Clorinde Balbi, and from her received valuable information on political subjects. *Son Excellence Eugène Rougon.*

RHADAMANTE, the sobriquet of a professor at the college of Plassans. He was supposed never to have laughed. *L'Œuvre.*

RICHOMME, one of the captains of the Voreux pit. He tried in vain to prevent a collision between the strikers and the troops, and even when bricks were being thrown he went between the two parties, imploring one and advising the other, careless of danger. He was one of the first to fall when the troops ultimately fired. *Germinal.*

RIVOIRE, a member of the firm of Piot and Rivoire. *Au Bonheur des Dames.*

ROBERT (MADAME), a regular customer at the restaurant Laure Piédefer. She was jealous of Nana's relations with Satin, and revenged her- self by writing anonymous letters to Muffat and to other lovers of her enemy. *Nana.*

ROBIN-CHAGOT (VISCOUNT DE), vice-chairman of the board of directors of the Universal Bank. He was selected for the position in the belief that he would sign anything put before him without making too many inquiries. *L'Argent.*

ROBINEAU, " second hand " in the silk department at " The Ladies' Paradise." As the result of a conspiracy among his subordinates, he was dismissed, and soon afterwards bought the business of M. Vinçard, a silk merchant, with money belonging to his wife. His capital was inadequate, but M. Gaujean, a silk manufacturer who had quarrelled with Octave Mouret, promised to give him unlimited credit. Robineau's intention was to break up a monopoly of the cheaper class of silks which Mouret had secured, but he soon found that each reduction in price which he made was met by a still larger one. As he had no other departments out of which to average his profits, ruin inevitably followed, and he attempted to commit suicide by throwing himself under an omnibus ; his injuries were not serious, however, and he ultimately recovered. *Au Bonheur des Dames.*

ROBINEAU (MADAME), wife of the preceding. " Daughter of an overseer in the Department of Highways, entirely ignorant of business matters, she still retained the charming awkwardness of a girl educated in a Blois convent."

Her small fortune enabled her husband to buy the silk business of M. Vinçard, and she assisted him in carrying it on. Their subsequent ruin affected her less than the attempted suicide of her husband, to whom she was devoted. *Au Bonheur des Dames.*

ROBINE, a regular attender at the revolutionary meetings in Lebigre's wine-shop. He sat for hours listening to arguments but never made any remarks. He escaped arrest. *Le Ventre de Paris.*

ROBINE (MADAME), wife of the preceding, lived with her husband in Rue Saint - Denis. No one ever entered their house, and even her personal appearance was unknown to her husband's friends. *Le Ventre de Paris.*

ROBINOT (MADAME), an acquaintance of the Deberles. *Une Page d'Amour.*

ROBIQUET, farmer of La Chamade. Being near the end of his lease, he ceased to manure the land, allowing it to go to ruin. He was eventually turned out as he did not pay his rent. *La Terre.*

ROCHART (MONSEIGNEUR), Bishop of Faverolles. He upheld the Sisters of the Holy Family in the matter of the succession to Chevassu's estate, but was beaten by Eugène Rougon, the Minister of State, who supported the claim of the Charbonnels. *Son Excellence Eugène Rougon.*

ROCHAS, lieutenant in the 106th Regiment of the line, commanded by Colonel de Vineuil. The son of a journeyman mason from Limousin, he was born in Paris, and not caring for his father's calling, enlisted when he was only eighteen. He gained a corporal's stripes in Algeria, rose to the rank of sergeant at Sebastopol, and was promoted to a lieutenancy after Solferino. Fifteen years of hardship and heroic bravery was the price he had paid to be an officer, but his education was so defective that he could never be made a captain. He held the old traditions that a defeat of the French army was impossible, and all through the campaign against Germany in 1870 he refused to believe in the repeated catastrophes. In the fierce attack by the Prussians on the Hermitage, he fought desperately against an overwhelming force, and up to the end encouraged his men by shouting that the victory was theirs. In the end he fell, mowed down by a hail of bullets. *La Débâcle.*

ROCHEFONTAINE, proprietor of a large factory at Châteaudun. He was desirous of serving as a Deputy, but did not secure the support of the Government, and, standing as an independent candidate, was defeated. Later, in consequence of the disgrace of M. de Chédeville, he became the official candidate, and in spite of a brusqueness of manner which made him unpopular, he was elected. *La Terre.*

RODRIGUEZ, a distant relative of the Empress, who made a claim upon the State for a large sum, which he said had been due since 1808. Eugène Rougon, the Minister of State, gave great offence to the Empress by opposing the claim. *Son Excellence Eugène Rougon.*

ROGNES-BOUQUEVAL (LES), an ancient and noble family whose estate, already much reduced by enforced sales, was declared national property in 1793, and was purchased piece by piece by Isidore Hourdequin. *La Terre.*

ROIVILLE (LES), members of Parisian society at whose house Baroness Sandorff occasionally met Gundermann. *L'Argent.*

ROSALIE, an old chair-mender at Rognes. The poor woman lived all alone, sick and without a copper. Abbé Godard came to her assistance. *La Terre.*

ROSE, a waitress in Lebigre's wine-shop. *Le Ventre de Paris.*

ROSE, servant in the household of François Mouret, was an old woman of crabbed nature and uncertain temper. She fell under the influence of Abbé Faujas, and encouraged her mistress in the religious observances which led to the neglect of her family. Later, when Madame Mouret's health became impaired, and she became subject to fits, it was chiefly Rose who threw suspicion on her master, encouraging the belief that he was insane and had inflicted injuries on his wife. *La Conquête de Plassans.*

ROSE, a peasant girl at Artaud ; sister of Lisa. *La Faute de l'Abbé Mouret.*

ROSE, maid-servant to Madame Hennebeau. She was not alarmed by the violence of the strikers, as, belonging to that district, she knew the miners, and believed them not to be wicked. *Germinal.*

ROSE, daughter of the concierge at the sub-prefecture at Sedan. She was a worker in Delaherche's factory, and he applied to her for information regarding the course of the battle, as she was in a position to hear the gossip of the officers and officials. When Napoleon III decided to request an armistice from the Prussians, it was Rose who furnished a tablecloth to be used as a white flag. *La Débâcle.*

ROSE, niece of Aristide Saccard's hairdresser. She was a pretty girl of about eighteen, whom Saccard sent to his son Maxime under the pretext of nursing him, but in reality with a view to hastening the course of a nervous disease from which the young man suffered. Aristide agreed to pay her a percentage on the fortune which he hoped to acquire at his son's death. *Le Docteur Pascal.*

ROUBAUD, assistant station-master at Havre. Born in the south of France, at Plassans, he had a carter for father. He had quitted the army with the stripes of a sergeant-major, and for a long time had been general porter at the station at Nantes. He had been promoted head porter at Barentin, and it was there that he first saw Séverine Aubry, the god-daughter of President Grandmorin, whom he married. This was the sole romance of his existence, and it was coupled with fortune, for apart from Séverine and her marriage portion of ten thousand francs, the President, now a director of the Western Railway Company, got him appointed assistant station-master at Havre. He proved an excellent official, and the only thing against him was a suspicion that he was affected by republican principles. For three years Roubaud's married life was a happy one, until a chance lie of his wife's gave him a clue to her former relations with Grandmorin. Driven frantic by jealousy, he forced her to reveal the truth, afterwards compelling her to become his accomplice in the murder of the President in the Havre express. The Roubauds established an *alibi*, though slight suspicion attached to them, and Denizet, the examining magistrate, endeavoured to fasten the crime on Cabuche. For political reasons it was not considered desirable that Grandmorin's character should be publicly discussed, and the inquiry regarding the murder was dropped. Roubaud was aware, however, that Jacques Lantier had strong suspicions, and tried to secure his silence by making him a friend ; a friendship which soon developed into a *liaison* between Lantier and Séverine. With the murder of Grandmorin, the disintegration of Roubaud's character began ; he gradually became a confirmed gambler, and having lost all his own money began to use that which he had taken from the body of his victim in order to establish a false motive for the crime. The relations between him and his wife became more and more strained, until they reached such a pitch that Lantier and she planned his murder. The homicidal frenzy of Lantier, to which Séverine fell a victim, ended the plot, but Roubaud and Cabuche, who arrived on the scene immediately after the murder, were arrested under what appeared to be suspicious circumstances, and, after trial, were sentenced to penal servitude for a crime which they did not commit. *La Bête Humaine.*

ROUBAUD (MADAME), wife of the preceding. *See* Séverine Aubry. *La Bête Humaine.*

ROUDIER, a regular attender at the political meetings held in the Rougons' yellow drawing-room. *La Fortune des Rougon.*

ROUGE D'AUNEAU (LE), lieutenant of Beau - François, leader of the band of brigands. He wrote a complaint while in prison. *La Terre.*

ROUGETTE, a cow bought by the sisters Mouche at the market of Cloyes. *La Terre.*

ROUGON, a young gardener who worked for the Fouque family, and afterwards married Adélaïde. Fifteen months afterwards he died from sunstroke, leaving a son named Pierre. *La Fortune des Rougon.*

ROUGON, *alias* SACCARD (ARISTIDE), born 1815, youngest son of Pierre Rougon, was educated, like his brothers, at Plassans and Paris, but failed to pass his examinations. His character was a combination of covetousness and slyness : his greatest desire was the acquisition of a rapid fortune, gained without work. In 1836 he married Angèle Sicardot, who brought him a dowry of ten thousand francs. As

Aristide did no work, and lived extravagantly, the money was soon consumed, and he and his wife were in such poverty that he was at last compelled to seek a situation. He procured a place at the Sub-Prefecture, where he remained nearly ten years, and only reached a salary of eighteen hundred francs. During that time " he longed, with ever-increasing malevolence and rancour, for those enjoyments of which he was deprived " by his lowly position. In 1848, when his brother Eugène left for Paris, he had a faint idea of following him, but remained in the hope of something turning up. In opposition to his father, he expressed Republican principles, and edited a newspaper called the *Indépendant.* At the time of the *Coup d'État*, he became alarmed at the course of events, and pretended that an accident to his hand prevented him from writing. His mother having given him private information as to the success of the Bonapartist cause, he changed the politics of his paper, and became reconciled to his parents. *La Fortune des Rougon.*

Early in 1852 he went to Paris, taking with him his

wife and daughter Clotilde, then a child of four ; his son Maxime he left at Plassans. Through the influence of his brother Eugène, he got an appointment as assistant surveying clerk at the *Hôtel de Ville*, with a salary of two thousand four hundred francs. Before entering on his duties, however, he changed his name to Saccard on the suggestion of his brother, who feared that he might be compromised by him. In 1853, Aristide was appointed a surveying commissioner of roads, with an increased salary. At this period great schemes of city improvement were under discussion, and Aristide by spying and other shady means got early information as to the position of the proposed new streets. Great chances of fortune were arising, but he had no capital. The death of his wife enabled him to enter into a plan proposed by his sister Sidonie, who had heard of a family willing to make a considerable sacrifice to find a not too inquisitive husband for their daughter. He accordingly married Renée Béraud du Châtel, and gained control of a considerable sum of ready money, in addition to the fortune settled on his wife. By means of a

cleverly contrived swindle, in which he was assisted by his friend Larsonneau, he got a fabulous price for some property acquired by him, and the foundation of his fortune was laid. From this time, he lived a life of the wildest extravagance, and, though his gains were frequently enormous, his expenses were so great that it was only with difficulty that he was able to prevent a catastrophe. *La Curée.*

He was appointed by Pauline Quenu's family council to be her " surrogate guardian." *La Joie de Vivre.*

After a last and disastrous land speculation, Saccard was obliged to leave his great house in the Parc Monceau, which he abandoned to his creditors. At first undecided as to his movements, he took a flat in the mansion in Rue Saint-Lazare, which belonged to Princess d'Orviedo. There he met Hamelin, the engineer, and his sister Caroline, with whom he soon became on intimate terms. Hamelin having spent much time in the East, had formed many schemes for great financial ventures, and Saccard was so impressed with these that he formed a syndicate for the purpose of carrying some of them out. With this view the Universal Bank was formed, and was at first very successful. By persistent advertising, and other means, the shares of the Bank were forced to an undue price, and then Saccard began to speculate in them on behalf of the Bank itself. The great financier Gundermann, with whom Saccard had quarrelled, then began a persistent attack on the Bank, selling its shares steadily day after day. Saccard continued to buy as long as he was able ; but the end came, the price broke, and he, as well as the Bank, which was now one of its own largest shareholders, was ruined. Since his previous failure, Saccard had not been on friendly terms with his brother Eugène Rougon, and, some time before the collapse of the Bank, had made violent attacks upon him in his newspaper. Consequently Rougon did nothing to assist him in the criminal proceedings which followed the final catastrophe ; he did not, however, wish to have a brother in jail, and arranged matters so that an appeal was allowed. Next day Saccard escaped to Belgium. *L'Argent.*

After the fall of the Second Empire, he returned to Paris, despite the sentence he had incurred. Some complicated intrigue must have been at work, for not only did he obtain a pardon, but once more took part in promoting large undertakings, with a finger in every pie and a share of every bribe. In 1872 he was actively engaged in journalism, having been appointed Director of the *Epoque,* a Republican journal which made a great success by publishing the papers found in the Tuileries. Covetous of his son's fortune, he hastened a disease from which Maxime suffered, by encouraging him in vicious courses, and in the end got possession of the whole estate. By a singular irony, Aristide, now returned to his original Republicanism, was in a position to protect his brother Eugène, whom in earlier days he had so often compromised. *Le Docteur Pascal.*

ROUGON (MADAME ANGÈLE), first wife of the preceding, was a daughter of Commander Sicardot. She brought her husband a dowry of ten thousand francs. *La Fortune des Rougon.*

Along with her daughter Clotilde, she accompanied her husband to Paris in 1852, and being an amiable woman without ambition she was quite satisfied with the modest position he at first secured. She died in 1854 of inflammation of the lungs. *La Curée.*

ROUGON, *alias* SACCARD (MADAME RENÉE), the second wife of Aristide Rougon, *alias* Saccard, was the elder daughter of M. Béraud du Châtel, the last representative of an old middle - class family. Having become seriously compromised, she was hurriedly married to Saccard through the agency of his sister Madame Sidonie, and a considerable sum of money as well as land was settled upon her. Wholly given over to pleasure and extravagance, she soon got deeply into debt, and her husband took advantage of this from time to time by inducing her to make over to him her property, in order that he might speculate with it. She engaged in a shameful *liaison* with her husband's son Maxime, which ultimately brought her great unhappiness, and she died of acute meningitis at an early age. *La Curée.*

ROUGON (CHARLES), born 1857, son of Maxime Rougon, *alias* Saccard, and of Justine Mégot, a maid-servant of Madame Renée Saccard. The child and his mother were sent to the country with a little annuity of twelve hundred francs. *La Curée.*

At fifteen years of age he lived at Plassans with his mother, who had married a saddler named Anselme Thomas. Charles was a degenerate who reproduced at a distance of three generations his great-great-grandmother, Adélaïde Fouque. He did not look more than twelve years old, and his intelligence was that of a child of five. There was in him a relaxation of tissues, due to degeneracy, and the slightest exertion produced hæmorrhage. Charles was not kindly treated by his stepfather, and generally lived with his great-grandmother Félicité Rougon. He was frequently taken to visit the aged Adélaïde Fouque in the asylum at Les Tulettes, and on one occasion, in 1873, when he chanced to be left alone with her he was seized with bleeding at the nose, and, under the fixed eyes of his ancestress, he slowly bled to death. *Le Docteur Pascal.*

ROUGON (CLOTILDE), born 1847, daughter of Aristide Rougon, accompanied her father and mother to Paris in 1852. After the death of her mother in 1854, she was sent to live with Dr. Pascal Rougon, her uncle, who had frequently offered to take her to enliven his silent scientific home. *La Curée.*

At Plassans Clotilde lived a quiet healthy life, much of it spent in the open air. She was not highly educated, but having considerable artistic talent was able to assist Doctor Pascal by making illustrations for his great work on heredity. At one period she developed strong religious tendencies under the influence of Martine, the doctor's old servant, who took her to church, and imbued the girl with her own bigoted ideas regarding the salvation of Pascal. Her grandmother, Félicité Rougon, who wished, for family reasons, to destroy Pascal's manuscripts on the subject of heredity, played on Clotilde's feelings, and induced her to assist in a search for the hated work. Rougon surprised them in the act, and subsequently laid bare to Clotilde the whole facts of the terrible family history. In time the mysticism of the Church gave place to passionate love between Clotilde and Pascal. The doctor felt, however, that she was sacrificing her youth for him, and

O

sent her to Paris to live with her brother Maxime. Soon afterwards, Pascal became ill, and died before she was able to return. A child was born some months later. *Le Docteur Pascal.*

ROUGON (EUGÉNE), born 1811, eldest son of Pierre Rougon, was educated at Plassans and Paris, and was called to the Bar. He practised in the local Court for a number of years, but with little success. Though of lethargic appearance, he was a man of ability, who "cherished lofty ambitions, possessed domineering instincts, and showed a singular contempt for trifling expedients and small fortunes." With the Revolution of February, 1848, Eugène felt that his opportunity had come, and he left for Paris with scarcely five hundred francs in his pocket. He was able to give his parents early information of the designs of the Bonapartes, and so prepared the way for the events of the *Coup d'État* of 1851, when the family fortunes were made. *La Fortune des Rougon.*

During his early days in Paris Rougon resided at the Hôtel Vanneau, kept by Madame Correur, and while there he made the acquaintance of Gilquin and Du Poizat, both of whom assisted him in spreading the Bonapartist propaganda. By his exertions in this cause he established a claim for reward, and he was appointed a member of the State Council, ultimately becoming its President. He fell into disfavour, however, with the Court on account of his opposition to a claim for two million francs by a distant relative of the Empress Eugénie. Finding that his position was insecure, he tendered his resignation to the Emperor, who accepted it. About this time he met Clorinde Balbi, an Italian adventuress, who endeavoured to induce him to marry her. Carried away for the time being, Rougon made overtures to her which she resented, and he was on the point of offering her marriage. Reflection on her somewhat equivocal position in society induced him to think better of this, and he offered to arrange a marriage between her and his friend Delestang. The offer was accepted, and the marriage took place. Soon after, Rougon married Véronique Beulin-d'Orchère. During his retirement Rougon was surrounded by a band of followers, the Charbonnels, Du Poizet, Kahn, and others, who in the hope of profiting by his return to office lost no chance of establishing a claim upon him. After the Orsini plot against the life of the Emperor, of which Rougon had prior information through Gilquin, the need for a strong man arose, and he was again called to office, being appointed Minister of the Interior. His harshness in carrying out reprisals against the Republican party, and even more, his recklessness in finding appointments for his friends, led to a public outcry, and his position again became undermined. Clorinde, who had never forgiven him for not marrying her, did much to foment the disaffection, and even his own band of followers turned against him. Always quick to act, Rougon again placed his resignation in the hands of the Emperor, who to his surprise accepted it. Three years later he was once more a member of the Corps Législatif, and having brought his principles into accordance with the more liberal views then professed by the Emperor, he gave his strong support to the measures giving effect to them. In consequence, he was appointed by the Emperor as a Minister without department, and commissioned to defend the new Policy. *Son Excellence Eugène Rougon.*

When his brother Aristide came to Paris, Eugène found a situation for him, but, fearing to be compromised by him, suggested that he should change his name to Saccard, which he did. There was no intimacy between the brothers, but Eugène occasionally visited Aristide at the great house built by him in the Parc Monceau. *La Curée.*

After Saccard's bankruptcy, Eugène refused to have any further connection with him, though he tacitly approved of the foundation of the Universal Bank. The Bank having failed, however, he did nothing to stay legal proceedings against his brother ; but, after a sentence of imprisonment had been passed, he connived at his escape from the country while the sentence was under appeal. *L'Argent.*

He continued to take a lively interest in Plassans, and it was by him that Abbé Faujas was sent there to counteract the clerical influence, which at that time was strongly Legitimist. He kept up a correspondence with his mother, whom he advised as to each step she should take in political matters. *La Conquête de Plassans.*

After the fall of the Empire, Eugène became a simple Deputy, and in the Assembly remained to defend the old order of things which the downfall had swept away. *Le Docteur Pascal.*

ROUGON (MADAME EUGÈNE), wife of the preceding. *See* Véronique Beulin-d'Orchère. *Son Excellence Eugène Rougon.*

ROUGON (MARTHE), born 1820, daughter of Pierre Rougon ; married in 1840 her cousin François Rougon ; had three children. *La Fortune des Rougon.*

She accompanied her husband to Marseilles, where by close attention to business they accumulated a fortune in fifteen years, returning to Plassans at the end of that period and settling down there. Her life at Plassans was a happy one until the household fell under the influence of Abbé Faujas. From the first she was in love with the priest, and as he gave her no encouragement in this, she devoted herself to church services to the entire neglect of her household and family. As time went on, her passion for the Abbé grew more extreme, and her health became undermined to a serious extent. She became subject to fits of an epileptic nature, and having injured herself in some of these, she allowed the injuries to be attributed to her husband, whom she had now grown to regard as an encumbrance. Though she was aware that he was not insane, she allowed him to be removed to an asylum, where confinement soon completed the work begun by her own conduct. The Abbé Faujas having resolutely resisted her advances, her health became still worse, and she died in her mother's house on the same night that her husband escaped from the asylum and burned down their old home. *La Conquête de Plassans.*

Rougon (Maxime), born 1840, son of Aristide Rougon. *La Fortune des Rougon.*

When his father went to Paris in 1852, Maxime remained at school at Plassans, not going to Paris till after his father's second marriage. From early youth he was of vicious character, and the idleness and extravagance of the life in his father's house only completed the training begun at Plassans. After carrying on a disgraceful *liaison* with his father's second wife, he married Louise de Mareuil, through whom he got a considerable dowry. *La Curée.*

After the death of his wife, six months after their marriage, he returned to Paris, where he lived quietly upon the dowry brought to him by her. He refused to join in any of his father's schemes, or to assist him in any way, and was consequently not affected by the failure of the Universal Bank. *L'Argent.*

After the war he re-established himself in his mansion in Avenue du Bois-de-Boulogne, where he lived on the fortune left by his wife. "He had become prudent, however, with the enforced restraint of a man whose marrow is diseased, and who seeks by artifice to ward off the paralysis which threatened him." In the fear of this impending illness, he induced his sister Clotilde to leave Doctor Pascal, and go to live with him in Paris, but in his constant fear of being taken advantage of he soon began to be suspicious of her, as he did of every one who served him. His father, who wished to hasten his own inheritance, encouraged him in a renewal of his vicious courses, and he died of *locomotor ataxy* at the age of thirty-three. *Le Docteur Pascal.*

ROUGON (MADAME MAXIME). *See* Louise de Mareuil.

ROUGON (PASCAL), born 1813, second son of Pierre Rougon, " had an uprightness of spirit, a love of study, a retiring modesty which contrasted strangely with the feverish ambitions and unscrupulous intrigues of his family." Having acquitted himself admirably in his medical studies at Paris, he returned to Plassans, where he lived a life of quiet study and work. He had few patients, but devoted himself to research, particularly on the subject of heredity, with special reference to its results on his own family. In the hope of alleviating suffering, he followed the Republican insurgents in their march from Plassans in December, 1851. *La Fortune des Rougon.*

In 1854 his niece Clotilde, daughter of his brother Aristide, went to live with him. He had frequently offered to take her, but no-thing was arranged till after the death of her mother, at which time she was about seven years old. *La Curée.*

His practice as a medical man extended to Les Artaud, and he attended his nephew Abbé Serge Mouret during an attack of brain fever. On the priest's partial recovery, he removed him to the Paradou, and left him in the care of Albine, niece of old Jeanbernat, the caretaker of that neglected demesne. Dr. Pascal was much attached to Albine, and deeply regretted the sad love affair which resulted from Mouret's forgetfulness of his past. He had no religious beliefs himself, and he urged Mouret to return to Albine, but the voice of the Church proved too strong in the end. *La Faute de l'Abbé Mouret.*

At sixty years of age Pascal was so fresh and vigorous that, though his hair and beard were white, he might have been mistaken for a young man with powdered locks. He had lived for seventeen years at La Souleiade, near Plassans, with his niece Clotilde and his old servant Martine, having amassed a little fortune, which was sufficient for his needs. He had devoted his life to the study of heredity, finding typical examples in his own family. He brought up Clotilde without imposing on her his own philosophic creed, even allowing Martine to take her to church regularly. But this tolerance brought about a serious misunderstanding between them, for the girl fell under the influence of religious mysticism, and came to look with horror on the savant's scientific pursuits. Discovered by him in an attempt to destroy his documents, he explained to Clotilde fully and frankly the bearing of their terrible family history on his theory of heredity, with the result that her outlook on life was entirely changed ; he had opposed the force of human truth against the shadows of mysticism. The struggle between Pascal and Clotilde brought them to a knowledge of mutual love, and an illicit relationship was established between them. He would have married her (this being legal in France), but having lost most of his money he was unwilling to sacrifice what he believed to be her interests, and persuaded her to go to Paris to live with her brother Maxime. Soon after her departure he was seized with an affection of the heart, and, after some weeks of suffering, died only an hour before her return. Immediately after his death his mother, Madame Félicité Rougon, took possession of his papers, and in an immense *auto-da-fé* destroyed in an hour the records of a lifetime of work. *Le Docteur Pascal.*

ROUGON (PIERRE), born 1787, legitimate son of Adélaïde Fouque, was a thrifty, selfish lad who saw that his mother by her improvident conduct was squandering the estate to which he considered himself sole heir. His aim was to induce his mother and her two illegitimate children to remove from the house and land, and in this he was ultimately successful. Having sold the property for fifty thousand francs, he induced his mother, who by this time was of weak intellect, to sign a receipt for that sum, and was so able to defraud his half-brother and sister of the shares to which they would have been entitled. Soon thereafter he married Félicité Puech, the daughter of an oil dealer in Plassans. The firm of Puech and Lacamp was not prosperous, but the money brought by Pierre

Rougon retrieved the situation, and after a few years the two original partners retired. Fortune, however, soon changed, and for thirty years there was a continual struggle to make ends meet. Three sons and two daughters were born, and their education was a heavy drain upon their parents' means. In 1845 Pierre and his wife retired from business with forty thousand francs at the most. Instigated by the Marquis de Carnavant, they went in for politics, and soon regular meetings of the reactionary party came to be held in their " yellow drawing-room." Advised, however, by their son Eugène, they resolved to support the cause of the Bonapartes, and at the time of the *Coup d'État* of 1851 Pierre was the leader of that party in Plassans. Having concealed himself when the Republican insurgents entered Plassans, he avoided capture, and after they retired he led the band of citizens which recaptured the town hall. This bloodless victory having been somewhat minimized by the townspeople, Pierre and his wife, with a view to establishing a strong claim for subsequent reward, bribed Antoine Macquart to lead the Republicans left in Plassans to an attack on the town hall. To meet this he prepared a strong ambuscade, and the Republicans were repulsed with considerable loss. As a result of this treachery, Pierre was regarded by his fellow-citizens as the saviour of the town, and the Government subsequently appointed him Receiver of Taxes, decorating him with the Cross of the Legion of Honour. *La Fortune des Rougon.*

He settled down quietly and took little part in public affairs, though his wife continued to hold weekly receptions at which members of the different political parties were represented. *La Conquête de Plassans.*

He became so corpulent that he was unable to move, and was carried off by an attack of indigestion on the night of 3rd September, 1870, a few hours after hearing of the catastrophe of Sedan. The downfall of the regime which he prided himself on having helped to establish seemed to have crushed him like a thunderbolt. *Le Docteur Pascal.*

ROUGON (MADAME FÉLICITÉ), wife of the preceding, and daughter of Puech, the oil-dealer. She was married in

1810, and had three sons and two daughters. A woman of strong ambitions, she hoped to better her social position by the aid of her sons, on whose education she spent large sums. Disappointed in this hope for many years, she and her husband retired from business with barely sufficient means to keep themselves in comfort. She, instigated by the Marquis de Carnavant (her putative father) urged her husband to take part in politics, and meetings of the reactionary party were regularly held in her " yellow drawing-room." While the success of the *Coup d'État* was in some doubt, she encouraged her husband in maintaining the position he had taken up ; and, having ascertained that the success of the Bonapartists was assured, she arranged with Antoine Macquart for the attack on the town hall, the repulse of which led to the rise of the family fortunes. *La Fortune des Rougon.*

After her husband's appointment as Receiver of Taxes, she continued her weekly receptions, but endeavoured to give them a non-political character by inviting representatives of all parties. Her son Eugène, now a Minister of State, kept her advised as to the course she should pursue, and on his instructions she gave some assistance to Abbé Faujas in his political " conquest of Plassans." *La Conquête de Plassans.*

In 1856 she interested herself in a lawsuit raised by M. Charbonnel, a retired oil-merchant of Plassans, and requested her son Eugène, the President of the Council of State, to use his influence on behalf of her friend. *Son Excellence Eugène Rougon.*

After the disasters of the war, Plassans escaped from her dominion, and she had to content herself with the *rôle* of dethroned queen of the old regime. Her ruling passion was the defence of the glory of the Rougons, and the obliteration of everything tending to reflect on the family name. In this connection she welcomed the death of Adélaïde Fouque, the common ancestress of the Rougons and the Macquarts, and she did nothing to save her old accomplice Antoine Macquart from the terrible fate which overtook him. After these events, her only remaining trouble was the work on family heredity which had for years occupied her son Pascal. Assisted by his servant Martine, she eventually succeeded in burning the whole manuscripts to which Pascal had devoted his life. Her triumph was then secure, and in order to raise a monument to the glory of the family she devoted a large part of her fortune to the erection of an asylum for the aged, to be known as the Rougon Asylum. At eighty-two years of age, she laid the foundation stone of the building, and in doing so conquered Plassans for the third time. *Le Docteur Pascal.*

ROUGON (SIDONIE), born 1818, daughter of Pierre Rougon. *La Fortune des Rougon.*

She married at Plassans an attorney's clerk, named Touche, and together they went to Paris, setting up business in the Rue Saint-Honoré, as dealers in fruit from the south of France. The venture was unsuccessful, and the husband soon disappeared. At the rise of the Second Empire, Sidonie was thirty-five ; but she dressed herself with so little care and had so little of the woman in her manner that she looked much older. She carried on business in lace and pianos, but did not confine herself to these trades ; when she had sold ten francs' worth of lace she would insinuate herself into her customer's good graces and become her man of business, attending attorneys, advocates, and judges on her behalf. The confidences she everywhere received put her on the track of good strokes of business, often of a nature more than equivocal, and it was she who arranged the second marriage of her brother Aristide. She was a true Rougon, who had inherited the hunger for money, the longing for intrigue, which was the characteristic of the family. *La Curée.*

In 1851 she had a daughter by an unknown father. The child, who was named Angelique Marie, was at once sent to the Foundling Hospital by her mother, who never made any inquiry about her afterwards. *Le Rêve.*

She attended the funeral of her cousin, Claude Lantier, the artist. Arrived at his house, "she went upstairs, turned round the studio, sniffed at all its bare wretchedness, and then walked down again with a hard mouth, irritated at having taken the trouble to come." *L'Œuvre.*

" After a long disappearance from the scene, Sidonie, weary of the shady callings she had plied, and now of a nunlike austerity, retired to the gloomy shelter of a conventual kind of establishment, holding the purse-strings of the Œuvre du Sacrament, an institution founded with the object of assisting seduced girls, who had become mothers, to secure husbands." *Le Docteur Pascal.*

ROUGON (VICTOR), son of Aristide Saccard and Rosaline Chavaille. Brought up in the gutter, he was from the first incorrigibly lazy and vicious. La Méchain, his mother's cousin, after discovering his paternity, told the facts to Caroline Hamelin, who, to save Saccard annoyance, paid over a considerable sum and removed the boy to *L'Œuvre du Travail*, one of the institutions founded by Princess d'Orviedo. Here every effort was made to reclaim him, but without success ; vice and cunning had become his nature. In the end he made a murderous attack upon Alice de Beauvilliers, who was visiting the hospital, and having stolen her purse, made his escape.

Subsequent search proved fruitless ; he had disappeared in the under-world of crime. *L'Argent.*

" In 1873, Victor had altogether vanished, living, no doubt, in the shady haunts of crime—since he was in no penitentiary—let loose upon the world like some brute foaming with the hereditary virus, whose every bite would enlarge that existing evil—free to work out his own future, his unknown destiny, which was perchance the scaffold." *Le Docteur Pascal.*

ROUGON (——), the child of Doctor Pascal Rougon and of Clotilde Rougon, born some months after his father's death. Pascal, a few minutes before he died, drew towards him the genealogical tree of the Rougon-Macquart family, over which he had spent so many years, and in a vacant space wrote the words : " The unknown child, to be born in 1874. What will it be ? " *Le Docteur Pascal.*

ROUSSE (LA), a peasant girl of Les Artaud, who assisted to decorate the church for the festival of the Virgin. *La Faute de l'Abbé Mouret.*

ROUSSEAU, one of the auditors of the Universal Bank, an

office which he shared with Lavignière, under whose influence he was to a great extent. *L'Argent.*

ROUSSELOT (MONSEIGNEUR), Bishop of Plassans, an amiable but weak man, who was entirely under the influence of Abbé Fenil. Having got into disfavour with the Government over the election of a Legitimist as Deputy, he was anxious to retrieve his position, and with this object agreed to appoint Abbé Faujas vicar of Saint-Saturnin's church. This led to a quarrel with Abbé Fenil, who, of course, resented the appointment. The Bishop being still in some doubt as to the standing of Abbé Faujas with the Government, went to Paris, where he interviewed Eugène Rougon, the Minister of State. Satisfied with the information which he received, he threw himself heartily into the political struggle then proceeding at Plassans, giving Faujas every assistance in carrying out his schemes on behalf of the Bonapartist candidate. *La Conquête de Plassans.*

ROUSSIE (LA), a woman who had formerly worked as a putter in the Voreux pit. *Germinal.*

ROUSTAN (ABBÉ), one of the clergy of Sainte-Eustache church. Madame Lisa Quenu consulted him as to her proposed course of action regarding Florent. *Le Ventre de Paris.*

ROUVET, an old peasant who lived in the same village as Zéphyrin Lacour and Rosalie Pichon. One of their pleasures consisted in calling to mind the sayings of the old man. *Une Page d'Amour.*

ROZAN (DUC DE), was a young man of dissolute life, who, after getting the control of his fortune, soon went through the greater part of it. He was the lover of Renée Saccard for a time. *La Curée.*

ROZAN (DUCHESSE DE), mother of the preceding. She kept her son so short of money that, till he was thirty-five, he seldom had more than a dozen louis at a time. Her death was largely occasioned by the knowledge of the enormous amount of debts her son had incurred. *La Curée.*

RUSCONI (CHEVALIER), the Sardinian Minister at Paris, a friend of Comtesse Balbi, and her daughter. *Son Excellence Eugène Rougon.*

S

SABATANI, a native of the Levant, who appeared in Paris after defaulting on some foreign Stock Exchange. He was a handsome man, and little by little gained the confidence of the Bourse " by scrupulous correctness of behaviour and an unremitting graciousness even towards the most disreputable." He began doing business with Mazaud by depositing a small sum as " cover " in the belief that the insignificance of the amount would in time be forgotten ; and " he evinced great prudence, increasing his orders in a stealthy gradual fashion, pending the day when, with a heavy settlement to meet, it would be necessary for him to disappear." When Saccard founded the Universal Bank, he selected Sabatani as the " man of straw " in whose name the shares held by the Bank itself were to be taken up. Sabatani soon increased his speculations to an enormous extent, gaining large sums, but after the collapse of the Universal Bank he disappeared without paying his " differences," thereby contributing largely to the ruin of Mazaud. *L'Argent.*

SABOT, a vine-grower of Brinqueville. He was a renowned joker, who entered into a competition with Hyacinthe Fouan, but was beaten by him. *La Terre.*

SACCARD, the name assumed by Aristide Rougon, on the suggestion of his brother Eugène. *See* Rougon (Aristide). *La Curée.*

SACCARD (VICTOR). *See* Victor Rougon.

SAFFRÉ (DE), secretary to Eugène Rougon, the Minister of State. *La Curée.*

SAGET (MADEMOISELLE), an old lady who had lived in the Rue Pirouette for forty years. She never spoke about herself, but she spent her life in getting information about her neighbours, carrying her prying curiosity so far as to listen behind their doors and open their letters. She went about all day pretending she was marketing, but in reality merely spreading scandal and getting information. By bullying little Pauline Quenu, she got a hint of Florent's past history, which she promptly spread through the markets, even going the length of writing an anonymous letter to the Prefect of Police. *Le Ventre de Paris.*

Saint-Firmin (Oscar de), a character in *La Petite Duchesse,* a play by Fauchery. The part was played by Prullière. *Nana.*

Saint-Germain (Mademoiselle de) was the owner of a princely house in Rue Saint-Lazare, which after her death became the property of Princess d'Orviedo. *L'Argent.*

Saints-Anges (La Mère des), superior of the Convent of the Visitation at Clermont. She saved from the cloister Christine Hallegrain, who had not a religious vocation, and obtained for her a situation in Paris as companion to Madame de Vanzade. *L'Œuvre.*

Salmon, a speculator on the Paris Bourse who passed for a man of extraordinary acumen by listening to everyone and saying nothing. He answered only by smiles, and one could never tell in what he was speculating or whether he was speculating at all. *L'Argent.*

Salneuve (De), a man of considerable importance in the Second Empire, whose influence was secured for Eugène Rougon by Clorinde Balbi. *Son Excellence Eugène Rougon.*

Sambuc (Guillaume), one of the francs-tireurs who carried on a guerilla warfare against the Germans in 1870. He was the worthy son of a family of scoundrels, and lived by theft and rapine. He furnished most valuable information to the French generals regarding a movement of the Prussians to surprise Beaumont, but his information was disregarded till too late. The francs-tireurs had a particular hatred against Goliath Steinberg, the German spy, and, instigated by Silvine Morange, Sambuc arranged for his capture, afterwards killing him by cutting his throat. *La Débâcle.*

Sambuc (Prosper), brother of the preceding. Of a nature docile and hard-working, he hated the life of the woods, and would have liked to be a farm labourer. He entered the army and became one of the Chasseurs d'Afrique. Sent to France to take part in the war against Germany, he shared in many weary marches, but saw no fighting, till the battle of Sedan, when his horse, Zephir, which he loved like a brother, was killed under him. He made his escape after the battle, and having been able to change his uniform for the clothes of a countryman, he returned to Remilly and got employment on the farm of Fouchard. *La Débâcle.*

SANDORFF, a member of the Austrian Embassy at Paris. He married Mlle. de Ladricourt, who was much younger than he. He was very niggardly. *L'Argent.*

SANDORFF (BARONESS), wife of the Councillor to the Austrian Embassy, who was thirty-five years older than herself. She was an inveterate speculator, and, as her husband refused to assist her, she found it necessary to have recourse to her lovers when her losses were greater than usual. She stopped at nothing to gain information, and at one time was on intimate terms with Saccard. Having quarrelled with him, she hastened the downfall of the Universal Bank, by giving information to Gundermann which caused him to continue his attack on the Bank. *L'Argent.*

SANDOZ (PÈRE), a Spaniard who took refuge in France in consequence of a political disturbance in which he was involved. He started near Plassans a paper mill with new machinery of his own invention. When he died, almost heart-broken by the petty local jealousy that had sought to hamper him in every way, his widow found herself in a position so involved, and burdened with so many tangled lawsuits, that the whole of her remaining means were swallowed up. *L'Œuvre.*

SANDOZ MÈRE (MADAME), wife of the preceding, was a native of Burgundy. Yielding to her hatred of the Provençals, whom she blamed for the death of her husband, and even for the slow paralysis from which she herself was suffering, she migrated to Paris with her son Pierre, who then supported her out of a clerk's small salary. In Rue d'Enfer she occupied a single room on the same flat as her son, and there, disabled by paralysis, lived in morose and voluntary solitude, surrounded by his tender care. Later, Pierre, who was now married, and was making a considerable income, took a house in Rue Nollet, and there Madame Sandoz passed her remaining years. *L'Œuvre.*

SANDOZ (PIERRE), a famous novelist whose youth was spent at Plassans, where at school he was the inseparable companion of Claude Lantier and Dubuche. The favourite amusement of the boys was walking, and together they took long excursions, spending whole days in the country. After the death of his father Sandoz went to Paris, where he got employment at a small salary at the *Mairie* of the fifth arrondissement, in the office for registration of births; he was chained there by the thought of his mother, whom he had to support, and to whom he was tenderly attached. Presently he published his first book : a series of mild sketches, brought with him from Plassans, among which only a few rougher notes indicated the mutineer, the lover of truth and power. He lived at this time with his mother in a little house in Rue d'Enfer, and there he received each Thursday evening his old friends from Plassans, Claude Lantier and Dubuche, and with them Fagerolles, Mahoudeau, Jory, Gagnière, now reunited at Paris, and all animated by the same passion for art. He was still obsessed by a desire for literary glory, and had thoughts of writing a poem on some vast subject, but at last he hit on a scheme which soon took form in his mind. With reference to it he said, " I am going to take a family, and I shall study its members, one by one, whence they come, whither they go, how they react one upon another—in short, humanity in a small compass, the way in which humanity grows and behaves. On the other hand, I shall set my men and women in a determined period of history, which will provide me with the necessary surroundings and circumstances, a slice of history—you understand, eh ? a series of fifteen or twenty books, episodes that will cling together although having each a separate framework, a suite of novels with which I shall be able to build myself a house for my old age if they don't crush me." The first of the novels met with some success, and Sandoz having resigned his appointment, and put his trust entirely in literature, married a young girl named Henriette, the daughter of middle-class parents, and removed his house to Rue Nollet. In course of time his circumstances became still more comfortable, and he again removed to a large house in Rue de Londres. When Claude Lantier fell into misery and despair, a gradual separation came about between him and his friends, but Sandoz remained true to the old companionship. He was one of the few mourners who attended the funeral of the unfortunate artist. *L'Œuvre.*

SANDOZ (MADAME HENRIETTE), wife of the preceding. She was an orphan, the daughter of a small shop-keeper, without a penny, but pretty and intelligent. She occupied herself much with the affairs of the kitchen, being specially proud of some of her dishes. Even later, when the family was more prosperous and had removed to a large flat in Rue de Londres, Henriette continued to take personal charge, out of affection for her husband, whose only fault was a tendency to gluttony. *L'Œuvre.*

SANQUIRINO (DUCHESSE), a lady of the Italian aristocracy, who resided at Paris. She gave Eugène Rougon very unsatisfactory information regarding Comtesse Balbi and her daughter Clorinde. *Son Excellence Eugène Rougon.*

SANS-POUCE, one of the brigands of the band of Beau-François. *La Terre.*

SAPIN, sergeant in Captain Beaudoin's company of the 106th Regiment of the line. " The son of a Lyons grocer in a small way of business, spoilt by his mother, who was dead, and unable to get on with his father, he had remained in the regiment disgusted with everything, but unwilling to be bought out." Later he became engaged to one of his cousins, who had a small dowry, and began to take an interest in life. During the march to Sedan, however, he became impressed with the idea that he would be killed, and this belief was realized during the fighting on 1st September, 1870. *La Débâcle.*

SAPIN (LA), a disreputable old woman at Magnolles who performed illegal operations and pretended to work magic. *La Terre.*

SARRIET (MADAME), sister of Madame Lecœur and of Madame Gavard ; mother of La Sarriette. *Le Ventre de Paris.*

SARRIET, usually called La Sarriette, was the niece of Madame Lecœur. She grew up in the markets and her sympathies were with the lower ranks of the people. At twenty she set up in business as a fruit-dealer, and took as her lover a young man named Jules, who was employed by her aunt as a porter. After the arrest of Gavard, her uncle by marriage, La Sarriette and her aunt divided his money between them. *Le Ventre de Paris.*

SARTEUR, a journeyman hatter at Plassans. He was afflicted with homicidal mania, and was confined for a time in the asylum at Tulettes. While there he was treated by Doctor Pascal Rougon, who effected a cure by hypodermic injections of a substance with which he had long experimented. Sarteur was released from the asylum, but the cure was not permanent, for a few months afterwards the unfortunate man became conscious of a return of his homicidal mania, and, to prevent its operation, hanged himself. *Le Docteur Pascal.*

SATIN, a friend of Nana from childhood, having, like her, attended the school of Mademoiselle Josse. She was a regular customer at Laure Piédefer's restaurant, where she met Madame Robert. She lived for a time with Nana, of whom she was intensely jealous, and in time gained control of the whole household. She died in the hospital of Lariboisière. *Nana.*

SAUCISSE (LE PÈRE), an old peasant of Rognes, who owned an acre of land which he sold to Père Fouan for an annuity of fifteen sous a day. In order to dupe the old man, he pretended to be in bad health. Later, terrorized by Buteau, he cancelled the agreement, and repaid half the sums he had received. *La Terre.*

SAUVAGNAT, a friend of Pluchart. He lived at Marchiennes. *Germinal.*

SAUVAGNAT, chief of the depôt at Havre, lived in a cottage near the engine depôt, which his sister Philomène kept for him, but greatly neglected. He was an obstinate man and a strict disciplinarian, greatly esteemed by his superiors, but had met with the utmost vexation on account of his sister, even to the point of being threatened with dismissal. If the Company bore with her now on his account, he only kept her with him because of the family tie ; but this did not prevent him belabouring her so severely with blows whenever he caught her at fault that he frequently left her half dead on the floor. *La Bête Humaine.*

SAUVAGNAT (PHILOMÈNE), sister of the preceding, was a tall, thin woman of thirty-two, who after numerous love-

P

affairs had settled down with Pecqueux, whose mistress she became. She had the reputation of drinking. A subsequent intrigue between her and Jacques Lantier excited the jealousy of Pecqueux to the point of murder. *La Bête Humaine.*

SAUVEUR (MADAME), a dressmaker, who numbered Madame Desforges among her customers. She frequented Mouret's shop, *Au Bonheur des Dames,* on the occasions of great sales, purchasing large quantities of stuff which she afterwards sold to her own customers at higher prices. *Au Bonheur des Dames.*

SAUVIGNY (DE), judge of the race for the Grand Prix de Paris. *Nana.*

SCHLOSSER, a speculator on the Paris Bourse. He was secretly associated with Sabatani, with whom he carried out many schemes to their mutual advantage. *L'Argent.*

SCOTS (H.R.H. THE PRINCE OF). *See* Écosse.

SEDILLE, a native of Lyons, who established himself in Paris, and after thirty years' toil succeeded in making his silk business one of the best known in the city. Unfortunately he acquired a passion for gambling, and a couple of successful ventures made him altogether lose his head. From that time he neglected his business, and ruin lay inevitably at the end. On the invitation of Saccard he became a Director of the Universal Bank. Like the other Directors, he speculated largely in the shares of the Bank; but, unlike most of them, he did not sell in time, with the result that he was completely ruined, and his bankruptcy followed. *L'Argent.*

SEDILLE (GUSTAVE), son of M. Sedille, the silk merchant. To the disappointment of his father, he despised commercial pursuits, and cared only for pleasure. In the hope that he might take an interest in finance, he was given a situation in the office of Mazaud, the stockbroker, where, however, he did little work, and soon engaged in speculations on his own account. The failure of the Universal Bank left him penniless, and deep in debt. *L'Argent.*

SICARDOT (COMMANDER), the father-in-law of Aristide Rougon. He had the strongest intellect of the politicians who met in Pierre Rougon's yellow drawing-room. He was taken prisoner by the insurgents at the time of the *Coup d'État. La Fortune des Rougon.*

SICARDOT, the name of Aristide Rougon's wife's family. He adopted this name when he went to Paris in 1851, using it for a considerable time before he again changed it to Saccard. *L'Argent.*

SICARDOT (ANGÈLE). *See* Madame Aristide Rougon.

SIDONIE (MADAME), the name by which Sidonie Rougon (q.v.) was generally known. *La Curée.*

SIMON (LA MÈRE), an old woman who assisted Séverine Roubaud in her housework. *La Bête Humaine.*

SIMONNOT, a grocer at Raucourt. His premises were raided by the Bavarians after the Battle of Beaumont. *La Débâcle.*

SIMPSON, an American who was attaché at his country's Embassy at Paris. He was a frequent visitor at the house of Renée Saccard. *La Curée.*

SIVRY (BLANCHE DE), the name assumed by Jacqueline Baudu, a girl who came to Paris from a village near Amiens. Magnificent in person, stupid and untruthful in character,

she gave herself out as the granddaughter of a general, and never owned to her thirty-two summers. She was much annoyed at the outbreak of war with Germany, because her lover, a young Prussian, was expelled from the country. *Nana.*

SMELTEN, a baker at Montsou. He gave credit for some time during the strike, in the hope of recovering some of his business taken away by Maigrat. *Germinal.*

SMITHSON (MISS), Lucien Deberle's English governess. *Une Page d'Amour.*

SONNEVILLE, a manufacturer at Marchiennes. His business was seriously affected by the strike of miners at Montsou. *Germinal.*

SOPHIE, a workwoman employed at Madame Titreville's artificial flower-making establishment. *L'Assommoir.*

SOPHIE, an old waiting-maid in the service of the Duchesse de Combeville, whose daughter, Princess d'Orviedo, she brought up. When the Princess shut herself up from the world, Sophie remained with her. *L'Argent.*

SOPHIE, daughter of Guiraude. Predestined to phthisis by heredity, she was saved, thanks to Dr. Pascal Rougon, who sent her to live with an aunt in the country, where she was brought up in the open air. When she was seventeen years old she married a young miller in the neighbourhood. *Le Docteur Pascal.*

SOULAS, an old shepherd at La Borderie, where he had been for half a century. At sixty-five he had saved nothing, having been eaten up by a drunken wife, " whom at last he had the pleasure of burying." He had few friends except his two dogs, Emperor and Massacre, and he especially hated Jacqueline Cognet with the jealous disgust of an old servant at her rapid advancement. He was aware of her numerous *liaisons*, but said nothing until she brought about his dismissal, when he told everything to his master, Alexandre Hourdequin. *La Terre.*

SOURDEAU, a bone-setter at Bazoches-le-Doyen, who was supposed to be equally good for wounds. *La Terre.*

SOUVARINE, an engine-man at the Voreux pit, who lodged with the Rasteneurs. He was a Russian of noble family, who had at first studied medicine, until, carried away

by social enthusiasm, he learned a trade in order that he might mix with the people. It was by this trade that he now lived, after having fled in consequence of an unsuccessful attempt against the Czar's life, an attempt which resulted in his mistress, Annouchka, and many of his friends, being hanged. His principles were those of the most violent anarchy, and he would have nothing to do with the strike at Montsou, which he considered a merely childish affair. Disgusted at the return of the miners to their work, he resolved to bring about the destruction of the Voreux pit, by weakening the timbers which kept out a vast accumulation of water. He accomplished that work of madness in a fury of destruction in which he twenty times risked his life. And when the torrent had invaded the mine, imprisoning the unfortunate workers, Souvarine went calmly away into the unknown without a glance behind. *Germinal.*

SPIRIT, an English horse which ran in the Grand Prix de Paris. *Nana.*

SPONTINI, a master at the College of Plassans. He came originally from Corsica, and used to show his knife, rusty with the blood of three cousins. *L'Œuvre*.

SQUELETTE-EXTERNE (LE). *See* Mimi-la-Mort. *L'Œuvre*.

STADERINO (SIGNOR), a Venetian political refugee, and a friend of Comtesse Balbi. *Son Excellence Eugène Rougon*.

STEINBERG (GOLIATH), a Prussian spy who was engaged in 1867 as a farm servant by Fouchard at Remilly. He became the lover of Silvine Morange, promising her marriage, but disappearing before the ceremony. It was said that he served also on other farms in the neighbourhood of Beaumont and Raucourt. During the war he was able to give important information to the German forces. In trying to regain his former influence over Silvine, he threatened to remove their child to Germany, and, to prevent his doing so, she betrayed him to Guillaume Sambuc and the francstireurs of his band, who killed him in the house of Fouchard, in the presence of Silvine, by cutting his throat, and bleeding him in the same manner as a pig. *La Débâcle*.

STEINER, a banker in Paris. He was a German Jew, through whose hands had passed millions. He spent vast sums upon Rose Mignon and Nana. *Nana*.

STERNICH (DUCHESSE DE), a celebrated leader of society in the Second Empire. She dominated all her friends on the ground of a former intimacy with the Emperor. *La Curée*.

STEWART (LUCY), was the daughter of an engine-cleaner of English origin who was employed at the Gare du Nord. She was not beautiful, but had such a charm of manner that she was considered the smartest of the *demi-mondaines* in Paris. Among her lovers had been a prince of the royal blood. She had a son, Ollivier, before whom she posed as an actress. *Nana*.

STEWART (OLLIVIER), son of the preceding. He was a pupil at the naval college, and had no suspicion of the calling of his mother. *Nana*.

SURIN (ABBÉ), secretary to the Bishop of Plassans, of whom he was a great favourite. He was a constant visitor at the house of M. Rastoril, with whose daughters he played battledore. *La Conquête de Plassans*.

SYLVIA, an actress who was admired by Maxime Saccard. *La Curée*.

TAB 214 THE

T

TABOUREAU (MADAME), a baker in the Rue Turbigo. She was a recognized authority on all subjects relating to her neighbours. *Le Ventre de Paris*.

TATIN (MADEMOISELLE), kept an under-linen warehouse in the Passage Choiseul, and was so seriously affected by the competition of Octave Mouret's great store that she became bankrupt. *Au Bonheur des Dames*.

TARDIVEAU (BARON DE), a character in *La Petite Duchesse*, a play by Fauchery. The part was played by Fontan. *Nana*.

TATAN NÉNÉ, a young girl of great beauty who had herded cows in Champagne before coming to Paris. She was one of Nana's friends. *Nana*.

TAVERNIER, an old doctor of Orleans, who had ceased to practise. Georges Hugon made a pretext of visiting him, in order to be able to join Nana at La Mignotte. *Nana*.

TEISSIÈRE (MADAME), a *mondaine* of the Second Empire. She was a friend of Madame de Lauwerens and of the Saccards. *La Curée*.

TESTANIÈRE (MADAME), a *protégée* of Madame Correur, who recommended her to Eugène Rougon, the Minister of State. *Son Excellence Eugène Rougon*.

TEUSE (LA), an elderly woman who acted as servant to Abbé Mouret. In addition, she cleaned the church and kept the vestments in order ; on occasion, it was said, she had even served the Mass for the Abbé's predecessor. She was garrulous and ill-tempered, but was devoted to Mouret, of whom she took the greatest care, and she was also kind to his weak-minded sister, Désirée. *La Faute de l'Abbé Mouret*.

THÉODORE, a Belgian who gave lessons on the piano to Clarisse Bocquet, and afterwards became her lover. *Pot-Bouille*.

THÉODORE, son of a pasteboard maker. He was to have married Nathalie Déjoie, but wishing to establish himself in business, demanded a considerable dowry. He afterwards married the daughter of a workman, who brought him nearly eight thousand francs. *L'Argent*.

THÉRÈSE, a former neighbour of the Lorilleux in Rue de la Goutte d'Or. She died of consumption, and the Lorilleux thought they saw a resemblance between Gervaise and her. *L'Assommoir.*

THIBAUDIER (M.), a banker at Caen. He had a daughter, Louise, but having married again soon after the death of his first wife, he troubled little about her, and was quite willing to consent to her marriage with Lazare Chanteau. *La Joie de Vivre.*

THIBAUDIER (LOUISE), daughter of M. Thibaudier, a banker at Caen. She was a slight, delicate girl, with an attractive manner, and Lazare Chanteau fell in love with her, though he was at the time engaged to Pauline Quenu. Pauline having magnanimously released him, they were married. Lazare's morbid mania having become more acute, and Louise being herself in poor health, their relations became strained, and the marriage was not a happy one. They had a son who was named Paul. *La Joie de Vivre.*

Louise died young. *Le Docteur Pascal.*

THOMAS, keeper of an eating-house at Montmartre. *L'Assommoir.*

THOMAS (ANSELME), a journeyman saddler at Plassans. He

married Justine Mégot, tempted by the annuity of twelve hundred francs which she received from Saccard. He disliked her child, the little Charles Rougon, who was degenerate and weak-minded. *Le Docteur Pascal.*

THOMAS (MADAME ANSELME), wife of the preceding. See Justine Mégot. *Le Docteur Pascal.*

TISON, keeper of a dram-shop at Montsou. *Germinal.*

TISSOT (MADAME), a friend of Madame Deberle. *Une Page d'Amour.*

TITREVILLE (MADAME) carried on the business of an artificial-flower maker, of which Madame Lerat was forewoman, and where Nana Coupeau was a pupil. She was a tall woman who never unbent, and the girls were all afraid of her, pretending to be engrossed in work whenever she appeared. *L'Assommoir.*

TOUCHE (M.), a townsman of Plassans who expressed disbelief in the success of the *Coup d'État. La Fortune des Rougon.*

TOUCHE, an Attorney's clerk at Plassans. He married Sidonie Rougon in 1838, and went with her to Paris, where he started business as a dealer in the products of the South. He was not very successful, and died in 1850. *La Curée.*

TOURMAL (LES), a family who resided at Bonneville and lived chiefly by smuggling and stealing. The father and grandfather were sent to prison, and the daughter, when shown kindness by Pauline Quenu, rewarded her by attempting to steal such small articles of value as she could conceal. *La Joie de Vivre.*

TOUTIN-LAROCHE (M.), a retired candle-manufacturer ; now a municipal councillor, and a director of the Crédit Viticole, the Société Générale of the Ports of Morocco, and other companies of doubtful standing. His ambition was to enter the Senate, and he clung to Baron Gauraud and Saccard in the belief that they could assist him. *La Curée.*

TRICON (LA), a well-known procuress, who numbered Nana among her clients. She had a passion for racing, and at the Grand Prix seemed to dominate the crowd. *Nana.*

TROMPETTE, one of the horses in the Voreux pit. It only lived a few months after being taken underground. *Germinal.*

TRON, a labourer in the farm of La Borderie. He was one of Jacqueline Cognet's lovers, and exhibited jealousy amounting to insanity regarding her. Having been dismissed by his master, he opened a trap-door through which Hourdequin fell and was killed. When he found that Jacqueline would not forgive him for this stupid murder, which ruined her prospects, he set fire to the farm buildings. *La Terre.*

TROUCHE (HONORÉ), brother-in-law of Abbé Faujas. Having been unsuccessful in business at Besançon, he followed Faujas to Plassans, where he went with his wife to live in rooms rented by the Abbé from François Mouret. He was of bad character and quite unscrupulous, but by the influence of Faujas he was appointed Secretary to the Girls' Home started by Madame Mouret and other ladies of Plassans. Having got a footing in the Mourets' house, he soon began to take advantage of his position, and little by little got possession of the whole premises. He did all he could to encourage the idea of François Mouret's madness, and after the unfortunate man's removal to the asylum was able with greater ease to carry out his schemes. Mouret having ultimately escaped from the asylum, returned to his home and set it on fire ; Trouche perished in the flames. *La Conquête de Plassans.*

TROUCHE (MADAME OLYMPE), wife of the preceding, and sister of Abbé Faujas. She accompanied her husband to Plassans, and contributed largely to the ruin of the Mouret family. Utterly heartless, she stopped at nothing, robbing Madame Mouret of money, clothing, everything that came within her power. Nemesis came with the return of François Mouret, who set fire to his house, causing the death of Madame Trouche as well as that of her husband. *La Conquête de Plassans.*

TROUILLE (LA), the nickname of Olympe Fouan. *La Terre.*

TRUBLOT (HECTOR), a young man whom Madame Josserand hoped at one time to secure as a husband for her daughter. He had, however, no thoughts of marriage, and, as he was averse to any risk of complications, his habit was to select his female friends from among the maid-servants

of his acquaintances. He was employed as correspondent in the office of Monsieur Desmarquay, a money-changer. *Pot-Bouille.*

V

VABRE, a notary of Versailles who retired to Paris with a fortune, part of which he invested in the house in Rue de Choiseul occupied by the Duveyriers, the Josserands, and others. He had unfortunately a hidden passion for gambling in stocks and shares, and when he died it was found that his whole fortune had been dissipated, even his house being heavily mortgaged. *Pot-Bouille.*

VABRE (AUGUSTE), eldest son of M. Vabre, carried on a silk merchant's business in part of the premises which belonged to his father. He married Berthe Josserand, but as he suffered much from neuralgia, and was, in addition, of a niggardly disposition, the marriage was not a happy one. An intrigue between Madame Vabre and Octave Mouret followed, and on its discovery she returned to her parents. For a considerable time Vabre refused to forgive his wife, but a reconciliation was ultimately brought about through the intervention of Abbé Mauduit. Vabre's fortunes were adversely affected by the extension of Madame Hedouin's business, known as "The Ladies' Paradise." *Pot-Bouille.*

The rapid success of Octave Mouret's business led to the ruin of Vabre, a result to which the extravagance of his wife also contributed. *Au Bonheur des Dames.*

VABRE (MADAME AUGUSTE), wife of the preceding. *See* Berthe Josserand. *Pot-Bouille.*

VABRE (CAMILLE), son of Théophile Vabre and his wife Valérie Louhette. *Pot-Bouille.*

VABRE (CLOTILDE), daughter of Vabre the notary, and wife of Duveyrier. She did not get on well with her husband, whom she hated, and her only passion was for music, which she practised to an inordinate extent. *Pot-Bouille.*

VABRE (THÉOPHILE), second son of M. Vabre, "a little old man of twenty-eight, a victim to coughs and toothache, who first tried all sorts of trades and then married the daughter of a neighbouring haberdasher." His life was shadowed by suspicions of his wife, with whom he constantly quarrelled. He was with difficulty prevented from making a scene at the marriage of his brother Auguste to Berthe Josserand. *Pot-Bouille.*

VABRE (MADAME VALÉRIE), wife of the preceding, *née* Louhette, was the daughter of a wealthy haberdasher. She did not get on well with her husband, who accused her, not entirely without reason, of carrying on a *liaison* with some one whose name he was unable to discover. *Pot-Bouille.*

VADON (MARGUERITE), daughter of a linen-draper at Grenoble, found it desirable to come to Paris for a time, and got a situation at "The Ladies' Paradise." She was a well-conducted girl, and ultimately returned to Grenoble to take charge of her parents' shop, and marry a cousin who was waiting for her. *Au Bonheur des Dames.*

VALENÇAY (BARON DE), *aide-de-camp* to the Emperor. He married the eldest daughter of the Comtesse de Brétigny. *L'Assommoir.*

VALENÇAY (MADEMOISELLE PAULE DE) was very rich

and extremely beautiful when at nineteen years old she married the Marquis Jean XII de Hautecœur. She died within a year, leaving a son named Félicien. *Le Rêve.*

VALENTIN, son of Guiraude, and brother of Sophie. His father, a journeyman tanner, died of phthisis, and Valentin, who had been in daily contact with him, developed the disease. Doctor Pascal Rougon prolonged his life for some time by hypodermic injections of a substance discovered by himself, but the respite was only temporary, for at twenty-one years of age Valentin died of hereditary phthisis. *Le Docteur Pascal.*

VALÉRIO II, a horse which belonged to M. Corbreuse and ran in the Grand Prix de Paris. *Nana.*

VALLAGNOSC (MADAME DE) belonged to an old family of Plassans. Left a widow with two daughters and one son, she found life difficult on the small remains of a former fortune. In order to assist his mother, the son, Paul, secured an appointment at Paris in a Government office. *Au Bonheur des Dames.*

VALLAGNOSC (PAUL DE), an old friend of Octave Mouret, whom he had known at Plassans. He belonged to an old family, but, being a younger son without money, was obliged to select a profession. He studied law, but meeting with no success, was obliged to accept an appointment in the Ministry of the Interior. He married Mademoiselle de Boves. *Au Bonheur des Dames.*

VALLAGNOSC (MADAME PAUL DE), wife of the preceding. *See* Blanche de Boves.

VALQUEYRAS (COMTE DE), a relation of Marquis de Carnavant, who lived in his house. *La Fortune des Rougon.*

He was a supporter of the Marquis de Lagrifoul, the Legitimist Deputy for Plassans, who visited him for a fortnight before the election which was dominated by Abbé Faujas. *La Conquête de Plassans.*

VALQUEYRAS (MARQUISE DE), in 1873, she was the only representative of a very old family. She was a widow with a little daughter of six, very rich, and equally parsimonious. When Doctor Pascal Rougon called on her to ask payment of his fees, he allowed himself to be put off, and even gave advice regarding the health of the child. *Le Docteur Pascal.*

VANDERHAGEN, the medical man employed by the Mining Company of Montsou. He was so much overworked that it was said he gave his consultations while he was running from place to place. *Germinal.*

VANDEUVRES (COMTE XAVIER DE), the last member of a noble family, had gone through a large fortune in Paris. His racing-stable was famous, as were his losses at the Imperial Club, while his ruin was completed by the vast sums which he spent on Nana. His final hope was centred on the race for the Grand Prix de Paris in which he was running two horses, Lusignan and a filly named Nana. Lusignan was the favourite, but Vandeuvres, having arranged his betting, caused the horse to be pulled, so that the filly might win. The ruse was successful, and Vandeuvres gained a large sum, but suspicions having been aroused, he was warned off the turf and expelled from the Imperial Club. Driven to madness, the Comte shut himself up in his stable, and, having set it on fire, perished among his horses. *Nana.*

VANDORPE, the head stationmaster of the Western Railway Company at Paris. *La Bête Humaine.*

VANPOUILLE BROTHERS, a firm of furriers in Rue Neuve-des-Petits Champs, who were practically ruined when Octave Mouret added a fur department to "The Ladies' Paradise." *Au Bonheur des Dames.*

VANSKA (COMTESSE), a well-known and rich *mondaine* of the Second Empire. *La Curée.*

VANZADE (MADAME), the widow of a general. She was an old lady, rich, nearly blind, and practically helpless. At Passy she lived, in a silent old house, a life so retired and regular that it might have been actuated by clockwork. As she required a companion, her old friend, La Mère des Saints-Anges, recommended Christine Hallegrain to her; but the girl, stifling in that dwelling of rigid piety, ended by running off with her lover, Claude Lantier. Madame Vanzade died four years later, and the bulk of her fortune went to charities. *L'Œuvre.*

VAQUEZ (JUDITH), an artist's model who lived in Rue du Rocher. She was a Jewess, fresh enough in colouring but too thin. *L'Œuvre.*

VAUCOGNE (HECTOR), husband of Éstelle Badeuil. At the time of his marriage, Vaucogne was a junior officer of customs, but when his wife's parents retired he took over their *maison publique*. He left everything to the care of his wife, and after her death the establishment ceased to be prosperous. In the end he was turned out by his father-in-law, and the business was given to his daughter Élodie, who showed all the family capacity for management. *La Terre*.

VAUCOGNE (MADAME HECTOR), wife of the preceding. *See* Éstelle Badeuil. *La Terre*.

VAUCOGNE (ÉLODIE), daughter of the preceding, and grand-daughter of M. and Madame Charles Badeuil. She was seven years old when her parents took over the *maison publique* of her grandfather, and she˙ was then sent to a convent at Châteaudun to be educated by the Sisters of the Visitation. Her holidays were spent with her grandparents, and she was supposed to be under the impression that her parents were carrying on a large confectionery business, but Victorine, a servant who had been dismissed for mis-conduct, had made her aware of the facts, and when, at eighteen years of age, she was asked in marriage by her cousin Ernest Delhomme, she

astonished her grandparents by joining with him in a desire to succeed to the family estab-lishment. *La Terre*.

VAUGELADE (DUC DE), at one time the master of Gourd, who was his valet. *Pot-Bouille*.

VENOT (THÉOPHILE), an old lawyer who made a speciality of ecclesiastical cases, and had acquired a fortune by serving the Jesuits. He had retired with a comfortable sum, and led an existence slightly mysterious ; received everywhere, saluted very low, even a little feared, as he represented a great and un-known force which he had behind him. An intimate friend of the Muffats, he did everything in his power to put an end to the *liaison* between the Comte and Nana, and, though no success attended his efforts for a considerable time, he was able when ruin seemed imminent to save Muffat from scandal and to console him by a return to the practice of religion. *Nana*.

VERDIER (BARON), proprietor of a racing-stable. Frangipane, one of his horses, ran in the Grand Prix de Paris. *Nana*.

VERDIER, a lawyer who had been for a long time engaged to Hortense Josserand. The marriage was put off from time to time, as he had got entangled with a woman from whom he found separation difficult. *Pot-Bouille.*

VERDONCK, a grocer at Montsou. His business was much affected by the competition of Maigrat, and he gave credit during the first week of the strike in the hope of getting back some of his old customers. *Germinal.*

VERLAQUE, an inspector in the fish - market at the *Halles Centrales.* Having fallen into bad health, he was allowed to find a substitute to keep the place open for him in case he should recover. Florent was appointed, and paid a considerable portion of the salary to Verlaque. *Le Ventre de Paris.*

VERLAQUE (MADAME), wife of the preceding. Florent assisted her after the death of her husband. *Le Ventre de Paris.*

VERNIER, an art critic who published an article on Fagerolles the artist. *L'Œuvre.*

VÉRONIQUE, maid-servant to the Chanteau family, was a tall, stout young woman of unattractive appearance and uncertain temper. She had been in the service of the Chanteaus for twenty years, and having

become necessary to them, took advantage of her position. From the first, Véronique resented Pauline Quenu's presence in the Chanteau household, and treated her as an intruder. In course of time, however, she came to see that Pauline was being despoiled of her means by Madame Chanteau, and her sense of justice made her take the young girl's part. The death of Madame Chanteau made a deep impression on Véronique, whose ill-will towards Pauline gradually returned. Her mind, not strong at best, became unhinged, and in a fit of temper she went into the orchard and hanged herself. *La Joie de Vivre.*

VIAL (ABBÉ), one of the clergy of Plassans. When his appointment became vacant it was promised to Abbé Bourrette, but was eventually given to Abbé Faujas. *La Conquête de Plassans.*

VIAL (MÉLANIE), second wife of Jean Macquart, to whom she was married in 1871. She was the only daughter of a peasant in easy circumstances, and was of a fine robust physique. She had three healthy children in as many years. *Le Docteur Pascal.*

VIAN, a wheelwright of Plassans, to whom Silvère Mouret was apprenticed. *La Fortune des Rougon.*

VICTOIRE, Madame Campardon's cook. She had been in the service of her master's father when Campardon was a baby, and though now old, and not over clean, they were unwilling to part with her. *Pot-Bouille.*

VICTOIRE (LA MÈRE), wife of Pecqueux, the railway stoker. She had been the nurse of Séverine Aubry, and later, as the wife of Pecqueux, who spent all his earnings on drink, she was leading a wretched existence in Paris by the aid of a little sewing, when, happening to meet her foster-daughter, the former intimacy had been renewed, and President Grandmorin took her under his protection, obtaining for her the post of attendant at the ladies' cloakroom. She occupied a room in the Impasse d'Amsterdam, which the Roubauds regarded as their head-quarters when they spent a day in Paris. Having become helpless as the result of a sprain, she was obliged to resign her post and seek admittance to a hospital. *La Bête Humaine.*

VICTORINE, cook in the employment of Nana. She married François, the footman. *Nana.*

VICTORINE, a servant in the employment of the Badeuils after they retired to Rognes. She was dismissed for misconduct, and in revenge told Élodie Vaucogne the occupation of her parents. *La Terre.*

VIGOUROUX, a coal merchant in Rue de la Goutte d'Or. He sold coke to Gervaise at the same price as the Gas Company. *L'Assommoir.*

VIGOUROUX (MADAME), wife of the preceding. She was a little woman with bright eyes who liked to laugh with the men. *L'Assommoir.*

VIMEUX, a miserable little sheriff officer, who was celebrated in the Canton for the bad usage he got from the peasants when he was obliged to serve summonses upon them. *La Terre.*

VINÇARD, a silk merchant, who, seeing that his business was likely to be seriously affected by the competition of " The Ladies' Paradise," sold it to Robineau, and took a restaurant at Vincennes. *Au Bonheur des Dames.*

VINCENT, a tavern-keeper in the neighbourhood of Montsou. *Germinal.*

VINEUIL (COMMANDANT DE), father of Gilberte. Retired from active service on account of his wounds, he was appointed Director of Customs at Charleville. His wife died of consumption, and he sent his daughter, about whose health he was alarmed, to reside for a time at a farm near Chêne-Populeux. He died soon after Gilberte's marriage to Maginot, the Inspector of State Forests. *La Débâcle.*

VINEUIL (COLONEL DE), brother of the preceding. In 1870 he commanded the 106th Regiment of the line, which formed part of the Seventh Army Corps. He was a man of fine appearance and character, and bore his part bravely through the disastrous campaign, until he was severely wounded on the battlefield of Sedan. Notwithstanding his wound, he remained on his horse till the end, when he was removed to the house of Delaherche, the husband of his niece Gilberte. By December his wound was cured, but crushed by his country's defeats, his mental depression was so great that he remained in a darkened room, refusing to hear news from the outer world, and associating only with his old friend Madame Delaherche, the mother of his niece's husband. At the end of December he died suddenly, horror-struck by an account of the surrender of Metz, which he chanced to read in an old newspaper. *La Débâcle.*

VINEUIL (GILBERTE DE), daughter of Commandant de Vineuil. She was first married to Maginot, and afterwards to Jules Delaherche. When she was nine years old, her father, alarmed at a cough she had, sent her to live at a farm, where she came to know Henriette Levasseur. Even at that age she was a coquette, and when at twenty she married Maginot, the Inspector of the State Forests at Mézières, her character had not changed. Mézières she found dull, but her husband allowed her full liberty, and she found all the gaiety she desired at Charleville. There she lived solely for pleasure, and Captain Beaudoin became her lover. In 1869 she became a widow, and in spite of the stories told about her she found a second husband, Jules Delaherche. On the eve of the battle of Sedan she resumed for the nonce her former relations with Beaudoin. Gay and irresponsible by nature, she

flirted with Captain von Gartlauben, a Prussian officer,
who was quartered on her
husband after the capitulation
of Sedan, while at the same
time she carried on a *liaison*
with Edmond Lagarde, a
young soldier who had been
wounded, and whom she had
assisted to nurse. *La Débâcle.*

VIOLAINE (LOUISE), an actress
at the Théâtre des Variétés.
She took the part in the
Blonde Venus originally
played by Nana, and secured
a great success. *Nana.*

VIRGINIE, sister of Adèle, for
whose sake Auguste Lantier
deserted Gervaise Macquart.
Gervaise, meeting Virginie in
a public washing-house, was
taunted by her on the subject
of her lover, and a terrible
fight between the two women
followed, Virginie being severely beaten. Gervaise did
not see her again for some
years, by which time she had
married M. Poisson, an ex-
soldier, who later became a
policeman. She professed to
have overlooked the fight
with Gervaise, but appears
to have been not without
hope that an opportunity of
repaying her injuries might
eventually arise. When the
Coupeaus gave way to drink,
Lantier, who had again es-

tablished friendly relations,
suggested that Virginie should
take the Coupeaus' shop and
buy a stock of groceries and
sweetmeats with a legacy she
had received from an aunt.
Partly moved by a desire for
revenge on Gervaise, she did
so, and Lantier retained with
the Poissons the place as a
lodger he formerly occupied
with the Coupeaus. Soon
after, he became Virginie's
lover, and, by paying nothing
for his support, while he
gradually ate the contents of
the shop, he accomplished the
downfall of the Poissons in
much the same manner as he
had already ruined the Coupeaus. *L'Assommoir.*

VISCARDI (SIGNOR), a Venetian
political refugee, and a friend
of Comtesse Balbi. *Son Excellence Eugène Rougon.*

VOINCOURT (COMTESSE DE),
mother of Claire de Voin-
court. She occupied at Beaumont a house adjoining the
bishop's palace. *Le Rêve.*

VOINCOURT (CLAIRE DE), the
daughter of an old family
of great wealth who lived
at Beaumont. Monseigneur
d'Hautecœur wished to ar-
range a marriage between
her and Félicien, his son ;
his plans were assisted by the
belief of Félicien that An-

O

gelique, with whom he had fallen in love, no longer cared for him. This belief having proved false, the proposed marriage between Félicien and Claire de Voincourt did not take place. *Le Rêve.*

VORIAU, a large black dog which belonged to Bambousse, the Mayor of Artaud. *La Faute de l'Abbé Mouret.*

VUILLAUME (M. and MADAME), the parents of Madame Pichon, whom they visited every Sunday afternoon. They were, later, much annoyed with the Pichons, whose family became, they considered, too large for their means. *Pot-Bouille.*

VUILLAUME (MARIE). *See* Madame Marie Pichon.

VUILLET, a bookseller of Plassans, who published a bi-weekly journal, the *Gazette de Plassans*, which was devoted exclusively to the interests of the clergy. *La Fortune des Rougon.*

W

WEISS, husband of Henriette Levasseur, and cousin of Otto Gunther. He got a situation in the refinery at Chêne-Populeux, almost in a menial position, but he gradually educated himself, and by dint of hard work raised himself to the position of accountant. A clear-headed man, he early saw the causes that were to lead to the downfall of his country, and expressed himself strongly regarding the unprepared state of the army. Weiss lived at Sedan, but in 1870 he had just bought a little house at Bazeilles, where he slept the night before the battle. He was frantic at the idea that the Prussians might pillage and perhaps destroy this dwelling so long desired and so hardly acquired, and when the attack was made he took an active part in the fighting. Captured by the Prussians, and being a civilian, he was at once condemned to be shot, and the sentence was carried out before the eyes of his wife, who had come from Sedan to look for him. *La Débâcle.*

WEISS (MADAME), wife of the preceding. *See* Henriette Levasseur. *La Débâcle.*

WORMS, a famous costumier, before whom the ladies of the Second Empire bowed the knee. Renée Saccard was one of his customers, and when she died owed him an account of two hundred and fifty-seven thousand francs (£10,280 stg.). *La Curée.*

Z

ZEPHIR, the horse ridden by Prosper Sambuc, who loved it like a brother. The animal received a mortal wound at the battle of Sedan, and fell on its rider, crushing under it his right leg. It lay upon him for some hours, but eventually, on his speaking to it, moved with a great effort sufficiently to allow him to escape. *La Débâcle.*

ZÉPHYRIN, a worker on the farm of La Borderie. He laughed at the agricultural machinery introduced by Alexandre Hourdequin. *La Terre.*

ZIDORE, a youth of seventeen, who was an apprentice zinc-worker. He was Coupeau's assistant at one time. *L'Assommoir.*

ZIZI, the pet name given by Nana to Georges Hugon. *Nana.*

ZOÉ, waiting-maid in the employment of Nana. She was entirely in Nana's confidence, and was always ready with shrewd advice, though there is no doubt she arranged matters so that a good deal of money came into her own hands. She ultimately took over the establishment of La Tricon, which she had long coveted, and, having large ideas, proposed to extend the business by renting a larger house. *Nana.*

ALPHABETICAL LIST OF PRINCIPAL SCENES.

ARROMANCHES, a small town on the Normandy coast, not far from Caen. It is about six miles from Bonneville, the scene of *La Joie de Vivre*.

ARTAUD (LES), a small village a few miles from Plassans (*q.v.*). Abbé Mouret was its priest during the events related in *La Faute de l'Abbé Mouret*.

ASSOMMOIR (Père Colombe's) was situated at the corner of Rue des Poissonniers and Boulevard de Rochechouart, which is a continuation of Boulevard de Clichy, in the northern district of Paris. *L'Assommoir.*

AUGUSTIN (RUE NEUVE SAINT), a street which joins the Avenue de l'Opéra a short distance from the Opera House. It is intersected by Rue Michodière, at the corner of which was situated Octave Mouret's great drapery establishment, known as "Au Bonheur des Dames." *Au Bonheur des Dames.*

BARENTIN, a small town on the Western Railway of France, about twelve miles from Rouen. It was at a point between Barentin and the previous station, Malaunay,

that President Grandmorin was murdered by Roubaud. *La Bête Humaine.*

BAZEILLES, a village about three miles south-east of Sedan (*q.v.*). It was the scene of some of the most important events in *La Débâcle*.

BEAUCE (LA), a fertile agricultural plain stretching between Chartres and Orléans, and intersected by the road from the latter town to Château-dun. The district is the scene of *La Terre*.

BEAUMONT, a town of about 3000 inhabitants, picturesquely situated on a height on the left bank of the Oise about twenty-five miles north of Paris. Its church, the scene of some of the principal events in *Le Rêve*, is an interesting building, dating from the thirteenth century. *Le Rêve.*

BONCŒUR (HÔTEL) was situated in the Boulevard de la Chapelle (*q.v.*). *L'Assommoir.*

BONNEVILLE, a village on the Normandy coast, about six miles from Arromanches. It is in an extremely exposed position, and many houses have been destroyed by the inroads of the sea. To prevent further damage, Lazare Chanteau constructed a breakwater, which was, however, washed away by the first storm. The inhabitants of the village were mostly engaged in fishing. *La Joie de Vivre.*

BORDERIE (LA), a farm on the plain of La Beauce, which belonged to Alexandre Hourdequin, whose father bought it after the Revolution. *La Terre.*

CAEN, a town of about 40,000 inhabitants, situated on the River Orne, about nine miles from the Normandy coast. Chanteau *père* carried on business there before he retired and went to live at Bonneville, and his son Lazare received his education at its college. *La Joie de Vivre.*

CHALONS, a town of about 24,000 inhabitants, is situated on the Marne 107 miles east of Paris. It is the head-quarters of the Sixth Army Corps, and was occupied by the Prussians in August, 1870. *La Débâcle.*

CHAPELLE (BOULEVARD DE LA) is a continuation of the Boulevard de Clichy, in the Montmartre district of Paris. In it was situated the Hôtel Boncœur, where Lantier and Gervaise Macquart found lodgings when they first came to Paris. *L'Assommoir.*

CHARLEVILLE, a town of about 17,000 inhabitants, situated about ten miles north-west of Sedan. It is close to Mézières, of which it really forms the commercial and industrial portion. *La Débâcle.*

CHARTRES, an important and interesting town, situated on the left bank of the Eure, fifty-five miles south-west of Paris. It is the principal town in the grain-producing district of La Beauce, and reference is frequently made to it in *La Terre.* In it M. and Madame Charles Badeuil carried on business for a number of years with considerable success. *La Terre.*

CHÂTEAUDUN, a town of 7000 inhabitants, situated on the left bank of the Loire, about eighty-four miles south-west of Paris. It is in the district of La Beauce, and is frequently referred to in *La Terre.*

CHOISEUL (RUE DE), a street which connects the Boulevard des Italiens, and Rue Neuve Saint-Augustin. It is parallel to Avenue de l'Opéra and Rue Michodière, being slightly to the east of the latter. *Pot-Bouille.*

CLOYES, a market-town in the district of La Beauce, about seven miles from Châteaudun and ninety-one miles south-west of Paris. It is frequently referred to in *La Terre*.

CROIX DE MAUFRAS (LE), a level crossing on the Western Railway of France, between Malaunay and Barentin, about nine miles west of Rouen. The crossing, which was looked after by Misard and his daughter Flore, was the scene of a terrible railway accident, and it was in the same vicinity that President Grandmorin was murdered by Roubaud. *La Bête Humaine*.

EAUX (PASSAGE DES), a steep lane which runs from Rue Raynouard at Passy down to the Seine. In an old house which abutted on the passage lived Mère Fetu, and in the same building was the room where Hélène Grandjean went to meet Doctor Deberle. *Une Page d'Amour*.

GOUTTE D'OR (RUE DE LA), a street in the Montmartre district of Paris. It enters from Rue des Poissonniers and runs parallel to and behind Boulevard de la Chapelle, which is a continuation of Boulevard de Clichy. The Coupeaus and the Lorilleux lived in Rue de la Goutte d'Or. *L'Assommoir*.

HALLES CENTRALES (LES), the great provision markets of Paris, are situated on the right bank of the river, and are directly north of the Pont Neuf, from which they are not far distant. *Le Ventre de Paris*.

HAUSSMANN (BOULEVARD) runs from east to west a short distance behind the Opera House. Its eastern end connects with the Boulevard des Italiens. *Nana*.

HAVRE (LE), an important seaport, which forms the terminus of the Western Railway of France, the line upon which Jacques Lantier was employed as an engine-driver. The Roubauds lived at Le Havre, and many of the principal scenes in *La Bête Humaine* were enacted there. *La Bête Humaine*.

LAZARE (RUE SAINT-) is in the neighbourhood of the railway station of the same name. In it was situated the Orviedo mansion, in which Aristide Saccard started the Universal Bank. *L'Argent*.

LILLE, an important manufacturing town in the north of France, near the Belgian frontier. Étienne Lantier was at one time employed in the railway workshop there. *Germinal*.

MALAUNAY, a station on the Western Railway of France, six miles from Rouen, and about midway between that

town and Barentin. It is referred to in *La Bête Humaine.*

MARBEUF (RUE), a street which
connects the Avenue des
Champs Élysées and the
Avenue de l'Alma. Eugène
Rougon lived there. *Son
Excellence Eugène Rougon.*

MARCHIENNES, a town in the
mining district of the north
of France, about thirty miles
south-east of Lille. It is
fre uently referred to in *Ger-
min l*

MET   a town of 55,000 inhabitants, is situated on the
Moselle, about 263 miles east
of Paris and about eighty
miles south-east of Sedan.
It was surrendered to the
Prussians on 27th October,
1870, and is now the capital of
German Lorraine. *La Débâcle.*

MÉZIÈRES, a small town of 7000
inhabitants, situated on a
peninsula formed by the
Meuse about ten miles north-
west of Sedan. Its situation
has prevented its extension,
and the closely adjoining town
of Charleville has become its
commercial and industrial
quarter. Mézières was three
times invested during the
Franco-Prussian War, and surrendered on 2nd January,
1871, after a bombardment of
three days. *La Débâcle.*

MICHODIÈRE (RUE), a street
which connects the Boulevard
des Capucines and the Rue
Neuve Saint-Augustin. At
the corner where it joins the
latter street was situated
Octave Mouret's great drapery
establishment, known as "Au
Bonheur des Dames," and in it
also Baudu carried on business.
The street is almost parallel
to the Avenue de l'Opéra. *Au
Bonheur des Dames.*

MOINES (RUE DES) was situated
at Batignolles, in the extreme
north-west of Paris. Madame
Lérat lived there. *L'Assommoir.*

MONCEAU (RUE), a street which
runs northward from Rue du
Faubourg St. Honoré. It is
a short distance to the northeast of the Arc de Triomphe,
and in it was situated Aristide Saccard's magnificent
mansion. *La Curée.*

MONTSOU, a mining village in
the north of France, about
ten kilometres from Mar-
chiennes (*q.v.*). It is the
scene of many of the chief
events in *Germinal.*

ORLÉANS, an important town
situated on the Loire, seventy-
five miles south of Paris. It is
referred to in *La Terre* and
Nana.

PARADOU, the name of a neglected demesne near Plassans
(*q.v.*). It was the scene of a
large part of *La Faute de
l'Abbé Mouret.*

PLASSANS, the name under which Zola disguised his native town of Aix. It is a place of about 30,000 inhabitants, and is situated eighteen miles north of Marseilles. Aix was at one time the capital of Provence, is the seat of an archbishop, and contains a university and an École des Art et Métiers.

In the Rougon-Macquart novels Zola made Plassans the cradle of an imaginary family, and throughout the whole series of books the town is constantly referred to. *La Fortune des Rougon,* etc.

RAUCOURT, a small town about six miles south of Sedan. It is frequently referred to in *La Débâcle.*

REIMS, an important town of 98,000 inhabitants, situated about 100 miles to the northeast of Paris. In 1870–71 it was occupied by the Prussians, who laid heavy requisitions upon it. The town is frequently referred to in *La Débâcle.*

REMILLY, a village about five miles south of Sedan. Old Fouchard's farm was situated in its vicinity. *La Débâcle.*

ROUEN, an important town of over 100,000 inhabitants, situated on the Seine, about eighty-seven miles from Paris and fifty-seven miles from Le Havre. It was the scene of the judicial inquiry regarding the murder of President Grandmorin. *La Bête Humaine.*

SEDAN, a town of 20,000 inhabitants, situated on the Meuse, about 170 miles northeast of Paris. It was the scene of one of the chief battles of the Franco-Prussian War of 1870, and capitulated to the Prussian forces on 2nd September of that year. The town is frequently referred to in *La Débâcle.*

VALOGNES, a small town in Normandy, not far from Cherbourg. It was the birthplace of Denise Baudu and her brothers. *Au Bonheur des Dames.*

VINEUSE (RUE DE), a street in the Passy district of Paris, at the extreme west end of the city. It is near the Trocadero Palace. Madame Hélène Grandjean and Doctor Deberle both lived in this street. *Une Page d'Amour.*

VOREUX, the name of a large coal-pit, situated about two kilometres from Montsou, on the road between that village and Marchiennes (*q.v.*). *Germinal.*